MW00595285

Praise for *Contagious You*

"Anese has found the key to a fundamental truth to being human: Your intentions, energy, and presence affect and influence everyone around you. You are contagious. As a leader, this is your most profound responsibility and opportunity. Understanding and working with this truth is the key to building healthy cultures and movements that catch fire. *Contagious You* will help leaders around the world create the cultures, communities, and impact they envision."

> —**Chip Conley**, Founder of Modern Elder Academy,
> author of *Wisdom @Work*, and Airbnb Strategic Advisor
> for Hospitality and Leadership

"There is something truly liberating in the realization that you have everything you need to be a force for positive impact in the world. The what and how of leading from your authentic self is where we can get lost. Lucky for all of us, Anese has everything we need to connect with our intentions, use our self-awareness meaningfully, and have the impact that is truly 'in service of.' Our organization would be lesser without her."

> —**Heather Currier Hunt**, Global Head of
> Learning & Development at IDEO

"*Contagious You* reminds us that each interaction, each choice moment, and each day is paramount in growing as a leader, both now and in the future. Anese Cavanaugh reminds us that we are all leaders in our own way and helps us find and connect with our Essential You. A game-changer for those looking for ways to lead in a way that inspires hope and change."

> —**Marshall Goldsmith**, *New York Times* #1 bestselling
> author of *Triggers, Mojo,* and *What Got You Here
> Won't Get You There*

"This book cracks the code on human energy. With insights and assessments, tools and practices, wisdom and wit, Anese teaches us how to cultivate and use our energy—the vital resource we all need to thrive in our personal and work lives."
—**Wayne Baker**, Professor of Management & Organizations and Faculty Director of the Center for Positive Organizations, University of Michigan Ross School of Business

"In an age when honoring relationships is more important than ever, Anese Cavanaugh offers an incredible, accessible guide for all those who are ready to show up to relationships as empathetic, empowered, energetic humans, ready to foster connection, lead with intention, and serve those around them, no matter who comes into their sphere."
—**Erica Keswin**, author of *Bring Your Human to Work* and Founder of the Spaghetti Project

"Anese's latest, *Contagious You*, is a gift to yourself and anyone in your span of care: your work team, your spouse, your children, your friends. When we show up in a manner that is life-giving, rather than life-draining, it creates the space for you and others to do their best, be their best. This book will help you accomplish what you want and inspire others to do the same. As we teach at Barry-Wehmiller, YOU are the message. Read this gem so you can be the best one!"
—**Bob Chapman**, author of *Everybody Matters* and CEO of Barry-Wehmiller

"Anese has taught me so much about what it means to lead in a present, mindful, and joyful way. In this generous book, she shares the secrets that have helped me and so many others bring our best, most exuberant, most contagious selves to work—and life."
—**Ingrid Fetell-Lee**, author of *Joyful* and Founder of The Aesthetics of Joy

"With all the challenges of burnout in health care today, *Contagious You* is a critical tool for helping you create and maintain an authentic and sustainable culture of engagement in your organization. From pixie dust to the neuroscience of trust, Anese empowers us to share our presence, intention, and love for what we do to create a culture of trust which allows us to provide the best team-driven approach to deliver amazing integrated care for those who need our services most."

—**Michael Lalich, MD,** Medical Director and Chief of Staff
of a large nonprofit integrated health care organization

"Contagious You is a powerful addition to Anese's already must-experience books and workshops, taking a deeper dive into unlocking your best self. This book is a great read for all who are ready for a change (big or small) and willing to invest in themselves. Anese offers a blueprint for understanding and implementing the best version of 'you.' For the last several years I've studied, implemented, and shared Anese's work with everyone I can. Her teachings are among the most impactful and transformational I have ever encountered!"

—**Katie Turner,** Head of Global Talent Development
and Org Capability for a Fortune 100 company

"In *Contagious You,* Anese Cavanaugh is enhancing the toolkit for those of us engaged in the work of expanding our own capacity. In her affable style, she reminds us that we cannot fix others, but we can ROCK ourselves; that our intentions, energy, and presence are all contagious all the time; and that when we take the time to improve how we are BEING within the world of our work, the lever of our DOING increases. Her question 'What kind of contagious do you wish to be?' is a stunning challenge that has to begin at the individual level to then spread throughout an organization and raise the vibrational level for all."

—**Corey Blake,** Founder and CEO, Round Table
Companies; Publisher, Conscious Capitalism Press

"Reading this book is like having an expert on organizational culture come over to your house, sit down on the couch, and tell you how to make the maximum impact in your life. Anese writes in a wonderfully down-to-earth, informative, and uplifting way. It is impossible to read this book and not come out of it a more powerful and effective person."

—**Kathie Nielsen**, Deputy Superintendent TUSD (retired) and Professor, Hope International University

"Anese Cavanaugh nailed it! *Contagious You* is a masterful representation of a 'HOW TO' do life in a way that will positively impact every person and situation that you encounter. This is a must-read if you are truly ready to BE a thoughtful, contagious leader and step into the greatness that is already within. Anese teaches that we are the silver bullet with easy-to-understand principles and lessons that are ready for immediate implementation. Prepare yourself to read the words that will change your life! (And be prepared to want to read it again after you finish.)"

—**Matt Beck**, CEO of Beck Investment Group

"We've all encountered those special people who light up a room, people we would follow anywhere if they asked. Anese Cavanaugh is one of those people, and *Contagious You* is her guide to becoming one yourself."

—**Blair Enns**, author of *The Win Without Pitching Manifesto*

"I remember when the word 'contagious' was reserved for being sick—Anese Cavanaugh spins the idea of being contagious a full 360 and transforms the very essence of the word into the equivalent of a Marvel superpower!

"This book will help you to truly engage and awaken yourself and most importantly realize the importance of being 'your best you' to elevate others.

"When I tell people, 'I have to take care of me to be the best I can be for you,' I am routinely met with puzzled looks—especially from other women. This book is the marker for changing this space and moving forward in your life—in all aspects of your life—feeling confident to 'own your magic' and truly be contagious."

—**Diane Cooper**, television executive

"A force multiplier for your personal leadership, this book is so timely you'll wish you had read it sooner. Cavanaugh is contagious as she helps us bring service and mindfulness together to create meaning in our organizations and lives."
—**Steve Krull**, CEO and Cofounder of Be Found Online

"If you are required to ever come in contact with other people, consider this required reading. In fact, I might make it a new deal-breaker that if you haven't done the work Anese so beautifully, articulately, and practically lays out in this book—then . . . well . . . I'm not interested. I spend my days speaking and consulting in organizations, and I know I will be buying cases of this book to help leaders everywhere take advantage of their contagious selves."
—**Mike Ganino**, author and Culture + Brand
Storyteller/Strategist

"As a 25-year veteran in financial services leading organizations in excess of 5,000 staff in over 100 countries, I thought I knew what a great leader looked like. And then I met Anese and read *Contagious Culture*. I am among the many friends and fans who have been asking for more, and this is it. There are so many leadership books out there, and NONE of them flip the industry on its head as this book does. Anese makes a powerful business case for the elimination of the term 'soft skills,' brings the most important components of being a successful leader together, and then puts it all into action. Leaders SERVE their teams. The word EMPOWERMENT is just wrong. This is not a book with sweeping statements and clichés we have all heard. This is the HOW TO reference book that I will keep at my side, and the resulting impact is material. If you buy only one book this year, you have found it."
—**Michelle (Mick) Lee**, Managing Director,
Financial Services + Hospitality (Fortune 200 company)
and Founder of WINiTforWomen.org

"My only regret after reading this extraordinary book is that I didn't read it when I was younger. No doubt, I would have benefited from these important lessons. I know that Anese Cavanaugh's work will help elevate those who read it and positively impact families, organizations, and communities that are impacted by the positive change it enables."

—**Mark J. Bernstein**, University of Michigan Regent and
President of The Sam Bernstein Law Firm, PLLC

"It's rare that one finishes a book and feels RARING to go, but this is one of those gems, equal parts poetic inspiration and technical manual for getting it done that will light and sustain the fire under your ass. It will make you feel like you've had one of those life-altering conversations with your wisest of friends, the one that slaps you upside the head with all her best lessons, while helping you stay upright as you shake the dust off your blind spots. Filled with paragraphs you'll highlight, sentences you'll jot down, and exercises that will make you go deep fast (and painlessly) to help pull up that version of yourself you've long known needs surfacing, this is a definitive guide to being a better leader . . . and human. It will motivate you, make you laugh, deconstruct tired unhelpful ways of thinking, and show you how to rebuild solid frameworks to deal with challenges big and small. Ultimately, it will make you want to show up and be the person you've always been meant to be, so you can inspire others to follow along, and in doing so, become more contagious themselves."

—**Andréa Vieira**, Cofounder of nailsaloon

"This book is a map for leaders to experience a sustainable shift in behavior that impacts their organization and naturally calls forth the best in others. Anese is part of a growing movement to reimagine business by improving ourselves so that employees naturally step into their own greatness. I like to think of the movement as a puzzle with different innovators adding their piece, eventually forming a new image of what business can and should be. *Contagious You* (and IEP) is essentially the last piece in the frame, and now Anese beckons us all to fill in what remains with our unique qualities of presence."

—**David Mizne**, Director of Best-Self Management at 15Five

"Ever experience something and go . . . OMG, I had no idea how badly I needed this! That's how *Contagious You* hit me.

"Compelled by a sense of moral imperative, our organization has been crazy busy pursuing an aggressive growth path to reach thousands of more youth across the country. As the CEO, I'd been so busy *doing* that I'd completely lost track of how I'd been *be-ing*. *Contagious You* helped me realign my energy with my purpose. This approach has challenged me to be more aware of how my energy impacts others. If I'm contagious, what am I spreading? Does my energy confine and contract or elevate and compel others in pursuit of our mission? When I lead with compassion and curiosity and intention, I influence more effectively and become a force multiplier. I now feel I have permission to be myself, to own my 'superpowers,' and to move from being overwhelmed with the responsibilities of being a leader to being 'response-able.' With daily grounding in my purpose, I discover new levels of leadership in myself and others. I emerge feeling clearer, tuned in, energized, on purpose, and in alignment. Damn that feels good."

—**Michelle Adler Morrison**, CEO Youth Guidance

"In a world filled with demands and distractions, it's easy to feel powerless over your work and your life. *Contagious You* reminds us that it's possible to live with intention, and gives us a methodology and tools to help regain control. Anese's work transformed my mindset and allowed me to design and live a life that fills me up—and sets me up to have a more positive impact in the world."

—**Marisa Smith**, Certified EOS® Implementer at 87plus

"*Contagious You* is the brilliant sequel to *Contagious Culture* and a must-read for anyone in a leadership role, striving for one, or just wanting to have a more positive presence in the world. Learning the IEP Method® has been key to my personal growth and development over the last several years. You ARE contagious whether you realize it or not, and this book is the perfect guide to teach you the steps to become a positive force in the world. I'm grateful for Anese and all the work she's done in this area, and my life and impact on the world is much richer as a result."

—**Eric Rieger**, President of WEBIT Services, Inc.

"If you have ever wanted to unlock the secrets of taking your connection to others and the world around you to the next level, *Contagious You* is for you. While reading these pages, Anese Cavanaugh became my guide in the realization that a life lived with intention and awareness can change everything."

> —**Lisa M. Brown, MD**, Ob/Gyn physician and Assistant Area Medical Director of wellness of a large nonprofit integrated health care organization

"Reading *Contagious You*, you'll be filled with a range of emotions, from reflection to curiosity to excitement. Through stories and practical tips, Anese will take you down a path to understand that the success you have in business and in life rests in the relationships you build. And the success you have in the relationships you build and the impact you have rests completely with YOU."

—**Hamsa Daher**, Executive Director of Small Giants

"This book is pure magic. As a surgeon, I am often in a position where leadership is not only expected but crucial. As with most physicians, my education focused on patient care with little (if any) training in leadership and development, management, or how to lead a team. *Contagious You* has opened my eyes to the importance of my own presence and awareness, and reinforced how important it is not only to project my own positivity but to live it myself. It is the single most applicable book I've ever seen to myself, my practice, my organization, my patients, and my personal life. I feel deeply connected with so many aspects such as healing, promoting health, and even transforming burnout into success! I am so excited to bring this book to my colleagues and organization to help inspire and energize our people from the inside out."

—**Aaron A. Centric, DO FAOCO-HNS**

"Anese is my spirit animal for living with intention, energy, and presence. Her influence has had a profound effect on my own personal ability to feel the way I want to feel, and have the impact I want to have in my life and work. *Contagious You* is not some dry reference book to be read once and put on a shelf. It's a living document, a user's manual for life that I plan to consult regularly. Reading it, I'm reminded of my power to influence any situation. If you're feeling at a crossroads, or simply want to have greater impact in your life, I highly recommend it. The principles within are universal, but what you do with them is up to you."

—**Alison Macondray**, advisor and partner to thought leaders and professional speakers, presentation design expert, former General Manager of Wired News

"*Contagious You* delves deeper into our personal impact that we can deliberately and knowingly make by choosing to show up for ourselves and each other; the power of first taking care of the leader in leadership. The seemingly magical results that can happen are deeply rooted in neuroscience, and Anese guides us through the indisputable changes that occur on a cellular level when we shift into our energetic best. The principles she introduces in the book are surprisingly simple and deeply profound. We are excited to delve into them with our leaders, and perhaps more importantly, use them to become better within."

—**Deb Bielek and Mary Spaeder**, Therapy Leaders for Ensign Services, Inc.

"*Contagious You* will change your way of thinking about leadership. Anese Cavanaugh brilliantly reveals the importance of growing more leaders to make a positive impact. If you lead a developing organization, this is a must-read."

—**Tom Walter**, Chief Culture Officer, Tasty Catering, serial entrepreneur, and author

"This book is a gift to restore leadership energy, presence, and intention. It is essential to connect to human beings, but the most important would be to self. This read permitted time to learn about myself and the absolute need for attention to all aspects of myself. For me, as a contagious leader in progress, the superpowers in this book serve as the foundation and building blocks for how to make choices, engage, breathe, find clarity, contribute, recover, and be confident daily. I am so grateful to have met Anese and experienced her confidence and contagiousness for being the best that I can be. This book reflects the need for taking time to appreciate others every day and receive their energy, breathe, give back, forgive, take care of me in order to serve others, and be grateful."

—**MZK, RN**, Chief Administrative Officer
of a large health care organization

"Anese Cavanaugh holds up the mirror for us to examine our leadership and ourselves in the most supportive, honest, and helpful way I have ever come across. *Contagious You* will help all of us be our best at leading, parenting, partnering, or simply being. If you want to make a bigger impact in your life, maybe you feel overwhelmed and are struggling, or just don't know where to start . . . you need this book."

—**Stephen Harms**, former Air Force officer, HR Business
Partner and Training Manager

"*Contagious You* is next level! If you have the desire to make a positive impact, then this book is an essential resource to get you there. Great news: How you take care of you and how you show up to make a positive impact with your teams is already present in you. How you make it happen is up to you. From the introduction to the assessments to the research to the last sentence, *Contagious You* is magic for all aspects of your life!"

—**Patricia Seagram**, Vice President, Human Resources
North Market, Henry Ford Health System

"Imagining all the energy we could collectively save and redirect into our businesses for those we serve is an exciting thought. *Contagious You* takes this thought from a dream into a realistic action plan to make it so. Not only does this work impact our businesses, our cultures, our families, and ourselves, but I have great hope for this book being shared in schools. If this work were taught in schools, the world would look, operate, and feel a whole lot brighter."

—**Heather Zara**, owner and CEO, Zara Creative

"Anese has written a tremendous follow-up to *Contagious Culture*. In her very personal and reflective work, *Contagious You* allows you to apply her magic formula of IEP (Intentions, Energy, and Presence) to your life through honest assessment, discovery of your 'superpowers,' and application of daily practices. Whether you get it intuitively, need the science behind it, or need the to-do list to follow, it is all in this book!"

—**Paul Spiegelman**, Cofounder of Small Giants Community

"We live in a world where we often feel like we have no control, whether it be at school, work, or home. However, we as individuals have a lot of control. Control over the way we feel, the way we make others feel, and the way we are able to positively impact the world. *Contagious You* entertains with scenarios that we all have faced out in the real world and helps us see these scenarios from multiple perspectives, specifically our own and how we show up. This book is a must-read not only for leaders, but for all those who strive to become kinder, better, happier, and ultimately the best version of themselves."

—**Jamie Pritscher**, Cofounder, nuphoriq and That's Caring

"Anese nails *Contagious You* as the perfect follow-up to *Contagious Culture*. As indicated by the title, it REALLY does focus on YOU, providing many scenarios, tools, and assessments to take your leadership to a whole new level. I especially appreciated the connection to modern brain research—it's more science than most recognize."

—**Gregory A. Franklin, EdD**, Superintendent of Schools, Tustin Unified School District

"We felt blessed with the gift of *Contagious Culture* in the early part of our organization's culture transformation. The deeper we go into this journey, the more evidence there is for the wisdom and insightful tools presented in *Contagious You*.

"People desiring to shape the culture around them will benefit from starting their journey within their own head and heart."

—**Nina Ramsey, SVP, CHRO**, Henry Ford Health System

"From her punchy chapter titles to her very real approach to everyday life situations, Anese inspires and teaches us how to decide who we want to be, then lays out the plan for inspiring others with our contagious spirit!"

—**Jill Young**, Business Coach and author of *In Courage*

"Anese reminds us of the impact we have on each other, and to *own* it. When we do (and it's not always easy!), we change lives (including our own!). *Contagious You* is a blueprint for mindfully finding our flow through self-awareness and self-care, which enables us to be of service to those around us. And isn't that what life is all about?!"

—**Rob Dube**, President, imageOne

"WARNING: This book is contagious! Do yourself a favor and buy two copies now. Here's one you're going to want to share.

"There's no denying it, this book brings me joy. Even after a major KonMari book purge session, I am making room on my nightstand for *Contagious You*. It's that important.

"Loved that this book crosses the line from leadership skills to personal well-being. That's what makes it so special. Anese has created practical tools to light your imagination on fire. More than a guide on what to do, this is a gift on how to be. After reading it, you'll show up better, more authentic, and so alive! People will sense that something is different, want what you've got, and tell you're magic. You'll routinely hear, 'what's your secret?'

"The only dust this book will ever encounter is the pixie dust that seeps from every page. This is the magic!"

—**Janette Lampe**, CFO (Chief Fun Officer) and
  Corporate Events Manager at a large health care
  organization

CONTAGIOUS
YOU

CONTAGIOUS YOU

UNLOCK YOUR POWER TO INFLUENCE, LEAD, AND CREATE THE IMPACT YOU WANT

ANESE CAVANAUGH

New York   Chicago   San Francisco   Athens   London
Madrid   Mexico City   Milan   New Delhi
Singapore   Sydney   Toronto

1 2 3 4 5 6 7 8 9   LCR   24 23 22 21 20 19

ISBN   978-1-260-45410-9
MHID   1-260-45410-X

e-ISBN   978-1-260-45411-6
e-MHID   1-260-45411-8

Library of Congress Cataloging-in-Publication Data

Names: Cavanaugh, Anese, author.
Title: Contagious you : unlock your power to influence, lead, and create the impact you want / Anese Cavanaugh.
Description: New York : McGraw-Hill Education, [2020] | Includes bibliographical references and index.
Identifiers: LCCN 2019030810 (print) | LCCN 2019030811 (ebook) | ISBN 9781260454109 (hardcover) | ISBN 9781260454116 (ebook)
Subjects: LCSH: Leadership. | Influence (Psychology) | Motivation (Psychology) | Organizational behavior.
Classification: LCC HD57.7 .C3888 2020 (print) | LCC HD57.7 (ebook) | DDC
658.4/092—dc23
LC record available at https://lccn.loc.gov/2019030810
LC ebook record available at https://lccn.loc.gov/2019030811

McGraw-Hill Education books are available at special quantity discounts to use as premiums and sales promotions or for use in corporate training programs. To contact a representative, please visit the Contact Us pages at www.mhprofessional.com.

Images in this book were created by Jef Lear.

DEVOTION

For all of us doing the best we can to be positively and usefully contagious in this big world of humans and impact.

CONTENTS

CONTENTS

FOREWORD

The Everyday Application of Energy

Let me begin with a very significant and sincere expression of gratitude to the woman who wrote this book: what I've learned from Anese Cavanaugh over the past 10 years, the way we've implemented it here in the Zingerman's Community of Businesses, the way it's resonated with nearly everyone I've taught it to, the way readers have responded to what I've written about it in my own books . . . all indicate that Anese is deserving of enormous appreciation. Her work and her insight have engendered an enormous amount of positive change for the people I work with, and those we serve. So Anese, let me simply start out by saying, *Thank you!*

Let me then back up a bit, to share some background. When my partner, Paul Saginaw, and I opened Zingerman's Delicatessen on March 15, 1982, we had two employees in a little 1,300-square-foot space at the corner of Detroit and Kingsley Streets in the Kerrytown neighborhood of Ann Arbor, Michigan. Now, 37 years later, the Zingerman's Community of Businesses is made up of a dozen unique businesses, each located in the Ann Arbor area. The organization overall now employs about 700 staffers (plus 300 more to help ship you food at the holidays).

Through the years, clearly, we've done a lot to increase our sales. But, behind the scenes, we've worked just as hard at developing our philosophy of business. We've spent thousands of hours studying business, read who knows how many books, attended other people's seminars, and started teaching lots of our own, all the while making sandwiches, bussing tables, picking up paper towels off the floor, and trying to make a positive difference in the lives our coworkers, customers, and community. Of all the ideas we've taken in, and all of those we've built on, I will say with great certainty that what we've adapted from Anese has become one of the most important elements of our organizational ecosystem. During the past decade we've turned Anese's teachings into an important part of our everyday organizational culture. It's had enormously positive impact.

Here's a quick anecdotal example. This afternoon I was at the weekly "huddle" in the kitchen at Zingerman's Roadhouse (our 200-seat, James Beard Award–nominated restaurant serving regional American food). To be clear, these aren't a bunch of yoga teachers or positive psychology professors. This is an hour-long meet up of line cooks, prep cooks, chefs, and a dishwasher or two . . . coming together for their weekly reporting and forecasting, and a quick, to-the-point conversation about what's happening in the kitchen. Their icebreaker this week, as it does most every week, included our standard question of: What's your energy? We use a zero to 10 scale. Energy is so incorporated into the culture that pretty much everyone here can comfortably converse about it. Newer employees, senior staff, people who don't speak English as their first language . . . they each pretty easily report their energy. Because we've been doing it so long, as they go around the room, folks have fun with it in a good way. People often take the scale into hundredths—"9.3," "9.66," or "8.8." One line cook, who's leaving soon for the summer to go work at a resort in Montana laughingly said she was so good today she's at an 11, and shares how much she's going to miss everyone while she's gone. One staff member says, "I'm at 8.5 or 9." The facilitator, another line cook, kindly shoots back, "We know you—you're not a 9 today." She adds with a smile, "We'll put in the notes that you're at 8.5." His response, "You're right. Thanks for calling me on it." He was smiling when he said it too.

I'm pretty sure that this was the only restaurant kitchen in the country where an interaction like that was taking place that afternoon. But I'm equally confident that it *could* be happening in hundreds or thousands of them. What the Roadhouse kitchen crew—and folks all over the Zingerman's Community—are doing almost daily, could be happening in any organization, in any part of the world. If it was, every single spot would surely be better for it. Banks, baseball teams, and bricklayers—all would benefit. It would help in Congress, and it would contribute just as positively at your local coffee shop. This mindful energy management—what Anese calls Intentional Energetic Presence (or IEP)—always, *always* makes things better!

Here's the bottom line: The work that Anese is sharing in this book (and in *Contagious Culture* before it) has the power to have an enormously positive impact on your organization. And really your whole life! Beyond the cost of this book, making the changes Anese is advocating will cost you next to nothing. But the benefits they can bring to your organization, to your own work, and to your life outside of work are—no exaggeration—enormous.

How do we use IEP here at Zingerman's? The icebreaker at the kitchen huddle at the Roadhouse is just one small example. Much more significantly, we've made positive energy a performance expectation. That's right—the stuff Anese is teaching is not just a bit of extra information, or fancy icing on your organizational cake. It's not human resources happy talk, or a pretty poster to put on the wall in the break room. It's a hardcore, real-life part of people's daily job duties—mine as well as the newest staff member we just hired to work the night shift. What does that mean in practice? If you're a great baker, but you bring bad energy every day . . . we need to talk. If you're an amazing accountant, but your energy is abrasive, we need to have a productive conversation about performance. While of course we coach folks who have suboptimal or negative energy on how to improve, we treat energy just as seriously as we would a bread baker whose dough doesn't rise, or an accountant who can't add. Energy (that is, IEP) is a critical part of every one of the 700 jobs at Zingerman's!

What do we get out of that? Better everything! Better service; better staff work experience. Less accidents in the workplace. Lower stress. More love. Better financials. Better food. And, because most staff take this learning into the rest of their lives, what happens to them outside of work starts to go better too. Which means that they feel better when they get to work! It's certainly one reason that we were included in Tracie McMillan's article in *Food and Wine* magazine called "19 Great Restaurants to Work For."[1] It's a very virtuous energetic cycle. And it's all built on what we learned from Anese.

What tips will you find in this beautifully wise book? There are so many. It's filled with literally dozens of ways that you can put Anese's approaches to work—super simple, easy-to-understand ways to use at work and in every other part of your life as well. (Mind you, they're simple, but I didn't say they were easy—changing a lifetime of habits can, to state the almost obvious, be really hard!)

One of my other intellectual mentors, Russian anarchist prince Peter Kropotkin wrote in his 1899 book, *Memoirs of a Revolutionist:*[2] "One must have some question addressed to the book one is going to read." I agree. And so would Anese. So, before you dive into the book, let me help you practice, with my own simple, in-the-moment, structure, what she's about to teach you in much greater depth in the rest of this tome. Based on the little bit I just shared with you about our own experiences at Zingerman's, or on what you knew about Anese's work before you bought the book, reflect for a few minutes on what you want to get out of it! As per everything Anese has written, setting your intention is sure to have a positive impact. I will *guarantee* that your experience will be infinitely better if you decide in advance the sort of impact you want it to have. What do you hope to learn? How are you hoping the learnings from the book will benefit you? How willing are you to open your mind and your heart to what Anese is advocating? The better you set your intentions, the better your learning and the bigger the benefit you'll get from the book!

Last thought before I let you get to your reading. Although I took it on as part of our growth about 20 years ago, I never loved the title CEO. Chief Executive Officer, to me, sounds grim—like you execute people for a living. But after getting to know Anese's work, I realized that the acronym was fine. It just needed a different interpretation. As per everything you're about to learn in this book, I believe that a much better explanation of CEO would be Chief Energy Officer. It's how, very happily, I've been looking at my own job for years now. The energy in our organization starts with me!

I'll end this short bit the way I began—with an enormous appreciation. Having already read the book you're holding in your hands, I can say with confidence that you're about to encounter 200-plus pages of life-altering material. I can't thank Anese enough. And the really good news? Thanks to Anese, I also know that meaningful appreciation like this, improves our energy! I feel better for it already!

Ari

Ari Weinzweig
CEO and Cofounding Partner
Zingerman's Community of Businesses
Ann Arbor, Michigan

Author of *Zingerman's Guide to Good Leading, Part 2: A Lapsed Anarchist's Approach to Being a Better Leader,* the full *Zingerman's Guide to Good Leading Series, Parts 1–4,* and other books

P.S.: The spirit of generosity is also a big contributor to the effectiveness of IEP. If you're interested to learn more about how we live what Anese is advocating, feel free to email me at ari@zingermans.com. I'd be happy to hear more about your own experiences and to share whatever I can of ours!

INTRODUCTION

We *Are* Contagious. How *We* Show Up
Matters. The Results Are In.

I wanted my last book to be called *Show Up*. My publisher and editor had other ideas, and we named it *Contagious Culture* instead. Of course, they were right. *Contagious Culture* turned out to be "the little book that could" that continued to build momentum and grow and attract people in ways I hadn't considered possible. Schools, health care systems, law enforcement programs, organizational development programs, and more adopted it and blended the work and principles into their way of being and practices in ways that fit their industry.

It didn't matter the size or company; the people who embraced that book wanted a culture that assimilated and celebrated the "soft stuff" and things like *intentions, energy, and presence* (IEP). The people in the organizations I met with and who were reading the book also wanted to create organizations that invited everyone to be "response-*able*" for the energy they brought to the table and the impact their IEP had on their culture. They knew what so many forget (or just don't know, yet): that happy, present, fulfilled human beings working together are what make any organization—*and* its bottom line—thrive. They also knew that energy and connection have a big return on investment (ROI), that purpose, love, and kindness (to self and others) is often the answer to some of the most complex questions, and that true success starts with each person showing up individually *and* together because each of them *wants* to.

These organizations held people as equally important as any tangible business result or financial impact—if not more important. They knew that the soft stuff was in fact magical titanium, netting better financial results, better customer care, better business outcomes, and happier engaged people at the end of the day.

They knew the importance of authentic and sustainable employee engagement—and the stats to go with it (see "The Cost of Disengagement" and "Some Interesting Numbers on Trust" at the end of this Introduction). They also knew that there was more to it than just *doing* culture and engagement and *doing* management and leadership; they had to *be* it. After all, in those engagement surveys that we all see, who are the people who are keeping their employees and each other engaged? They are. We all are. On both sides they saw their responsibility to create an organization that nourished engagement for their employees and also for themselves.

Low and behold it worked. People reported feeling happier not just with their work but with their professional and personal relationships, and with their lives. High-risk employees began taking more ownership for their impact and career (or exited with dignity); leaders who'd previously "left dead bodies" everywhere they went became more pleasurable to work with. Executives considering leaving their organization found new ways to love and lead in it instead (and stayed); teams worked more collaboratively together; teachers felt less stress, more present, and more excited going into their classrooms.

Reports of more and more honest, clean, and direct conversations occurred. Deals were closed; promotions were had; money was made; disempowering stories were learned from and changed; divorces were more peaceful and intentional (some were avoided all together). People got out of their own way, replacing the Drama Triangle with accountability and purpose. Many shared of significant weight loss and improvements in health, and even their therapists asking them what they were doing to create these shifts. Some of the more heart-wrenching outcomes came from people going through incredibly difficult life events, like the woman who shared that working her IEP supported her through the death of her husband.

No realm of life or business has been off-limits in terms of impact and possibility for those who were willing to dare to engage.

How did they do it? What were they doing? They did the work I outlined in *Contagious Culture*. Not only did they achieve better cultural, business, and collaboration success, but also their personal lives were positively impacted. Which makes sense and can be expected, because as we say in this work—it's all one life, and it starts with *you*. And that's where this book comes in.

After my first book, I heard countless stories from readers, revealing themes of how it impacted their lives, such as:

- **A fuller, more credible presence** (like the executive who became more trustworthy with her team, within a month, simply by shifting her awareness, intentions, and presence)
- **A richer quality of life and relationships** (like the leader who left one of our sessions and redesigned her marriage with the spouse she'd been ready to divorce two days before)
- **More space** (like my client who went from having no room for lunch or breaks or to hear himself think, to getting workouts in and taking a three-hour window of nonnegotiable white space each week)
- **More grace** (like the attorney who felt the only way he could be successful was by being a hard-ass to all, and therefore alienating everyone, but who eventually learned how to expand his range and became a "Velvet Hammer" and more pleasurable to be around—especially for his wife and kids)
- **Better financial results** (like the team who closed a seven-figure deal after doing the "Five Steps to Intentional Impact" from the IEP Method® before the client meeting)
- **And leadership that was more powerful, helpful, and positively contagious** (like the Director who went from being overwhelmed and not taken seriously by his firm to Partner in under a year while making only three simple changes in his

presence—and they weren't the changes he originally thought he needed to make)

All of these people were the answers to their own problems. But they wouldn't have known that going in. They needed awareness. And they needed to work it.

So they did. But they needed more. And this is where the book you are holding in your hands comes in.

It's All About You

More than three years after the release of *Contagious Culture*, I continue to receive feedback and questions about being contagious, my concept of Intentional Energetic Presence®, and the IEP work (the methodology I created to support people in showing up better, which I will share later in this book). I've listened earnestly and have identified overall themes to what people took away from the content.

The first theme was "surprise, excitement, ownership, and action." People were surprised by what a personal *inside-out* approach creating culture actually was and how much their own IEP and self-care impacted their environment and results. "I *am* the culture? How I show up matters? Taking care of myself is a leadership skill? I'm my best bet for creating the culture and life I want? And I am contagious?" Great! They were on their way.

The first half of *Contagious Culture* focused on the reader as leader; only in the second half did I dig into "culture." This was intentional. After all, I am the culture (as are you, he, she, and they)—*and* I control me. Most were excited; some were relieved. If *they* were the culture, that meant they had the power to shift it. They didn't have to be just at the effect of their culture or the people around them; they could be the effect. These people applied the principles and quickly saw results not only at work, but at home.

With this realization, a puzzle piece that had been missing as they'd spent all sorts of time, energy, and money on different cultural initiatives and training fell into place. No matter how many things they *did* to make their culture great, if they led and presented in a way that had people feeling not safe, not inspired, not connected, not real, exhausted, or like they *had* to show up (versus *wanted* to show up), or if people held the culture "out there" as something that was everyone else's responsibility (not mine!)—they wouldn't have a great culture.

Different questions emerged from this awareness: "How are we truly showing up? What culture are we creating by how we do so? Are each of us owning culture? How *do* we want to lead? Whom do we want to be together? Am I contributing to things going better or worse? Am I being intentional about what I want to create? What behaviors will we tolerate, or not (even if the bad behavior is coming from our biggest rainmaker)?"

The ideas of organizational hostages, hiring and firing for the energetic good of all, the leadership trifecta, the super seven for cultural health, and the IEP Method® as it applied to individual leadership and the organization as a whole all took hold. And voilà! New awareness, small (and big) shifts, and a whole new ball game.

Of course, in all of the feedback, there were still those who just wanted the "punch list" on what to *do* about culture—not how to *be* it. They thought they had the "being" handled. (They didn't, especially those who were most focused on securing "the list.") They thought the punch list would be the magic pill. (It's not.) In these cases my work became about helping people realize that the punch list is only as good as the *intentions, energy*, and *presence* of the person executing it.

Another theme that's emerged over the years is "What about *them*?" "How do I make my spouse (or boss, friend, mother-in-law, partner, or colleague) read this book? How do I work with the person who is the 'lowest vibration in the room,' who thinks culture is about foosball tables and 'doing' values, who shows up terribly and is leaving dead bodies everywhere he or she goes? But I work for him (or she makes us a ton of money, or they're related to the founders, or they're my family, or I'm married to them) so we're stuck?" This theme was bigger than I anticipated. These readers were applying it, *and* they were spending a ton of time and energy trying to navigate people who weren't. Bummer.

And, finally, the "What's next?" theme. "Things are getting more intense; we're getting busier; demands are higher; I'm stressed; I feel overwhelmed; I'm lonely . . . What now?" Or "Got it; we're rocking it; I'm working my IEP in big ways; I want more, gimme"! And "I'm sorry, but, again, what do I do about 'that guy'?"

The questions and requests for topics that I cover in this new book were heartfelt and enthusiastic. Ironically, and maybe no surprise, one of the biggest requests was to write a book to "change George." ("George" is the "lowest vibration in the room," and I'll stop you there—you can't fix or change him. But don't worry; I have a plan. Keep reading.)

Requests for a book on IEP and relationships, impact, speaking, sales, marketing, parenting, divorce, teaching, and more were made. All feedback pointed me to go deeper into the power of our individual (and ultimately collective) contagiousness, and the essentialness of getting it handled and pointed in the right direction.

Forget culture, forget business, forget results, forget "George," forget everything—take care of *you*, and you have a better chance of dancing with everything else *and* contributing more.

More *with* less.

More impact, presence, meaning, and leadership. *Less* drama, noise, burnout, and blame.

While *Contagious Culture* attracted many different industries in business, what it really attracted was humans. Humans who wanted to have more impact, feel better working together, and feel and be better at home, too. Humans who wanted to lead, connect, be valued, be real, and be happy.

There was more work to do here that honored the *you* in the culture.

You are the culture in every system you are a part of. What you "put out there" and how you show up creates the culture. And *you* can't be your best culture if you're exhausted, burnt out, busy, blaming everyone else for culture, leaving dead bodies behind, constantly on the defense, or not *owning* the culture. This book is written to give *you* more personal and individual support to show up well, feel good doing it, and inspire others to lead better too. After all, culture is only a bunch of *you*s together.

If you've already read *Contagious Culture: Show Up, Set the Tone, and Intentionally Create an Organization that Thrives* and you're wondering if you should read this one now, the answer is *yes*. While we talked about you in that book, there was so much more to discuss. And in the three years since its release, not only have readers shown me where they want and need more, but the work has grown significantly. So while this book will enrich ideas shared in the first one, and vice versa, the content in this book is new and works beautifully with *Contagious Culture*.

Throughout this book, you'll meet people like Max (whom you'll learn about in Chapter 1—his people kept quitting *him*, not the company); Lester and Matt (whom you'll meet in Chapter 3—their leadership trust and credibility was being diminished by behaviors and presence issues totally within their control and easily remedied); Team X (in Chapter 4, who almost bombed a major deal but used the IEP Method to identify team issues and closed the deal beautifully at the last minute); Casey (in Part 3, who learned how to manage her "leadership bully" by more effectively holding her space and ultimately surpassing her in the organization); and many more humans and organizations that have shown up in bigger, better, and more peaceful ways (and sometimes *not*) because they did their work (or *not*).

All to say, here we are.

Check Yourself Before You Wreck Yourself

If you are one of those people reading this book for "them"—meaning you think this is all good and dandy and you get it, but you want *them* to get it and you're looking for some new tricks to make it happen. Or you're hoping George will finally get it and you'll get him out of your hair once and for all. Or you really want to integrate this more but don't think others on your team will bite. Here are a few things to consider.

One . . . I've found that the minute I think I already know something or think something is *not* for me or is really for everyone else (especially if I'm feeling self-righteous about it), I'm in the danger zone. It's a sign for me to pay extra attention. There's likely a blind spot and an opportunity that will change my game. If I'm willing to look, I can usually find a place where I'm not having the impact I want or I'm feeling pain—and trace it to the very idea or principle (or human) I'm resisting.

Two . . . If you are reading this for your team or organization, I get it. And please read it for you as well. One of the biggest questions I get is "How do I get others to do this?" Answer: You don't. You be it. They catch it. Voilà. You're contagious—they'll get it. Don't worry about them; it will come. At some point you may think, *Yeah, but not everyone is going to do this, believe this, be this, or even read this book! They might even think I'm woo-woo for talking about it! How do we do this if not everyone is on board?* That's true. You may be right. And no worries. A small amount of people can have a very large impact. *You* are mighty. Embrace. Embody. Adopt. Apply.

Three . . . If you are reading this with your team, good. The more, the merrier. When we work with organizations to integrate these ideas into their culture, they often find it doesn't take a lot of people to create change. Even the "naysayers" and skeptics can shift just by *being* in a different kind of energy and community. It's not uncommon for a skeptic to become an advocate. We've found that if we can get even 30 percent of the team or organization playing, it is *plenty* of mass to create a positive culture change. (And if 30 percent seems like a stretch, revisit point two above.)

If you get pushback, no worries. Let your knowingness be stronger than their doubt and keep doing you. (A skill we'll be discussing in Part 2.) Smile, bubble up, remember that your Intentional Energetic Presence is a superpower, and you're just getting started! Own it.

Let's Talk About You for a Minute

Some of you coming to this work are already bought in. Hungry for more even.

Some of you are on the fence, not sure if this energy, presence, and contagious stuff is for you. But you're curious. You're here.

Some of you resist this work entirely, even poo-pooing it or diminishing it, because what it takes to truly bust through your current leadership impact and presence may be very uncomfortable for you to be with; *energy, presence, vibration, feelings, vulnerability, soft stuff—in leadership? Where's the exit?* But . . . your people are *hoping* you might reconsider.

Some of you will be having none of this. Either it's not your cup of tea, or you don't care. It's OK. When you decide you want people to follow you because they *want* to versus *have* to, or when you get tired of walking around encountering resistance everywhere you go, this book will still be here.

And, of course, some of you are brand new to all of this. Welcome.

You care. A lot. About leadership and being your best. Wherever you landed in my assumptions above (I'm talking to you too, George), you care and you want to do and be better.

You have a full life. Maybe you have a partner, spouse, kids, aging parents, friends, dog, job, team, exercise routine, goldfish, etc., and you're trying to do it all. You want to lead, command respect, create great morale in your company, nurture others in their own development, have more energy, be fitter, be better, and be happier with the mounting pressure you feel in your life. And then you get to deal with "George," the guy who sucks the life out of the room and leaves dead bodies behind him everywhere he goes (often leaving you with cleanup duty). How do you do it?

I don't know exactly what you want or need, or what's right for you (though I might have some ideas), but I do know that what you desire is possible, and your challenges solvable, *if* you're willing to do the work and own your magic.

Wherever you are right now—top of your game, as CEO of a huge organization; middle of your game, being led *and* leading others at the same time; just getting started in your game and trying to figure out how to take the next step (or what the next step even is); or don't even know what your game is yet but know you want it to be a good one—this book will help.

Set your intention now for what you want to get out of this conversation. I'll do everything on my end to show up, do my part, and give you my best on these pages.

What We're Doing Here

The world needs more of you and your magic. And it needs it now. Some of the traditional ways of leading, while classic and important, aren't enough anymore. I'm going to give you new ones. (Everything I give you will only amplify your other leadership skills.)

Having a *big* impact requires that we show up. Showing up requires that we take a minute and show up for ourselves. This book offers that minute.

Take a breath, bask in your badassery for being willing to pick up a book that calls you "contagious," and trust that our meeting now is divine as we lean into another way of *thinking about, doing,* and *being* in leadership.

Nothing I offer will apply to only one domain of your life.

And nothing I share will be dependent on other people doing something for you or changing who they are or how they show up.

My intention? To help *you* access more of yourself, expand your leadership presence and range, accelerate your effectiveness, create more influence on the things and people you care about, navigate George with rigor and grace, create more space and ease in your own life, and inspire those you love and lead to step up with you.

Me and My 411

Who am I? I'm a mom, sister, daughter, friend, dog rescuer, and a lot more. I'm also a leadership and cultural advisor to business leaders and executives, having worked in many different spaces, including design and innovation, health care, education, hospitality, finance, government, tech, and more. I've served as an executive coach, advisor, teacher, speaker, and writer since 2002. I have training and credentials in coaching, leadership, intuitive work, relational health, and more. I have a degree in kinesiology, which is the science of the mechanics of human movement. And more than all this, I am just me.

I am a mom to a 14-year-old and 19-year-old, both of whom I love more than air and who've grown up with this work. I co-parent with their dad. We have a collaborative, caring, and respectful relationship.

(This, by the way, is a result of many of the principles and frameworks I'll share in this book. Yes, good news, this book is not just for business; it's for your personal life too!)

The IEP work has grown organically and significantly over the years. It doesn't matter the industry, age, gender, geography, or level of leadership—the results are indicative of the courage and willingness of people engaging in this content to show up for themselves and serve.

Common feedback we get from people includes, "I didn't know how good good could feel," or "I didn't realize that I wasn't happy or was having a negative impact," or "I didn't know that I was the common denominator in all my ails"; "until I did and owned there was so much more I could do/be/have." And "This work follows me home and everywhere I go. It makes me a better human (for me, my kids/spouse/people)." The more I teach this work, the more I experience these statements to be true for myself as well.

In this book I'll share new learning and work I've done in the field since the release of *Contagious Culture,* including working in education, with law enforcement, with the Navy, in health care, in design, in finance, in tech, with foster care, and yes, of course, in corporate culture and more. I've navigated sheep (literally and figuratively), taught others to teach this methodology, worked with government agencies, taught in colleges, spoken on stages around the world, participated in a think tank, worked with women in research, and on, on, and on. All while momming my "babies," honoring my own life and leadership, tending to my well-being, running my organization, and putting these principles to the test throughout. It's been a productive and heartfelt couple of years, and I'm excited to share new awarenesses, stories, and science in this work that I hold will support you in creating more value.

As with anything I write or speak about, this is all from the heart, offered without attachment to how you use it, or even *if* you use it. Use this as it resonates and at your pace.

I'm excited to be in this conversation with you. Thank you for reading my stuff and for being in the dance of *human* with me. And thank you for who you *be* in the world.

Play the game; choose your cause; lead . . .
Always with love,

Anese

P.S.: A few things you should know as we move forward . . . I write like I talk. I make up words. I sometimes pretend that you are sitting right here with me. I dream about you. I sometimes question if I should write books about being (positively) "contagious" and "showing up" (well) when I fall down in these areas all the time. Many of the stories shared here are mine. Some of them belong to others. I've purposefully blended a combination of professional and personal stories because it's all *one* life. All stories are real. Some have been modified to honor confidentiality; some are composites to give you the most relevant points and also honor the privacy of the people and organizations involved. For all of you who have shared and allowed me to tell your story—thank you. And for all of you who have contributed to mine; the good, the bad, the ugly, and the oh so doggone gorgeous—thank you.

How to Partner with This Book

This book is intended to be an active conversation. I want you thinking *with* me. In every chapter, you'll find inquiry or fieldwork. Do it. It will make these ideas even more personal to you. I've divided this book into five parts to help you tackle your stuff in your own authentic way. Use it as it serves you most. A reminder to read this book through the lens of *you*—not through the lens of what others may, or may not, be doing well. Do your own work. It will pay off.

You can read from start to finish, or dabble and dip in and out as you feel called. (Though I do find letting it build from front to back is helpful with this content.)

- **Part One: You.** Get in there. All you.
- **Part Two: Presence.** Own it; build it; protect it; use it.

- **Part Three: Relating**. Because relationships are everything and then some.
- **Part Four: Leadership**. Because if not you, who? (Besides, with Parts 1 to 3 under way, it gets easier from here.)
- **Part Five: Impact.** Because this is the whole darn point, right? Impact for you, impact for those you lead and love, and impact for our world.

Ready? Let's get contagious.

THE COST OF DISENGAGEMENT

FACTOID 1

Actively disengaged employees cost the United States an estimated $483 billion to $605 billion each year in lost productivity.[1]

FACTOID 2

As of 2016, 33 percent of U.S. employees are engaged at work, 51 percent are not engaged, and 16 percent are actively disengaged. (*Note:* In the world's best organizations 70 percent are engaged at work.[2])

FACTOID 3

When compared with business units in the bottom quartile of engagement, those in the top quartile realize improvements in the following areas: 41 percent lower absenteeism, 24 percent lower turnover (in high-turnover organizations), 59 percent lower turnover (in low-turnover organizations), 28 percent less shrinkage, 70 percent fewer employee safety incidents, 58 percent fewer patient safety incidents, 40 percent fewer quality incidents (defects), 10 percent higher customer metrics, 17 percent higher productivity, 20 percent higher sales, and 21 percent higher profitability.[3]

FACTOID 4

Only 21 percent of employees strongly agree their performance is managed in a way that motivates them to do outstanding work, 22 percent of employees strongly agree the leadership of their organization has a clear direction for the organization, and 15 percent of employees strongly agree the leadership of their organization makes them enthusiastic about the future. (*P.S.:* 51 percent of U.S. employees say they are actively looking for a new job or watching for openings.[4])

FACTOID 5

"According to Gallup polls, a full 50 percent of employees who quit cite their manager as the reason. People might join a company for the compensation, growth opportunities, or mission, but they frequently leave because they don't have a good relationship with their manager."[5]

Who do you think is keeping them engaged (or not)? (Hint: YOU.)

Some Interesting Numbers on Trust

- In its 2016 global CEO Survey, PwC reported that 55 percent of CEOs think that a lack of trust is a threat to their organization's growth. But most have done little to increase trust, mainly because they aren't sure where to start.[6]
- In a 2016 study conducted in the United States, data showed that people at high-trust companies had 74 percent less stress than people at low-trust companies, 106 percent more energy at work, 50 percent higher productivity, 13 percent fewer sick days, 76 percent more engagement, 40 percent less burnout, 11 percent more empathy for—and 41 percent less depersonalization of—workmates, and 41 percent greater sense of accomplishment.[7]

Behaviors That Create Collaboration and Trust or Protection and Aversion in Engagement

- Concern for others, being truthful about what's on our mind, stimulating discussion/curiosity, painting a picture of mutual success, and being open to difficult conversations are all oxytocin-producing behaviors. (Oxytocin is a feel-good hormone that elevates our ability to communicate, collaborate, and trust others.[8])

- Not trusting others' intentions, being focused on convincing others, others not understanding, pretending to be listening, and having emotions that detract from listening are all cortisol-producing behaviors. (Cortisol is a hormone that shuts down the thinking center of our brains and activates conflict aversion and protection behaviors.[9])

All of these points relate to how we show up with each other, how we create contraction or expansion in relationships, and how we use our contagiousness for good . . . or not.

We are the common denominator.

We are contagious.

CONTAGIOUS
YOU

PART 1

CONTAGIOUS YOU: CLAIM YOUR POWER

CHAPTER 1

You Are Contagious. Own It.

Your contagiousness is a superpower.
With great power comes great response-ability.

Claim it. Work it. And use it for good.

Have you ever noticed you can be in a great mood, feel on top of the world, on your game, ready to rock your day, and thinking people are amazing—until you run into *that* person, and suddenly you're exhausted, the world seems dimmer, and people aren't so great after all? Or you can be in a foul mood, feeling tired, irritated, and like everything is hard—and then you run into that *other* person, and suddenly life feels good and bright and people are wonderful again? Have you noticed you have the ability to influence other people's outlooks, decisions, and moods—not necessarily through the words you say, but through your presence and the intentions behind your words? Or that you can change the mood of a room by the energy you bring into it (for good or bad)? Or that you can be in a meeting that feels great and productive but you have one negative person in there—and before you know it, the whole meeting sucks?

Have you noticed you can "vibe" with someone right off the bat, liking and trusting that person instantly—or feel repelled by him or her just as fast? And have you ever noticed the feeling you get when you stand in front of a group, sense the energy in the room, and feel strong and powerful (or anxious and small)?

3

Have you ever noticed that a smiling person can make you smile? Or that a scowling person can bum you out? Or that one kind word can shift your mood, fill you up, and have you paying that kindness forward all day to everyone you meet?

In my experience most of us can relate to these scenes in our lives. Why? Because we are human. And we're contagious. Our intentions, energy, presence, and state of being are all contagious.

We put energy out there; we take energy on. This happens at work, at home, at the coffee shop, on the train, and everywhere else we go. Whatever we put out there and whatever we take on affects our ability to influence, lead, and create the impact we want.

So the real question becomes: What kind of contagious do you want to be? What do you want to put out there? What do you want to take on? And in service of what? Let's go.

Max and the Magic Culture List

I'd just given a keynote to a group in an industry essential to our future about "Creating a (Positively) Contagious Culture." I got off stage, signed books, said my hellos, and was in a conversation with an audience member when *that guy*, we'll call him "Max," showed up.

Cutting to the front, interrupting our conversation, smirking, with a quick clip to his voice, he offered me this: "Anese, you did a good job. All the people here needed to hear your message. I already knew it, but they needed it, so good job." He shook my hand and planted. I could feel the "but" coming (you know the energy of "but," right?). So could the person I'd been talking with. Her energy shifted, and she stepped back. She seemed to get "smaller," tentative. She watched us with what felt like a blend of curiosity and frustration.

"I have some feedback for you, Anese. Anese, I hope you can take it." Abrasive *with* a smile. I took a breath and secured my space. "Anese" (was he attempting to bond by using my name?), I would have liked it more if you would have talked about culture and how to create it. You know. You mentioned it, but you went 'culture light' on us. I was waiting for you to tell us what to actually *dooo*. It'd be much more powerful if you just told us how to *dooo* culture. We need a

4

punch list, not a talk about how we show up. We need action, Anese. Not the soft stuff. Where's the list?"

Gruff. Passionate. Standing for his point.

I got his point.

He'd missed mine.

I'd experienced him in the room that morning and also in a meeting the day before. His arms crossed, brows furrowed, ongoing sidebars while others spoke, a curt condescending tone in the room when he talked, cutting people off, interrupting my discussion now. The culture he was creating was palpable. And contagious.

Max was *that* guy.

And he wanted *the list.*

People want *the list*: the Culture Change Checklist, the Relationship Fixer, the Trust Builder, the Leadership Enhancer, or the Lose Ten Pounds list—all magically bulleted shortcut lists of things to do to create the results they want. I get it.

Unfortunately, as amazing as any "list" may be, if we show up badly—if our intentions, energy, and presence are not on point—that list is nothing special and can even do more harm than good. There are not enough action steps, checklists, to-dos, or cultural perks in the world to override how we make people feel and the energy we create with ourselves and other human beings.

The "soft stuff" that Max was so desperate to discount is what actually sets the tone.

It's the gold.

(Fret not. I'll give you "the list" later in this book. However, you won't need it by the time we're done here.)

I took a breath, held my space, and located some gratitude for him in my system.

"Max, I love this question!" (I did.) "I understand your request. I can give you the 'punch sheet'; that's easy. Happy to. However, a punch sheet will only take you about 10 percent of the way there."

"Huh? Come again?"

"In this work, and I bet your people would agree, we've found that the other 90 percent is what counts most. The 'soft stuff.' It's how *you* make people feel. It's how you set the tone for optimal productivity,

5

thinking, and contribution. It's the quality of your presence, the container you hold with them, the safety you create. How you show up in a room: your intentions, your energy, your regard, *that* is the culture. *You* are the culture."

"Great! Got it! Here's my card, Anese; send me that punch list!" He gave me his card, shook my hand, patted my shoulder, gave me a big smile (I think he winked), and he was off.

The woman I had been talking to, one of Max's employees, looked at me and said, "Of all the people in that room, I wish he would have heard you. Max is the reason people in our organization keep quitting. Maybe you should write a book that teaches *us* how to handle the 'Maxes' better."

Setting the Tone

You walk into a room and either you can set the tone and bring the energy up, or you can trash it. Quickly. You can create the space for honesty and vulnerability, or you can get people to armor up fast. You can be in a conversation and make it awesome, or a drag. You can talk about another human being and make that person sound and feel like the most amazing person in the world, or the worst. You can stand in front of people and feel powerful and real, or scared and fake. You can give your kids courage and belief, or freak them out. You can make your staff feel seen and cared for and championed, or like a vehicle to get stuff done for you. You can make your loved ones and partner feel grand, or small. You can look at your calendar and be overwhelmed and busy, or grateful and on purpose. You can make any situation feel like the end of the world, or like the beginning (even though it may be intensely painful or horrible in the moment). You can be an invitation to engage, or a repellent.

How? With your *energetic presence* and what you bring into that room, conversation, or situation. Research shows that we decide within a *tenth* of a second if we like people, trust them, and sense they're competent. Some people say it's 7 seconds (I even found someone who says it's 27), but the research that I found most consistent and resonant says it's 1/10 of a second.[1]

For example, in one study done on "first impressions" at Princeton University, Janine Willis and Alexander Todorov[2] ran a series of experiments investigating the minimal amount of time it takes for people to make trait inferences from looking at an unfamiliar face. They explored participants judging for *attractiveness, likability, trustworthiness, competence,* and *aggressiveness.*

What did they find? "For all five of the traits studied, judgments made after the briefest exposure (1/10 of a second) were highly correlated with judgments made *without* time constraints; and increased exposure time (1/2 of a full second) did not significantly increase the correlation. Response times also revealed that participants made their judgments as quickly (if not more quickly) after seeing a face for 1/10 of a second as they did if given a longer glimpse."[3]

Even more, when exposure time was increased from one-tenth to one-half of a second, participants' judgments only "became more negative, response times for judgments decreased, and confidence in judgments increased." Increasing it further to 1 second (1,000 milliseconds) generally only boosted confidence in the initial judgments; however, it also allowed for more differentiated trait impressions.

At the end of the day, all correlations for the five traits were high, but trustworthiness was the highest (with attractiveness right behind it).

So what does this mean?

We have one-tenth of a second! We generally make our first impression (and perceive others) within one-tenth of a second, we assess most accurately and quickly for trustworthiness and attractiveness, and the longer we have with our exposure further increases our confidence in judgment while facilitating even more impressions.

One-tenth of a second, seven seconds, whatever! How we show up matters, and it creates impact faster than we realize!

And wait; there's more . . .

In addition to what's happening with our brains and quick decision making, the heart and our electromagnetic fields are at play too. Emotional energetics research (by the HeartMath Institute) states:

The heart produces by far the body's most powerful rhythmic electromagnetic field, which can be detected several feet away by sensitive instruments. Research shows our heart's field changes distinctly as we experience different emotions. It is registered in people's brains around us and apparently is capable of affecting cells, water and DNA studied in vitro. Growing evidence also suggests energetic interactions involving the heart may underlie intuition and important aspects of human consciousness.[4]

Bottom line? There are things happening in our brains, hearts, physiology, and the collective energetic field that help us set the tone, manage our contagiousness, and intend our impact. (I'll talk more about the "science of showing up" in Chapter 8.)

You can design for impact and show up *intentionally* by cultivating what I call your Intentional Energetic Presence® (IEP). Our intentions, energy, and presence all work together to influence what's happening in any situation. We are at every moment creating our experience, setting the tone, and cocreating the energetic field with any human we engage with.

Just as someone with positive IEP can walk into a room, light it up, and make it feel amazing, someone else can walk in, low vibe with negative and yucky energy, and bring the whole house down. We get to decide which vibe we'll take on. We can *be* contagious and spread the good (or the nasty), and we can also *choose* not to be the victim of someone else's contagiousness (the good or the nasty).

This is a decision. It takes awareness. Self-care. And a *decision to choose* what experience we want to create and what tone we want to set.

We set the tone—every day.

We set the tone for the office on Monday morning, in the meeting we have that we're scared to lead, and in our feedback session with our boss or employee, as we begin that new client project, and as we prepare our sales report or annual taxes. We set the tone at home, at our parent-teacher conference, for the conversation with our kid, for the conflict we're navigating with our spouse, and as we do the dishes. And we set the tone throughout the rest of our lives, for the conversation we have at Sunday brunch with girlfriends, as we get on the packed early-morning flight, as we respond to news and current events, as we decide how to engage in social media, as we intend our day before we even get out of bed. We set the tone. Everywhere. We create the experience. We become a force for good, or bad.

And if we didn't set it? And someone else "got there first," we can absolutely change it. The person with the strongest purpose and intention, cleanest presence, and highest vibration wins.

I'm going to teach you how to be *that* person.

So, What Is "Contagious"?

*"People will forget what you said, people will forget
what you did . . . but people will never forget
how you made them feel."*
—MAYA ANGELOU

The *Oxford English Dictionary* defines "contagious" as "(1) (of a disease) spread from one person or organism to another, typically by direct contact, and (2) (of an emotion, feeling, or attitude) likely to spread to and affect others."

Simply put, contagious means *something*, a disease or an emotion, feeling, or attitude that can be spread from one person to another by direct or indirect contact that is likely to spread and affect others. For good or bad.

Great news, this is all your choice. And whatever you decide will be contagious.

After doing this work for over twenty years, this is my formula for contagious:

$$\frac{\left(\text{actions}\right)}{\left(\dfrac{\text{emotions} \times \text{intention}}{\text{presence} \times \text{self-care}}\right)} = \text{CONTAGION FACTOR}$$

FIGURE 1.1   Contagion Factor Formula™

9

The more clear, positive, and helpful the emotion and intent, and the greater the presence and self-care—the higher the vibration and the more good it will do.

The more ambiguous or negative the intent and emotion, and the lesser the presence and self-care—the lower the vibration and the less good (or more bad) it will do.

With no emotion, no intent, no presence, no self-care . . . *meh*.

And of course, the action happens on top of all of it.

This plays out all the time. That guy sitting next to you in your meeting (that sucked) yesterday was contagious (crossed arms + eye rolls/boredom × intention to get out of here/exhausted negative vibe = energy suck). The lady next to me in the hotel lobby where I'm currently holed up writing this chapter is contagious (fortunately in a really great way: smile/happy to see another human/positive energetic vibe = lucky me). The woman who mad-dogged me at the gym today, contagious. Me smiling back at her saying "Good morning!" and not catching her vibe, but rather changing the field with mine, contagious. There's no getting around it.

We're either catching stuff from others or putting it out there for them to catch, and usually a lot of both.

Our emotional states, attitudes, presence, characteristics, and ultimately our actions are all contagious. Courage is contagious, busyness is contagious. Kindness and accountability are contagious, as are complaining and blaming. Vulnerability and risk taking, judgment and contempt, apathy and abdication, positivity and gratitude, negativity and entitlement, generosity, greed, grit—you name it—they're all contagious.

Our contagiousness impacts our ability to connect with, lead, and influence others.

It can be used for good or for evil.

It can be spread intentionally or unintentionally.

It's never ending; it doesn't stop.

It applies to all of us.

How are you contagious? What do you put "out there"? What impact do you create by the way you show up? Are you an invitation? Are you life-giving or soul-sucking? Do you feel good to be around?

Do you create breath and expansion for people? Do you create resistance and contraction? Do people feel safe with you, or do they feel careful? Are you full of possibility? Or are you Debbie Downer?

The leadership is in how we decide to use our superpowers here.

The Real Remedy Is Not to Fix "Them"

What happened with Max in my opening story is not a new problem. Max is not a bad guy. In fact, I love this story, as it demonstrates a common speed, lack of awareness, and earnest quest to have the magic pill that handles impact and culture.

We've all been Max (you might even be someone's Max right now and not even know it): self-focused, distracted, moving fast, "busy," complaining, sucking the air out of the room, having unintended impact, being negatively contagious . . . There's rarely poor intent. Being Max is human. And often Max just needs a minute . . .

In our go-go-go world, taking the time to consider our impact or that "I may be the issue—or at least contributing to it" is often considered a luxury—if it's considered at all. The idea of "how I show up energetically," or "that I create the culture with my presence," is outside what people have traditionally focused on, let alone been rewarded for, in building their business and culture. Add to this that the soft stuff, and even our self-care, has a huge impact on our presence, trustworthiness, and credibility and we're into new territory for leadership development and culture work.

Max was *being* the culture in that room. Max was contagious. He was contagious in our conversation too. This scene was a microcosm of the bigger context of Max and that particular team. After spending just a few hours with the members of the team, I understood why they'd brought me in.

The remedy was not to spend their energy on changing "Max." It was to nourish and strengthen their own leadership awareness, presence, and abilities so that they could lead more powerfully, stay on track, give clean feedback and direction, and influence the Maxes of the world more effectively.

While they'd initially wanted me to "get through" to Max, I really needed to get through to the rest of the team in a new way.

Contemplating feedback for that group on the way to the airport that afternoon, I got a call from another high-level executive I'd worked with the month before. She was "done" with the soft stuff and energy and hearing about showing up with her people. She *got it*. She wanted me to just tell her what to *do* to fix her team and her culture so she could be "done with all this culture stuff" and get down to business once and for all. She was frustrated. Shouldn't it be fixed by now?

Nope. Not at all.

She was still showing up "badly" and in a way that was creating resistance for people (for personal reasons the team was not privy to), and the team members, despite integrating the IEP work in many other ways for themselves and with each other, were still trying to figure out how to work around her. The defensive and punitive ways she'd handled feedback in the past had them terrified to give it to her now, and she wasn't honoring her agreements with them to change it. Her trust and credibility were at an all-time low, and sensing this just made her more determined to "make it go away." Add to this that her fellow directors and employees had a really hard time "holding their space with her," and, no, this situation wasn't going anywhere good anytime soon. As long as this dynamic was in play, they'd never "fix" the culture.

There was more work to do here. While I could continue to work with her personally on this, I was clear that the members of the team needed additional tools as well to support them in being able to manage themselves and navigate her better. This was similar to what I'd seen earlier that day with Max.

Again, the solution was not to "fix" her; it was to engage the others, who were open to doing the work, with more tools. If they could get even a small group of them holding a healthy vibration on the team, they'd be able to determine productive next steps and more effective ways to stand in the feedback and hold their space. They'd also be more enrolling as a positively contagious invitation than as a team trying to "work around" her.

It didn't guarantee that she'd change, but short of her deciding to show up better, it would be their best bet. See, here's the beauty . . . you don't have to have everyone on board to make a positive leadership or cultural change (and definitely not to make your own life better or easier)—you just need you. One person can do a lot. It's lovely if everyone is on board, and way easier for sure, and in my experience I've found that *one* person can make a huge difference and having even 30 percent of your team on board is enough to start the positively contagious revolution.

Being positively contagious, holding your space, and doing your work does not guarantee Max comes on board, but it does guarantee that *you* are better equipped to lead and rise above (if you so choose). It's also the best chance you've got at being an invitation for Max to shift, and creating a healthy dynamic, culture, and life. Because you can't "fix" Max. But you can rock you.

Here's the thing . . . your present-day results and circumstances are a product of the decisions you've made, work you've done, ways you've shown up for yourself and others, the quality of your leadership, and your ability to manage your contagiousness to this point.

Your impact on this planet, your ability to influence others and to create what you want (money, trust, love, that promotion, solid results, authentic relationships, loyal employees, an awesome culture, a kickass business model, great abs, more joy), depends on the decisions you'll make, what you'll do, who you'll be, how you'll take care of yourself, and how you'll lead moving forward.

Contagious Culture gave readers a head start in setting the tone for a healthier and more positively contagious culture.

Contagious You will help you unlock more superpowers for being an even bigger force for your life.

Wait. This Is on Me? I Create the Culture?

After working with countless people, teams, organizations, and industries, I've learned that leadership and culture are something that we *be*, not that we *do*. The being, which I hold as our intentions, energy, and presence, is like food coloring in water—you can't separate the being from the doing. It infuses and colors everything. It's contagious. The doing is important, absolutely—but the being is what people respond to and are inspired or repelled by. At the end of the day, if we lead intentionally with the being and doing working together well, we're more likely to have a positive impact.

It is easier to put culture out there—to hold culture as something to be done or something that everyone else is responsible for. Holding culture as internal—something that you are and that you are accountable for—can be confronting. It requires you to be present and aware. It requires connection with others. It requires vulnerability. And it requires self-reflection and accountability posing the questions: "How am I showing up to create the experience I'm having? How am I contributing to my situation? What help might I need?" And "Might I be like Max?" It also offers that whether you love or don't love your culture, life, relationships, or results—it's on you. You are cocreating it.

This is a tremendous gift and superpower, and like any good superpower it comes with opportunity, and also great responsibility.

How we show up, how we own our leadership, how we treat people, how we honor and take care of ourselves, how we get support where we need it, how we think, how we take responsibility for our energy and presence, and how comfortable we can be with our discomfort—this is all part of good leadership.

Leadership is not solely related or limited to formal roles or rank in your organization. You do not have to be formally deemed "leader" to lead. When I speak of leadership, I am speaking to any human who is leading their life. Period.

Good leadership creates good culture (at work, at home, and everywhere in between).

To be a good leader we want to be *usefully* contagious (not just positively, but usefully). There are skills, tricks, frameworks, methods, and all sorts of good to support us in leading well and in being so. And considering our usefulness and the impact we create through our contagiousness is a solid place to start.

The foundation of this all starts with our intentions, energy, and presence and our IEP. Our impact begins with how we show up.

No matter what I do, what I teach, what I write, what framework or model I create, or how I work with anyone—including myself and my own team—I don't know a better way to create healthy leadership and congruent living than to start with each of us individually taking responsibility for who we are being, our IEP, what we do, the tone we set, and the culture we create with all of it.

We Impact, and Are Impacted by, Contagiousness Every Day

It's not often that we talk about energetic presence, or intention, or vibrational energy, or contagiousness in leadership and impact. Yet we are dealing with it all the time, in every moment. In my experience it's the "thing" that is often "off" about people or situations that people have a hard time identifying or giving feedback on. It's intangible but it packs a punch.

If you've ever been in a meeting and you've felt the room get tense or the energy drop—you know vibrational energy, energetic presence, and contagiousness.

If you've ever been in a good mood, talked to someone who was not, and then felt yourself get tired, contracted, or somehow affected by their presence—you know vibrational energy and contagiousness.

If you've ever walked into a room and felt magic, a buzz, a vibe, or a frequency that said "Yes!" without even knowing why yet—you know energy, presence, and contagiousness.

If you've ever walked into a room and felt heavy and tired and like you wanted to get out fast—you know energy, presence, and contagiousness.

You know energy. You experience it. You project it yourself. It is ever present. And it is contagious.

It doesn't matter what you call it, only that you're aware of it and know how to work with it.

How Vibrational Energy, Energetic Presence, and Contagiousness Play Out

Jack walks into the room for a meeting with six other business leaders. The energy is good. They're all excited to be there. There's one guy, Bob, who's not excited to be there at all. They feel him. The other five, and Jack, are good to go. Jack takes note, asks Bob how he is ("Fine"), and keeps going. Within five minutes, three of the original happy six are lower energy. Within 12 minutes, the meeting is flat. By the time they leave an hour later, that meeting sucked—big time. (Proving Bob's point that meetings are useless. Hmmmm.)

Bob was contagious. He powerfully impacted six other beings with his presence. They matched his energy. Ironically, they're not aware of what actually happened—except that "the energy was low" and "meetings blow."

Carrie wants to have more impact. She makes a point in every meeting to show up, speak up, give her opinion, and make sure people know that she's there and that she's contributing. It's not going so hot. When we do her feedback, via an interactive 360-style process, we find that her presence is experienced as aggressive and distracting; it creates "chaos." She's confused. That's not her intention.

We get clear on her intentions. Part of the reason she speaks up is because she wants to be *seen as* valuable, not because she wants to be value-added or to serve. Ah, easy! The next meeting Carrie goes into, she practices pure presence—being in the room fully focused on being of service and only speaking when she can share something that will truly help. She speaks up one time. The energy in the room flows. People are calm, speaking with presence and as needed. Carrie gets four texts afterward praising her for how helpful she was in the room and how powerful her presence was.

Carrie started out being contagious in a way that was self-serving and negative and created resistance. With some awareness and a small tweak in intention, her contagiousness shifted to being positive and of service.

Julie gets together with her girlfriends for dinner. She's excited to see them. She's feeling good. They sit down. Order drinks. Do a quick round of catch-ups. The vibe is good. And then . . . Jody kicks in. She is talking about Sara. Sara's not there. The vibe shifts. Jody starts complaining. The other three join in—one by one. The energy gets yucky. This lovely meal has turned into gossip, complaining, and a tense contracted conversation. Everyone leaves feeling dirty.

Jody was contagious—her girlfriends caught it and spread it.

Steve and Sara are at the airport. Their flight gets delayed. Then delayed again. Ruh roh! They watch as people react. One group reacts with blame, anger, agitation—one guy kicks a pole and says, "You guys *suck*!" The other group reacts with, "C'est la vie! Travel! Let's get a glass of wine and figure out next steps. And oh, by the way—thank you, airline people, for trying to help."

Sara and Steve have a choice to make—how shall they respond? What experience will they create for themselves? What reaction will they catch? What will they spread? They choose "C'est la vie!" and go for wine. They have a lovely delay.

Company Z is going through some changes. Big ones. Scary ones. They'll mean shifts in personnel, locations, and policies. They're not sure how big yet. These changes will also mean some ambiguity for a while (maybe forever). Ambiguity breeds contagion; good or bad, healthy or toxic. Which types grow fastest are up to the people leading (aka *you*). Some people choose to go down the path of pain—negativity, blame, gossip, and spreading the worst-case scenario story. It spreads fast. It doesn't take long. Before you know it, the situation is worse, and since humans are evidence-gathering machines, the fear goes viral.

There's another smaller group of people, though, that decide to do everything they can to "help things go right"—or at least better. They "hold their space" (not participating in the negativity), get curious, and ask people for clarity when they hear assumptions being made. They also point out the possible gifts and focus on staying present and creating results. While this group starts out smaller, they grow together as a team and create a much better experience for themselves.

In the end, when the ambiguity clears up a bit and things have settled, the people in the first group—the negative—are exhausted and depleted and are carrying their heavy stories everywhere they go. The people in the second group—the positively contagious who chose to create a healthier experience—are energized and grateful and are looking forward to digging in and getting to work.

Both groups were contagious—one positively, one negatively. They all chose what they wanted to take on and put out. The experiences of the two groups were significantly different—even though they had the same circumstances to deal with.

Familiar? Each of these scenarios has a "choice point" in which the people around the lower contagions could choose something different. In some cases they did, and in others they were negatively "infected."

This happens every day—at the grocery store, coffee shop, your kids' school; among teachers, doctors, nurses, staff; and with your clients, vendors, team members, and your boss. It's also in your family dynamics; among your friends; on social media; in politics, business, current events, natural disasters, and financial ventures. Just look around you—feel around you—and you'll feel it; everything is contagious.

You catch and spread what you are committed to.

What are you committed to?

If you want to lead well, influence others, and create results, it matters that you are aware of your commitments. It also matters how you use your contagiousness, how you shift it, and how you protect yourself when people throw their stuff your way (which is why we're having this conversation).

Your Contagiousness Is a Superpower

We're talking about superpowers here. Did you know you have them?

Your first superpower?

Being contagious. Yep.

You *are* contagious. I *am* contagious. So is everyone else.

We can't help it—we just are. (There is science behind this—lots of it! Our brain, heart, coherence, and collective energetic fields all create contagiousness—more on this later.)

Being contagious is also a coachable skill. Just like sports stars have their coaches to help them focus on performance and recovery, contagiousness in leadership can be coached.

We invite or repel people with our contagiousness.

We create what we want, or what we don't want, with our contagiousness.

We have control of *ourselves* and *our own contagiousness.*

We have no control of theirs. We do have the power to decide what we'll "take on" and "catch."

The ability to do this is another superpower. These superpowers are some of the most fundamental leadership assets we'll ever have. We must use them well.

Here's your first lesson, Superhero: At the root of your contagiousness are your intentions, energy, and presence, and your Intentional Energetic Presence (your IEP). You control all of these things. They're yours; nobody can do them for you; no one can take them away. Make any of them better, and you level-up your ability to create influence.

Here are three questions to ask yourself to upgrade your results and contagiousness factor.

Start now. (This is part of the IEP Method® we'll dig into in Part 2.)

- What experience do I want to create? (This can be with a project, conversation, workout, anything.) Why? What's important about this to me? (What and whom does it serve?)
- How am I showing up? Are my intentions, energy, and presence supporting my desired experience? (The intention is what you want to have happen, the energy is the energy and stamina you're bringing to it, and your presence is how present you are and what you're projecting in this moment.)
- What's the littlest (or biggest) thing I can do to shift things in the right direction? (This may be a small tweak in IEP, or a decision you need to make, or a breath you need to take. It could also be a time-out, a truth that needs to be spoken, a mindset shift, or accessing gratitude—anything.)

Powerful little questions—do not underestimate them.

Meet "George" and "Mary"

When I wrote *Contagious Culture*, I set out to show the world that we are the culture. (By the way, if you have not read that book, I invite you to grab a copy. It will help you in the areas of leadership and culture in ways that this book will not, just as this book will support you in ways that one will not. I wrote them to be BFFs and work together forever.) Culture is not only created out there—it is mostly created in here (within each of us). How we show up in our intentions, energy, and presence (our IEP) creates that culture.

As people read that book, they were excited, surprised, often relieved, and sometimes challenged, to step into "I am the culture" and to show up in a way that created the culture they wanted to be a part of. They realized that this impacted culture everywhere—not just in their organization, but in their family, on the soccer team, in their community, in the classroom. Anywhere there were humans to be impacted or working together, culture was created. And they were the culture.

Two things happened (*very* generally speaking). The first group (most people) who read the book were excited, embraced it, and ran with it, building and strengthening their IEP and optimizing their leadership presence and impact. We'll call this group "Mary" (or "Marvin"). The second group (by my estimation about 20 to 30 percent of readers) thought the book and this idea of "I am the culture" didn't apply to them, called it "soft stuff" and "fluff," and went about their merry way. We'll call this group "George" (or "Georgette").

The Marys really wished the Georges would reconsider their "This doesn't apply to me, and it's silly" stance because in most cases it was the Georges who were making the Marys' lives harder. Marys were having to work around Georges. (Sometimes Marys were even married to Georges so it was extra personal.) This is not surprising. It lines up with what I've seen in my work with leadership and cultural change: People who can most benefit from this content are often the most resistant. And often the ones who adopt it readily and want more of it, don't need it as much, use it for optimization, and ultimately end up needing it even more to handle the Georges of the world.

At the end of the day, it doesn't really matter who said or did what—what matters is that whether we're showing up as George or Mary, we are all contagious. We can use that contagiousness for good or evil, to create magic or pain, and to help things go better or worse.

While *Contagious Culture* focused on you and the culture, this book is focused more deeply on *you, you, you*, which of course will serve your culture even more.

George or Mary?

George

What I've noticed in this work is that George (or Georgette) often doesn't know he (or she) is George and so they don't reach out for help or even pick up books to support them on being more positively contagious. I've also learned that we all have a little George in us from time to time, and that the Georges of the world, also have a little Mary in them from time to time. Either way, in the land of awareness it's helpful to know.

So how do you know?

Let's talk to George first . . .

George, I love you. We have some work to do in this book. But first, let's chat.

George, you are the person who comes up to me after keynotes to say (or leaves thinking), "This doesn't apply to me; I've got this. My team needs this." And "So how do I create a healthy culture? I need the list" after you've sat in a room with me, not present, rolling your eyes, having side conversations, and texting your heart away because this isn't for you. Meanwhile your team and at least three people in the audience (and maybe even your spouse) have told me how grateful they are you're going to get exposure to these ideas and please make sure you "get them" because you are the person they're struggling with. (Only you think this doesn't apply to you, George.)

If this is at all familiar to you—or triggering—as you read this, then *yay*. I've hit a button, which means there may be gold here. The questions to ask yourself now are: "Is this me? Might I be George? What do I want/need?"

The first sign will be this one: This scenario made you slightly uncomfortable. And if you were actually in a room with me over the past few years, you may now be wondering "who ratted me out?"

21

Even more, if you're sensing you may be George, this may feel a little tender. (That's good; let's do this.)

Other ways to know if you're George:

1. **You're not having the impact you want to have right now in your life or career—or both.** This might mean you're not growing at the pace you want to grow; you haven't gotten the promotion yet; or you're not being accepted into a program or business circle you want to be a part of. It could also mean you still don't have the relationship you want; your kids don't want to hang out with you; or you haven't hit "that" goal yet—still.

2. **People don't talk to you proactively or openly.** They may be careful around you. They don't seek out opportunities to engage. They talk about you behind your back (maybe you hear about it or just sense it). They don't want to hang out with you. You may chalk this up to "I'm too cool" or "I'm a leader" or "I'm intimidating"—but that's not it. They're avoiding you or being careful with you for a reason.

3. **You don't feel the way you want to feel.** You're tired, burnt out, not inspired, or resenting your work schedule or the humans in your life. You don't have joy or energy or excitement. You feel alone. (This doesn't mean you are George, but this is often reported by George when he and I sit down together and get *real*.)

4. **People follow you/work with you/hang with you/stay married to you because they have to, not because they want to.** This relates closely to #2, but is deeper. They're on your team because you're their boss. They go to dinner or lunch with you because they have to. They do their job because you pay them. But, oh, guess what? They're not giving you 100 percent or their best creativity. And they're definitely not going to go out on a limb with you. You might feel like they're on your team, but they don't have your back and they're not fully engaged. They don't answer your calls after work hours because they don't have to, and they don't want to.

5. **Your culture is not great, or not ideal, and you blame everyone around you for it.** You don't own it. You think it's all externally driven—not about you. (You got them the free lunches and put in the Ping-Pong table after all; what the heck?) You may feel superior about this and wonder why people can't just do their jobs—after all, you don't pay them to be happy.

6. **People avoid or resist you.** They push back on your agendas, react unenthusiastically to your ideas, turn down your invitations, and give you that obligatory"yes" only because they have to.

Is this you? Don't freak out—because every single one of these scenarios and points can totally be figured out and can be changed *quickly*, if you're willing to make that decision and do a bit of work around it.

The beautiful thing about being George is that *you* are in the power seat.

Mary

Hi love, you're doing it. You're showing up well. You're having great impact. You know you're contagious and do everything you can to be positively so. You might still relate to or answer "yes" to some of the questions above for George—but you're on your way. You have awareness and desire. Go, Mary!

Here maybe are some things you're dealing and dancing with.

Well, first, if you read the George scenario and it was familiar or made you sad or super-excited that I'm talking to George because you really want to have a better relationship with George—maybe you've been spending a lot of time, energy, and bandwidth managing him or her or them or your emotions around all of it; well, *hello*.

Here are some other indicators:

1. **You're exhausted, Mary. Wiped out.** Running around being positively contagious and finding the gifts in things and managing the negative vibes that go with life and just surviving day-to-day—forget thriving—it's exhausting.

23

2. **You actually are very clear that you are Mary because you know George, and he is tough.** You work with George— maybe you work for him or he works for you. Or maybe he's a client, or he's just an audience member, or he's that grumpy checker at the grocery store who every time you see him and get stuck in his checkout lane you walk away feeling crappy. Despite all your efforts to "go high when he goes low"—it ain't working. You need a stronger "bubble" and more resiliency just to navigate your days.

3. **You have so much to do—a "richly scheduled" life** (not "busy" because you read *Contagious Culture* and we're good here). It is rich and full, and how the heck are you going to keep this up? You have kids, work, workouts, yoga, food prep, the PTA, your leadership team, the neighborhood watch, dating maybe, a marriage to nourish (maybe), or an ex-spouse to co-parent with (maybe). You have a house or apartment to run, a schedule and finances to manage, and bad habits to break (maybe, but damn, Anese, they're all I've got!!). You also have a team to manage and inspire, friends to keep engaged, and in all of this, people you love and lead to make feel seen, valued, and important. Where is the time, energy, and band-width to do this all well? (There's no perfect formula here, and I'll share some of my tricks for navigating these as we go.)

4. **You want to have *more* impact. Do more good in the world. Make more money. Have more time. You just want to be better.** I'm with you. Let's do this thing. So much for us to talk about. This book, and me? We're going to be your new best friend. Buy a highlighter and journal, please, and treat this book as a living document. On it!

5. **You're daunted by all the negativity and challenge in the world right now (and who are we kidding, always?).** Political crises; global warming (or the fight about it); fires and other natural disasters; education; diversity; gender inclusiveness; political correctness; social media and "neighborhood watch" apps where people just put the "ick" into the

threads hiding out in their virtual camouflage and anonymity; the future your kids are growing up in; your retirement fund (or lack of) *and* college fund for kiddos (or lack thereof); homelessness; hunger; abuse; and on and on and on . . . It's daunting. You feel the weight of the world in responsibility. You can only do so much. And if it feels a little like "why bother?" and being "contagious," who cares? But I promise you, it all matters; it all counts; that *little* thing you do *is big*. There is support for you here.

6. **Your boundaries suck or leave a lot to be desired.** You have a hard time saying no; you really want to please; you want everyone happy. Oh, and you're a rock star with serious multitasking and problem-solving skills so everyone comes to you because you will not let anyone down. (Unless you're in the emergency room or on exhaustion leave—and even then they allow computers in hospitals, right?)

Any of these indicate that you could be Mary (or George) or even a bit of both. There are more indicators (listed in the assessment in Chapter 2), and we get it, right?

Your job, right now, is to simply claim where you are. No muss, no fuss, no drama. It's just information.

Here's the thing. Once you claim your contagiousness and own it—you are the sole owner of your superpower—*no one* can take it away from you. Especially if you nourish it, amplify it, protect it, optimize it, grow it, use it with intention, use it for good in the world, and spread it big time.

Because that's what being contagious is all about.

Claiming Your Contagiousness

Ready to claim it, baby? It's big.

We are all George or Mary at different times.

I personally have absolutely been Mary (more and more as I choose and practice). And guess what? I've also been George. (As recently as yesterday. I told you, work in progress.)

25

Having awareness, claiming our contagiousness, and owning our impact are the first steps in using our superpowers for good. We've got to love up the good and the bad, the light and the dark. Nothing I write or teach—ever—is about only being happy and light, rah rah and perfect. No. No "spiritual bypassing" when you hang out with me. The good, the bad, the beautiful, the ugly—we honor all parts.

Seventy percent of this work is in awareness. If you have awareness, you have power. No awareness? You have suffering and struggle. Ignorance is bliss only because you don't realize how much pain you're in (or what a Georgette you are) until you have awareness. Once you have awareness, you get to decide to change things. It may be painful, but suffer and struggle no more. Because while pain is inevitable and part of life and change—suffering and struggle is supremely optional.

So . . . awareness first.

CHAPTER 2

Awareness Is Power. Work It.

*The truth will set you free, especially if you
are willing to own it, work it, and change it.*

Consider this the "chapter of *you*." (You get your own chapter!!)

Awareness is power, so before we go one word further I want to amplify that power.

First, we're going to talk about where you *might* be right now in your life. This means doing some assessing, which will help us gauge where you are, identify patterns and themes, and help you determine what you most want to focus on.

Once we know where you are, then I'm going to give you six activities and assessments that tie into claiming your contagiousness.

You can do each activity as you wish and when you wish, and I invite you to come back to them. I suggest you grab a journal—make it your *Contagious Me Journal* for this book. There are *no* right or wrong answers. Answer from your heart and realize your answers will change over time.

First *you*. See what resonates and gets sparked by this little story.

YOU

That you even picked up a book called *Contagious You* means you're curious about being contagious, care about leadership and how you show up, and want to do more good with your life . . . which means you are in the business of creating positive impact.

You have a full life. You care about people, your family, those you love and lead, making good things happen, and doing solid work.

You care about leadership and continuing to up your game. You're dealing with things entirely out of your control: people, places, predicaments, politics, power misplacement, pubescent teens (whoops, that's me), and probably some persnickety party poopers throughout.

And life is tricky. You're giving it all you've got, and even still, it doesn't feel like enough. And you want more—more time, more energy, more space, more impact, more money, more lean muscle mass, more health, more love . . . all while being a trusted leader who helps other people create more too.

Am I close?

Perhaps you've done your DiSC® personality test, your Myers-Briggs Type Indicator® (MBTI®), your Simpli5®, your BIG5, your Kolbe Indexes, and a bunch of other assessments to gauge who you are. Maybe you've gotten Six Sigma certified, had that conflict mediation rectified, and participated in four leadership development programs (this year alone!). You've invested in cultural initiatives galore, engaged in coaching, had heart-to-hearts with your team, and read more books (or started to) than you can name. You've spent a ton of time, money, energy, and resources getting yourself, your team, company, career, family—or all of the above—together.

Still, many of these things have just made you *busier*, not *better*. Your kids want more of you, your spouse is missing you, and your boss *and* your direct reports keep asking you to stretch (in directions that seem to compete). Even complete strangers tell you what they need and how busy they are. It's relentless.

And you? You just want to sit down for a minute. You want to do good work . . . and live your life. That promotion would be great, and more respect and credibility as a leader? Dandy. You'd love it if people referred to you as an inspiring badass and if your family experienced you as the devoted parent and spouse you *intend* to be. The physique and energy you had years ago (when you had time to tend to yourself) would be fantastic. And to actually call your friends back within a month, and even *see* them, without feeling the pressure and pull of family, career, and life would be divine. It's not a lot to ask, right?

You know as a leader in your organization you set the tone; people look to you for answers, mentorship, strength—and this creates a little more pressure. Heck, a lot more.

You go back and forth feeling clear, on fire, in service of, and on purpose. You've got this. You're killing it. And then, bam! That one little thing (maybe it was just a thought you had) jacks your whole jam. Your "worry mind" wakes you up at 4 a.m.; lots to do, keep up with, show up for. Again. And again.

Perhaps you're feeling at your edge, exhausted, depleted, burnt out. Perhaps you're wondering what's next. Perhaps you're wondering how the heck you're supposed to keep up with the accelerating pace of your life and the never-ending increase of demands on your time, energy, and resources.

You have more ways to connect than ever, more resources, more tech, more toys, and maybe more invitations to dinners, meetings, and opportunities to contribute. Yet you feel more isolated than ever, lonely even. Are you alone? (No.)

You're magnificent. And you're tired. You wonder if anyone can tell.

And how did you get to this position anyway? You worry people will find out you have no clue what you're doing.

And that's just *you*.

Because, wait for it, you also have George. George (or Georgette or G) makes your life harder, if not blatantly—energetically. George walks into the room and your heart sinks. Georgette sits in your meetings, looks irritated all the time, and sucks the air out of the room every time she opens her mouth to speak or sigh loudly. G is the "lowest vibration in the room." In two seconds flat, G can take a human, or even a whole team, from soaring, happy, and creative, to exhausted, deflated, and ready to quit, simply with his or her presence. G loves to talk about how hard things are, how busy she is, how unlikely the latest ideas and initiatives are to work. G loves to complain. G makes you feel careful when you don't even know why.

29

When you see G on your calendar, you brace for "trudgery" (and the meeting is not even for a month!). When G walks into the room, people get quiet.

When in a meeting with you, G's not actually there. He's on his phone, arms crossed, sidebarring, scowling, not *present*, and definitely not adding any magic or ease to the mess. G's people have even started coming to you with complaints, asking for support on how to handle G. There may even be a "G Support Group" (true story). It's awkward because G may be your colleague and tough to give feedback to. (This all just adds hours of drama to your life.) G might be your boss, CEO, business partner, teammate, or employee who didn't *seem* like a George when you first met. But he is. She is. And now you may be stuck with G either because you'll get fired if you push back. Or you'll get sued or be financially impacted if you get rid of George.

So you keep on keeping on. It's not a *huge* deal; you "stay in your own lane" and even have compassion for George. (At some point, you've probably been George too.) But it's one more thing to manage. Argh.

So not only do you have your own leadership to up-level, life to lead, relationships to nourish and care for, kids (and dogs) to raise, and *you*. You are also dealing with the Gs of the world! Not to mention global warming, politics, finances, diversity, cultural tension, world hunger, sex trafficking, school shootings, gun control, homelessness, pollution, social media, natural disasters, quarterly projections, and . . . yes, I know the list is not near complete.

It's a lot. Even worse, *none* of it is in your control. Damn.

Are you exhausted yet? Stick with me. If any of this resonates, hits a nerve, *or* piques your curiosity—we are on track.

Awareness Is the Beginning (and the Key to It All)

First let's take a moment to step away and get real about where you are and what you need. In my work with people I find that awareness is about 70 percent of the battle with the other 30 percent being what we choose to do with it. Without awareness I don't know what my problem is (or that I even have one), and there is often pain, struggle, ambiguity, suffering, busyness, and repeating patterns that don't serve. But . . . once I have the awareness, I am in a position of power as I can *choose* to change what's not working. Awareness and grounded clarity are power. With awareness, I'm more than halfway there. That other 30 percent may be the harder work, *and* my choices can set me free.

The questions I pose in these assessments, along with those in the Introduction and Chapter 1, will give you a solid foundation for working this content. This awareness will help you connect with the stories and resources in the book more effectively. Answer your questions honestly; they are only for you. (And if you skipped the Introduction, no big deal; go back and get your full value out of this book.)

Before we dig in, let me address the fact that self-assessments are tricky, even flawed. Some days we are jamming and on top of the world; some days we feel like we can't do anything right. Some days we don't even know how we feel. In some situations and with specific people, we may lead beautifully, and some people or situations may push our buttons so hard that we can't lead well enough to save our lives. Not to mention that we are often way off when we assess ourselves in comparison to what others see. (More often than not, we're actually doing better! And yes, sometimes worse.)

So, yes, there are no perfect self-assessments. For these assessments I'm asking you to zoom out and think generally in terms of the majority of your duties, interactions, relationships, activities, attitudes, presence, and mindset. We're going for the "overall" answers here. To give you a more rounded perspective, I've also included an assessment you can have your people complete for you. Use these as a journal of sorts, making notes as you go (especially for any questions or situations that really poke at you or stand out). These assessments are designed to come back to again and again to track change.

Note: When we first started doing this work with organizations, we'd collect pre- and post-measures to gauge people's happiness, presence, satisfaction, success, and other metrics. They often gave higher scores at the beginning of the program than at the end. What? What kind of a return on investment

(ROI) is that? Turns out, a great one. They hadn't known what those things actually meant to them when we started. After our work together, their awareness, effectiveness, genuine presence, and happiness went up. Like a fish in water that doesn't know what water is because it lives in and breathes it every day, people often don't realize how happy or unhappy, full or empty, effective or ineffective, present or distracted, or exhausted or in pain they are until they have space to breathe, reflect, and consider what's true for them. They need to "get out of the water" for a minute. This work gets them out of the water and creates space so they can see, decide, and be from a place of conscious choice.

All this to say two things:

1. Your score may drop over time as you learn more about what these things *truly mean* to you in this book. (This is not a bad thing; it means your awareness is going up!)
2. You need to get out of the water.

Let's go.

Assessment 1

Part A: Personal Foundation Work

Let's delve into you a bit. Please answer these thoughtfully. Keep track of the dates you take all of these assessments. If you work with this book, these numbers will shift over time.

Use a 0–10 scale with 10 being super-true and 0 being not true at all.

___ 1. The way I show up supports me in creating the results I want.

___ 2. The *energetic presence* I bring to my life and people is positive, helpful, proactive, and leadership-like.

___ 3. I talk to myself in ways that are kind, life-giving, and helpful.

___ 4. The way I take care of myself (physically and emotionally) sets me up for success.

___ 5. I am happy.

___ 6. I am intentional—I proactively consider what I want to create and then go for it.

___ 7. I know I am the author of my life, captain of my ship—my leadership is up to me.

___ 8. The way I regard other human beings makes my life happier, easier, and more peaceful.

___ 9. I know what I need to have present in my life to show up as my best. I have rituals and agreements with myself to support me.

___ 10. I know why I lead, what I stand for, and what I am in service of.

___ 11. I am clear about what I need to do to move forward in my career and life.

___ 12. I am in integrity with myself and others. (I honor time, agreements, truth, and my core values.)

___ 13. I am willing to do the work to make myself better.

Total Score: _____ /130

(**Goal:** Your goal is to score high here. Items you score low on indicate areas to work on and nourish in order to strengthen your foundation.)

My motivation for reading this book and doing this work is: (Check any that apply and add as desired.)

- ❏ Be a better leader; more intentional, respected, inspiring, effective, caring, etc.
- ❏ Have people like me more.
- ❏ Handle "George" better.
- ❏ Be less "busy" and exhausted.
- ❏ Have more positive impact.
- ❏ Get a promotion/grow my business.
- ❏ Make more money; create more time and space.
- ❏ Be a better parent/friend/spouse/human/partner.
- ❏ Make a (positive, helpful) dent on this planet with my life (legacy).
- ❏ Do and be my best (in my ongoing quest for growth).
- ❏ Tend to questions 1–13 above, especially number(s): _____
- ❏ Other_____

If you are still thinking that *being contagious* and that intentions, energy, and presence are for everyone else. Or if you're still doing culture versus being it. Or if you're still sitting in rooms with your arms crossed while your people (and/or spouse, kids, direct reports, or bosses) pray you'll ask yourself these questions and reconsider how you're showing up because they love you, and they're also a little scared of you or worried for you—I offer you the questions in Part B. (These are also helpful if you work with George and want to offer him a self-assessment or have a coaching conversation.) I realize some of these may be hard to answer. Go with your gut. Your first response is usually right on (especially if you didn't like it). If you're feeling extra brave and collaborative, ask others for feedback as it resonates.

Part B: Impact Foundation Work

Circle the answer where I've given you choices. Fill in where I've given you blanks.

- Am I having the impact I want to have?
  YES / NO
- Am I creating the results I want to create?
  YES / NO
- Do I feel the way I want to feel?
  YES / NO
- Do people follow me, work with me, hang out with me, and stay partnered with/married to me because they want to or have to?
  WANT TO / HAVE TO
- What is the experience I generally create with my presence?
  AWESOME / CRAPPY
- What do I want my leadership presence to be?
  INSPIRING / OBLIGATORY
- Who in my life would be happy/grateful/delighted/relieved if I were to work on my energetic presence and impact with them?

  _____

- What might I be able to bring to the world, my organization, and/or my industry from a place of greater intention, presence, and impact?_____
- What have I got to lose if I give this a real go? What's to gain?

  _____

- What support do I need? _____

Journal any thoughts or ahas you had while answering questions in Parts A and B. If you have a sense of what's missing (i.e., why something is a 6 and not a 10, or a "no"), capture that as well.

Assessment 2

The Cost of Being Contagious

Your contagiousness is costing you. I promise. And how much? What is the cost of your being contagious in a negative way? Of getting sucked into other people's "stuff"? Of being completely self-obsessed about your own stuff? How much time do you spend worrying about things, making assumptions, grappling with decisions, making up stories, being unclear, getting in your own way, or not getting your way? What's the cost of drama and gossip and stress in your organization? Or of abdication and blame?

Your contagiousness either amplifies and positively builds the field and your impact or detracts and contracts, breaking down your field and impact. Our contagiousness costs us precious time, energy, money, connection, sleep, self-trust, results, peace—or all eight. Fortunately, they all work together. These are your most precious resources. Think about it.

Time . . . once it's gone, you can't get it back. It's gone forever.

Energy . . . your emotional, mental, physical, spiritual, vibrational—your energy is your life force. It is precious. Spend it intentionally.

Money . . . need I say more? This one is obvious, right? Or is it? Here's something people often miss that is not obvious: "good profit" versus "bad profit." You can make money, tons even, but have it be so energetically exhausting or misaligned with your values that the energetic and spiritual cost results in bad profit.

Connection . . . we all need it, want it, and thrive on it. I believe that love is unlimited—we have unlimited amounts to give. But if we're not taking care of ourselves, if we're showing up toxic, if we're living in scarcity, if we're not loving ourselves and each other, this one is harder to access. The answer to everything is love. (Yes, even in Corporate America.) Tapping connection, especially when things are hard, is magical. But in our drama, this special resource is often forgotten or unhealthy.

Sleep . . . if you're up worrying about drama, things you can't control, how you showed up in yesterday's meeting, what may or may not happen in tomorrow's, you're robbing yourself of precious *zzzz*'s.

Self-trust . . . every time we break an agreement with ourselves to show up well, be real, honor our senses of what's right, or engage in self-care and self-kindness, or whenever we get hooked into something we know we shouldn't, we put a little dent in our personal impeccability. (Great news is that it works very quickly the other way too.)

Results . . . are where the rubber hits the road. Where you create your intended results—or not. You are always getting a result—the question is, is it the one you want? And if it's not, how honestly can you honor your disappointment, and then how quickly can you make this "loss" a productive learn?

Peace . . . internal, external. This one is on you to define. Clarify it and create it.

Great news! If you address any of these, they tend to positively impact the others. So pick what resonates, or what "pinged" you hardest reading this, and dig in.

Behavioral Energy and Impact

Below is a list of behaviors and habits that have energetic impact, influence our contagiousness, and are common areas of focus (there are many more).

Please rate these items on a scale of 0–10 where 0 = I don't do this at all—I feel great and am energized by the lack of this issue in my life! And 10 = I spend a significant amount of time and energy on this—it is an energy suck for me.

___ 1. Getting sucked into other people's "stuff"
___ 2. Being obsessed with my own performance and perfection
___ 3. Worrying about things
___ 4. Making assumptions and making up stories
___ 5. Being unkind to myself (treatment, self-talk, judgment, breaking promises to self, etc.)
___ 6. Saying *yes* when I really want to say *no*

___ **7.** Keeping secrets or being out of alignment with personal integrity

___ **8.** Grappling with decisions

___ **9.** Gossiping, not engaging directly, or talking behind someone's back

___ **10.** Procrastinating (on anything)

___ **11.** Blaming others (people or things)

___ **12.** Judging others (people or things)

___ **13.** Triangulating between people

___ **14.** Not feeling happy about my work

___ **15.** Not feeling happy about my relationships

___ **16.** Not feeling happy about my health or fitness

___ **17.** Being negatively contagious, making messes that need to be cleaned up, or creating resistance in others

___ **18.** Going it alone—because no one else can do it as well as I can

___ **19.** Going it alone—I don't ask for help, even though I know I can

___ **20.** Denying joy, pleasure, or play

___ **21.** Not being clear about my intentions and desires

Total Score: _____ **/210**
(**Goal:** Your goal is to score low here. Items you score high on provide good information for energy leaks, indicating focus areas to optimize your energy and impact.)

Please capture anything that feels important to you here. You will apply this information on the next page as we put this all together.

Notes:

_____

_____

_____

_____

_____

_____

Measuring the Cost/Benefit of Contagiousness

What is the impact of your contagiousness and the scores on previous pages in the following areas? The way we show up on that list impacts each of the primary areas that follow at a deeper level. For example, if I scored high in the previous section, it's likely impacting my time, energy, money, connection, sleep, self-trust, results, and/or peace. However, if I scored low, I might find that my low scores provide me with extra resources and energy. For example, if I'm great at saying no and staying out of drama, that adds an extra hour to my day and pep in my step, so I'm even happier with my time.

Please rate from 0 to 10 how happy you are with where you are at for each of these. 0 = not happy at all; 10 = ecstatic, couldn't be better!

Time   _____

Energy   _____

Money   _____

Connection   _____

Sleep   _____

Self-trust   _____

Results   _____

Peace   _____

Total Score: _____ /80

(**Goal:** Your goal is to score high here. Low scores? Great! I am so happy for you! Now you know where to focus!)

Notes:

_____

_____

_____

_____

_____

_____

Assessment 3

Self-Awareness: Desires, Impact, and Resourcefulness

Please answer with your first thoughts as you read each question. Don't overthink it; one to two sentences or three paragraphs is great. Whatever comes to you.

1. What is the quality of your intentionality, energy, and presence and your Intentional Energetic Presence? (As you understand it now; more to come.) What are you creating in your life through how you are showing up?

2. Where are you not fully resourced right now? How does this impact your decisions, mindset, self-talk, physical well-being, heart, generosity, compassion, clarity, and ability to serve others?

3. Where can you love yourself better, taking care of your well-being, energy, and presence?

4. Where are you afraid of being judged or "doing it wrong"? Where are you hard on others (judgmental, critical, blaming)? What's the connection you see here?

5. Where are you taking on other people's negative contagions, "matching" their vibes, or being influenced—or even designed—by their energy or expectations of you?

6. Where might you have given up? What do you need to believe about yourself (and humans) in order to step back in?

7. How do you feel in your current role right now? How drained or energized are you? What is the quality of your relationships? What are you excited about? What do you dread?

8. What do you believe about your ability to "up-level"? How confident do you feel that you can improve your leadership, become more present, successful, trustworthy, influential, credible, inspiring, and happy?

9. Who is someone who would be really happy you're asking yourself these questions? What is *one* relationship you want to improve over the course of this book?

10. How important is all of this to you? What's important about it?

Assessment 4

George or Mary or Mary/George?

In Chapter 1, I spoke about George and Mary and some of the qualities and challenges they might have. Below are 10 indicators for each of them.

Circle each statement you relate to. (Circle = 1 point.) Are you George, or Mary, or both? Let's find out. **Note:** *If you desire a refresher on some of these components, go back and look at the details of each. If the statement doesn't apply, leave it alone.*

I Am (or Might Be) George

1. I am *not* having the impact I want to have right now in my life or career—or both.
2. People *don't* talk to me proactively or openly; they're "careful" around me.
3. I *don't* feel the way I want to feel.
4. People follow me/work with me/hang with me because they *have to*, not because they want to.
5. My culture is *not* great, or not ideal, and it's *not* my fault. *They* don't get it.
6. People avoid me, resist my ideas, and/or act out of obligation.
7. People fear me, and this is a *good* thing; I get stuff done! ("If they don't like my style, they can leave. After all, you want me to be authentic, right? Well, I'm an authentic jerk." #truestory.)
8. I *generally* feel dissatisfied, ineffective, cranky, and/or lonely, and it's *not* my fault.
9. What I have will *never* be enough; what he/she/they did will *never* be enough; I want more. There is no time for smelling the roses. (I hire people for that!)
10. The soft stuff is silly! No time. Let's get down to business. Show me the money!

GEORGE POINTS: _____

41

I Am (or Might Be) Mary

1. I'm exhausted. Wiped out. I'm doing my best, and there is so much to do.
2. I know George(s), and engaging with him is *tough*. He's the hardest part of my day.
3. I have a richly scheduled life (not "busy"), maybe too richly scheduled. I could use some optimization here.
4. I love my life and creating impact. I want to do and be even more. I'm on a continuous quest for being my best self. (More time, money, and freedom would be lovely too!)
5. I'm daunted by all the negativity and challenge in the world right now. I feel overwhelmed frequently, yet do my best to remain positive and helpful. (I'm not sure how much longer I can keep this up authentically; I need new tricks!)
6. My boundaries suck, or leave a lot to be desired. I avoid confrontation and saying no.
7. I am aware of my presence and impact, and can manage and shift it at will.
8. I believe that life happens *for* me, not *to* me, and that while I can't control anything or anyone else, I can control myself. I am the captain of my ship.
9. I am grateful for all I have. I appreciate the present moment and celebrate big and small wins. Everything counts. And I smell the roses—I love them.
10. I care deeply about creating stellar business results *and* being a leader people are inspired to work with. I know that the soft stuff *is* the secret sauce that saves *time, energy*, and *money* and helps optimize *creativity, collaboration*, and *human potential*.

MARY POINTS: _____

I'm GEORGE. I'm MARY. I'm a Little Bit (or a Lot) of Both

Scoring guide:

- If you scored fewer than 2 points total in *either* the George or Mary category: OK! Rare! Read on anyway. I'll bet there's still something good for you in here. (Definitely have your people take Assessment 5B, below, for you.)
- If you scored 3–5 points in either: Good to have you here; let's go.
- If you scored 5+ points in either: Thank goodness we met! Clear your schedule! Start reading now! You and those you love and lead are counting on you. Plus, we're going to have so much fun. Don't stop reading (and applying) until you feel a shift.

You can come back to this assessment again and again. It will change.

Notes:

_____

_____

_____

_____

_____

_____

_____

_____

_____

_____

_____

_____

_____

_____

_____

Assessment 5A

How (Positively) Contagious Am I? (Self-Assessment)

Answer these questions for yourself using a scale of 0–10, where 0 = not true at all and 10 = totally true!

___ 1. When I walk into a room, people are happy to see me.

___ 2. I am asked to be involved in decision making and in meetings.

___ 3. People seek me out for advice.

___ 4. When there is a crisis or tender moment, people look to me for leadership and support.

___ 5. I generally bring up the vibration of a room or meeting.

___ 6. I am aware of the intentions, energy, and presence I bring into a room. I can reboot and command my intentions, energy, and presence as needed to serve whatever is happening and soothe myself in times of stress or conflict.

___ 7. People sense I am good at managing stress, staying open, helpful, and calm in any situation. It feels good to be around me.

___ 8. I am a contributor to any space I am in whether that is a meeting, a conversation, a project, anything. People are glad when I am there.

___ 9. People know I value their time, attention, and energy by how I show up with them, honor agreements, and honor time.

___ 10. People work with/hang out with /stay in a relationship with me because they *want* to, not because they have to.

___ 11. People like having me on their team.

___ 12. I show up in a way that makes people feel seen, cared for, valued, important, and safe.

___ 13. I feel I am positively contagious in our organization/team/relationship. People feel better, more inspired, and happier being around me.

___ 14. I know that I am responsible for my own experience and how I feel—no matter what is happening around me.

__ **15.** I am a detractor in the room; people feel careful around me—not safe and often judged.

__ **16.** My presence, attention, body language, and behavior are often distracting and not a contribution.

You're looking for high scores in items 1–14, while 15 and 16 are designed to give you another frame—for these you want lower scores.

Total on 1–14: _____ /140 (**Goal:** High)

Total on 15–16: _____/20 (**Goal:** Low)

Notes:

_____

_____

_____

_____

_____

_____

_____

_____

_____

_____

_____

_____

_____

_____

_____

_____

_____

_____

_____

Assessment 5B

How (Positively) Contagious Am I? (Peer Assessment)

Ask your people to answer these questions using 0–10 as a guide. (You are "X.") For a solid feedback pool, I'd ask at least five to six people: your biggest fan, a colleague or team member, your boss, your nemesis, a direct report, and your choice. Note that you can revisit these over time. All of these just provide information, and you are likely going to start seeing themes. If your interpretation or scoring in 5A is way off from theirs in 5B—you've likely hit gold, as awareness and clarity are power. You go, you!

___ 1. When X walks into a room, people are happy to see X.

___ 2. I want X to be involved in decision making and in meetings.

___ 3. I seek X out for advice.

___ 4. When there is a crisis or tender moment, I look to X for leadership and support.

___ 5. X generally brings up the vibration of a room or meeting.

___ 6. X's presence is a gift in any room X is in. We feel better knowing X is here.

___ 7. X seems to have a great handle on managing stress, staying open, helpful, and calm in any situation. It feels good to be around X.

___ 8. X is a contributor to any space X is in whether that is a meeting, a conversation, a project, anything. I am glad when X is in the room.

___ 9. I feel like X values my time, my attention, and my energy by how X shows up with me, honors agreements, and honors time.

___ 10. I work with/hang out with/stay in a relationship with X because I *want* to, not because I have to.

___ 11. I would choose to have X on my team again and again.

___ 12. X makes me feel seen, cared for, valued, important, and safe.

___ 13. I feel X is positively contagious in our organization/team/relationship. I feel better, more inspired, and happier being around X.

___ **14.** X has command of X's experience so that any situation can become (even slightly) better because of X's IEP and how X embodies it.

___ **15.** X is a detractor in the room; I feel careful around X—not safe and often judged.

___ **16.** I feel like we need to manage X and X's presence and attention. X's body language and behavior are distracting and not a contribution.

You're looking for high scores in items 1–14, while 15 and 16 are designed to give you another frame—for these you want lower scores.

Total on 1–14: _____ /140 (**Goal:** High)

Total on 15–16: _____/20 (**Goal:** Low)

Now look at 5A and 5B. Do you see any gaps in what you think versus the feedback you received from your people? If so, smile. You now have more specific areas to focus on.

Notes:

_____

_____

_____

_____

_____

_____

_____

_____

_____

_____

_____

_____

_____

Assessment 6

Final Assessment: Put It Together

This is where you name, claim, and start your (next level) leadership game. Ready?

Answer the following before you move on to Chapter 3.

1. What are the themes I see here?
2. Do I care? Why or why not?
3. What do I care the most about; what is most important to me to shift?
4. Where am I relieved? Where am I surprised? Capture any other predominant emotions that may be coming up for you as well.
5. What three things do I see now are my highest-leverage changes to make? (I can work on these throughout this book.)
6. What three things are my lowest-hanging fruit? (I can do these right now with awareness.)
7. What is my intention now? What do I want to get out of this book, and what experience will I create for myself reading it?

OK, now that you've claimed it, it's yours.
Ready to increase your credibility, success, and influence?
Let's get it.

CHAPTER 3

More Credibility, Success, and Influence Is Within You. Get It.

You are your most powerful advocate. Lead.

Do you ever wish for a "magic button" or a "silver bullet" or a "reset lever" to help you find your answers, restart a situation, fix a relationship, turn you into a rock star leader, or simply make things all better?

I'll never forget Lester, a gentleman I met at a session I led in Texas, who wished for the "silver bullet" (his words) to make him a better dad and leader, lose 20 pounds, and stop his struggles with his team. He waited an hour after the session to ask me for it, and when I told him *he* was the silver bullet, he walked away deflated and perplexed. (Only to come back the next morning stoked, because he'd realized if *he* was his own silver bullet, he could do something about that!)

Or Cheryl, an executive in Chicago who was excited about this work because after she did it, she'd never have problems again, ever—this would be her "reset button." Afterward, she'd do everything "right." (Little did she know this work would make her her own reset button.)

Or Casey, who wanted a "magic button" to make her nemesis just go away or at least be nicer to her. (You'll see what actually happened in Chapter 10.)

49

Or Jack, who kept hoping that someone else would swoop in and lead because he was way out of his comfort zone but didn't want to say so. He hoped someone would save him. So he waited. And waited. And waited. (Not actually asking for help.) Until he was miserable and the initiative failed.

External Solutions and Magic Buttons

Can you relate? I know I can.

Who doesn't want a quick fix or a magic button? Or someone or something else to do it?

Leadership is tricky. It is a natural default to want to be led, to want someone else to give us the answers, to have someone else tell us what to do, to have that magic button that fixes things. It is easy to give our power away, abdicate, and comply—thinking that someone outside ourselves knows better or has our answers. And while we may receive guidance or support, ultimately we *get* to be our own advocates. No one outside of ourselves can do this for us. We have to lead our game. After all, if not you, who?

You are your own silver bullet (or pixie dust, magic button, reset lever, captain of your ship, hero, master of your domain, or whatever metaphor works for you).

One of my favorite things about doing this work is watching the difference in results between the people who embrace this idea and those who don't.

The difference is magnificent.

Here's what I know . . .

We can have what we want—and more. *If* we're willing to do the work to create it.

Want more credibility? It's on you.

Want better leadership presence? You.

More creativity and flow? You.

More money and prosperity? You.

Fitness? You.

50

Success? You.

Better relationships? Yep, you.

Culture? You got it—you.

Being more positively contagious? You guessed it.

Once you've claimed your contagiousness (Chapter 1) and assessed where you are at (Chapter 2), the next step is to fully own that only *you* can decide to be the accountable boss of you. A decision is needed here.

What will you decide?

Our outcomes are a result of the decisions we make, the work we do, and how we show up.

If our company puts us through training or coaching, but we decide not to integrate it—it's on us.

If we want to be a better writer or speaker or presenter but decide not to get feedback or guidance—on us.

If we want to be a better spouse or partner but don't engage or, even better, wait for our spouse or partner to make the first move—on us.

If we want to be healthier, fitter, leaner, faster, but decide to eat junk food and not exercise or make time for sleep—on us.

If we want a better business, stronger client relationships, clearer agreements, more white space, healthier culture, better . . . anything—on us.

Do the work.

Make time for integration, follow through, and apply.

Hire the editor or coach; get the hard feedback. Make it better (and better).

Stop waiting. Start leading. Do the more vulnerable stuff. Get in there.

Make the time and effort to eat well, exercise, sleep, and love your body up.

Take the time to clarify intentions and agreements, communicate clean, hold boundaries, pick up the phone, ask for what you want and need, stop complaining, and own the process.

Of course, collaborate, get help, get coaching, consult experts, ask for the care and support you desire—do whatever you need to do to shine; you are not alone. *And* it's on *you.*

If you want it, go for it.

The only question is, *Are you willing to do the work?*

And an even more important question that will fuel your work is, *Why? What is the desire that will make this all worth it?*

Want It . . . Love It . . . Do the Work

And what if you don't know your desire? What if you're not clear about what you want? This is not uncommon. I've found that we humans often get so busy in our lives—handling survival, dynamics, and the day-to-day—that we can lose touch with our desires or not realize they've shifted. As we shift and grow, so will they. It's useful to check in.

This is when taking a "minute" to step back and get clear about desire, and about what you want to create *now*, is precious fuel for moving forward, creating impact, being inspiring, and feeling energized throughout.

So how do you do it?

The Want Dial and the Why

Being a leader can be hard. Being your own advocate? Oh, geesh. Yeah . . . sometimes it's hard.

You know what will make it easier? Knowing *why* you're doing it. In Chapter 5 we'll dig into the Essential You, which is where your values and purpose live. The Essential You fuels impact. Before we go there, let's handle some basics in the land of want. Please turn on your "Wanting Machine" right now. Got it? Great. Can't find it? No worries, you had it when you were younger—you may have put it away as you grew up and were told to stop asking for things. Find it, dust it off, and turn it back on now. Thank you. There is a dial on your Wanting Machine. Notice what the dial is set at (0 is nada; 10 is the top). Got it? Great. Breathe.

Now what do you want? (No filtering, no judging, no "figuring it out"—let your intuition inform you here.)

Turn up the dial; want it more.

What's important about it to you? What will it give you? What will it allow you to do (or be)?

You have to start here.

Desire—heartfelt, soulful, authentic desire—is fuel.

Here are some things that are hard, that are fueled by desire:

- **Leadership.** People make difficult decisions, take brave risks, and go into daunting, uncharted territories in service of making something they care about happen. All the time. It doesn't matter if it is in service of finding the cure for diabetes, providing paychecks, feeding kids, stopping sex trafficking, making the world better, or providing a roof over your head—there is a reason why you lead, why you work, why you do what you do. There is a *why.* Find it.

- **Divorce.** People go through the incredibly difficult, heartbreaking process of divorce and break-ups to create a healthier environment for their kids and themselves; to be more free and authentic; to honor their values, themselves, their soon-to-be exes; and for their well-being, truth, and spirit.

- **Health.** People engage in fitness and health programs, stop smoking, and take on new (or eliminate old) behaviors so they can feel good in their bodies, keep up with their kids, have a healthier pregnancy, be around for their grandchildren, and feel great at their college reunion. I had a mentor who stopped smoking—cold turkey—so she could do deeply meaningful, hugely impactful work in a system that could not allow her to smoke anywhere around the compound. Lifelong smoker, cold turkey quitter (#purpose).

There is a bigger reason, a bigger "why," for doing what we do than just doing what we do. If there isn't, our goals and intentions can fall apart fast.

If our why is strong enough and the thing we want is important enough—we will do it. The more connected we are to our why, the more sustainable our leadership becomes. Especially when it gets hard to do the work.

So what do you want and *why?*

In my work with clients I've noticed this can be a tricky question. It can be hard to want. It can also be hard to determine what you want. But it's there. And if it isn't clear right away, giving ourselves the space and permission for this question can unlock answers we may have tucked away. Answers that have been buried in the busyness of our lives or that we've just not had the courage to claim yet. So whatever this "want dial" brings up for you, it's perfect. Allow it and keep exploring.

The want dial is a primer for getting clear about what's most important and giving ourselves full permission to claim it and focus in. The most important elements of this exercise are presence, full permission, and honest questions (and answers).

Here are a few to prompt your want dial:

- What would make me happy? What would be pleasurable?
- How do I want to serve? What kind of impact do I want to make?
- How do I want to spend my time? If money were no object, what would I do for a living?
- How much money do I want to make? What freedom would this give me?
- How do I want my relationships to feel? My body? What do I need to make that so?
- What kind of leader, parent, partner, friend, human, do I want to be? What would that look like?

If you are having a hard time connecting with this idea or accessing what you want, start small—start with "a cup of coffee," or "a day off," or "a new pencil." Then work your way up: to have a better relationship, to run a 5K, to be a better parent, to get a promotion, to impact 10,000 people next month, and so on. You'll come up with a list. When you have all the "wants" out in front of you, go back and circle the top five to focus on for now.

It is not uncommon to start this exercise feeling stuck, to slowly identify wants, and then to be unable to stop. I give people seven minutes to do this. They write their wants on paper and then go back and prioritize. Our record is 86 wants in seven minutes from someone who took the first three minutes to really tap the want dial. People walk away awake to desire and with three to five areas of focus to really go for.

Have at it.

The "Want It/Love It Up" Five-Step

Now that you know what you want, we can go deeper to lock it in and bring it closer to reality. Do the five-step (Figure 3.1).

❶ See it.

❷ Want it.

❸ Know it.

❹ Decide it.

❺ Love it.

FIGURE 3.1   The "Want It/Love It" Five-Step

- **See it.** Envision yourself doing it or being it, see the result of it, and see the people around you benefiting from it.
- **Want it.** Connect with the feeling of having this thing. Feel where success lives in your body, the energy of having it, the feeling of connection and aliveness that comes with it, the importance of it. Really feel this. Feel it? Great, now turn the want dial up. Want it more. Breathe. Good.
- **Know it.** What will this do for you? What will it give you? What will you be able to do because of this? Who will you become? Now, tap into what will happen if you don't create this. What's the cost? Feel that. Now come back to what's possible when you've created it. Stay there.
- **Decide it.** Once you see it, want it, and know it—it's time to decide to create it. No kidding. Make the full-body decision to make it so. It's on you to lead.
- **Love it.** Now all you have to do is love it up, partner with it, stay conscious in it, and get ready to do the work.

55

The "Do the Work" Five-Step

Once you have the model in place for finding what you want, the next step is doing the work to get there.

Here are five steps (Figure 3.2) to being your own silver bullet and the awesome accountable boss of you.

❶ Own it.

❷ Mind it.

❸ Nourish it.

❹ Do it.

❺ Be it.

FIGURE 3.2. The "Do the Work" Five-Step

First, *take full* **ownership** *for your experience and results.* Your decisions, choices, and way of being have brought you to this point. Yes, of course, there are things completely out of your control (these can sometimes even be tragic events) that you did not create. And the way you decide to be with them, take care of yourself, and get support in transitioning through them is part of what will move you to the next place successfully.

Second, *check your* **mindset** *in how you're relating to each of the unexpected events.* Doom and gloom, judgment and blame, taking your marbles and going home. Or can you find a better way to think about it? A reframe to the "thank you" or "gift" of it? Can you shift the way you're holding the reality of it, identify how you're contributing to it, and identify the littlest thing you can do or be to move forward?

Third, *take excellent care of yourself,* **nourish** *your vibe, and eliminate anything from your life that is not serving you in being your best.* Pay attention to your nutrition and self-care; your self-talk and self-kindness: your use of alcohol or TV or anything else you might do to "check out" or "numb out" to avoid the pain; the people you hang out with and quality of conversations you have; the excuses you make; the support you engage; and the space you create *proactively* to be able to show up better.. (We'll talk more about this in Part 2— it's *Big.*)

Fourth, *show up and* **do** *it.* Claim it. Step in and do something about what you want to see change in. Take accountability for it and do the work. Since you see it and want it—it's up to you. You can use the IEP Method to help make this so. (More on this in Chapter 5.)

Fifth, **be** *it.* Finally, with all this *do*ing is the *be*ing. Being the boss of you requires that you be the boss of you. You own *you.* Hold this energetically; stand in it; be it; take full responsibility for it. People will feel it in your presence. Show up in a way that holds and communicates intention, leadership, and accountability. Own your leadership.

Run yourself through these five steps in any situation you're grappling with. You'll likely find many new solutions, ideas, wants, and ways of "doing" and "being" to support you in making your desires a reality.

"Silver Bullet" Blind Spots

Think you already are your own silver bullet and pushing all edges? In my experience we all have sneaky corners we hide out in, often in our unconscious, where we're not fully being the boss of us and going for what we want.

Check yourself against these to see if you might have any blind spots here:

- You want more trust and credibility in your leadership, and you are waiting for someone to give it to you or for something to happen that just makes it so. You're too busy to actually think about what you might be doing that's hindering your growth here. (Gold mine.)
- You have been dieting and working out forever—or not—and just can't seem to lose that last 10 pounds.
- Your relationship with your colleague, friend, or family member is strained, maybe it has been for years, and you're hoping that something will magically just shift it.
- Your culture is not great. You dread going to work, feel careful and not safe in your environment, and hold your cards close to get through the daily "thunderdome" that is your culture.

- You want that promotion, gig, art exhibit, book deal, contract, clients—you name it. But you can't make time to be less "busy" or tired and do the work required. You *hope* it will just eventually happen.
- You have money problems in your business (or life, period); things are getting scarier by the day. The pipeline is low, the checking account even lower. You're spending more than you make; you can't fill your programs. Money drops; stress rises; you feel powerless.
- Your retirement and savings are not so stellar right now. "I'll save when," "I'll do this when," "If only when" has become a steady inner conversation.
- Your marriage is hurting. Maybe you've been together 2 years or 20, and ouch. It's not great. You hope things will just get better. "This is a phase," you say.
- There is something in your life, anything, that you want to make happen, create change in, or feel better about. *If only . . .*

These are nine scenarios I find to be common challenges, intentions, and places of hope (and waiting) among people I meet.

There are core things to honor in each of these:

1. They're scary places to be in.
2. The emotion (and struggle) is real.
3. They are often influenced by external factors in making the changes.
4. While external factors are always at play, what's even more powerful is that every single one of them is most dependent on *you*—the person with the challenge, the desire, the need.
5. They require a decision. The decision to get in there and do the work.

The only person who can make that decision is you.

You must be your own advocate. The sooner you understand and own this idea—the sooner your trust, credibility, and influence will go up.

Why? Because people feel the vibe of *ownership* just as much as they feel the vibe of the lack of it.

And your own intentions become contagious.

Matt

Matt was a director at his firm. He'd hired me to work with him on his leadership presence and building trust and credibility with his team. His ultimate goals were to have more impact, build real connections, grow his confidence levels, and ultimately get a promotion into senior leadership.

He was smart and had a great heart and clear intentions. Initially, I didn't think we had too much work to do. As far as I could tell, our work together would be about optimizing what he was already doing and bringing his leadership presence to new levels. Until we got into the process.

I noticed that Matt showed up two to four minutes late for every call. Sometimes it was just one minute. But 1 minute or 20, he was late.

I also noticed that he was often exhausted, even on a Tuesday at 10 a.m. He liked to talk about his exhaustion and cite it as an excuse for not being totally present, or "on it."

I noticed he used a lot of language like "can't," "try," "they," "busy," "not in my control," "I hope," "sorry," and sometimes, "not my problem."

But he deeply wanted to build trust and credibility with his peers.

When I work with people, their time integrity is nice for me, but it's *not* for me—it's for them. If they've said they want to build trust and credibility with others, they have to build it with themselves first. Time integrity is low-hanging leadership fruit. Every time Matt was late, broke his word with himself to be on time, or made an excuse, he put a chink in his field of trust and credibility—with himself. Which of course was energetically communicated to everyone around him.

When we don't own our integrity within ourselves, we are not trustable with others. (Even if they don't know why they don't fully trust us, they'll feel something is off.) If we make excuses for why we're not showing up well, it weakens the field and our credibility even more.

I see this almost every day. People are confused about why they don't have a better business or culture or leadership credibility, and it is often related to how they are showing up in even the littlest of ways. Being late (for *anything*) or breaking agreements (even *little* ones), making excuses, talking about being "so busy" or exhausted or overwhelmed, not being present (and even worse *pretending* to be)— these are some of the most common diminishers of personal trust and credibility, and they cost people and organizations dearly, daily. Period.

(Pause for a minute: do *you* like to hear about how exhausted people are, or how overwhelmed or busy or "out of it" they are, from anyone? Let alone your boss, partner, vendor, or employee? Let alone as an excuse for why they've dropped the ball on something? What's the energetic impact of that? Does it inspire trust, credibility, any of the good "feels?" Likely not. Is it something you want to catch energetically? Is it a helpful kind of contagious? Nah? OK, just checking.)

During one Tuesday coaching session, Matt once again used exhaustion as an excuse for being late and not honoring a commitment with his team. Twenty minutes into the conversation, he stated that he just couldn't be his best today for our work together because he was "too worn out."

"Matt, it's Tuesday morning at 10 a.m. How are you exhausted already?"

Matt had attended a BBQ on Sunday that had involved lots of craft beers and hot dogs. He'd enjoyed many of them. He'd gotten back late that night, ditched his IEP practice of proactively setting up his week, and was still in energetic catch-up mode by Tuesday morning. On top of this, because he was so tired and his decision-making muscles were weak (this happens when we're depleted), when someone on his team asked him to do something he couldn't possibly get done on time (or well), he still agreed to it in an effort to please his team member. Ultimately, he only put more pressure on himself and set everyone up for failure.

His intentions were not bad; he'd just gotten himself "behind it all." His nutrition, presence, and taking a pause were his quickest ways back.

"Matt, are those craft beers, hot dogs, and you giving up 'getting in front of your week' with sleep and intentions and presence of mind worth your next promotion and leadership credibility?"

"Nope."

Matt learned how his relationship with time, his integrity with himself, his self-care, and his inability to hold space and make thoughtful decisions (largely due to his fatigue and self-care) all affected his trust, his credibility, and his ability to lead. While nuanced and little things to tweak, they were in the way of his creating the impact he desired.

His language was also affecting his ability to be impactful. Anytime we catch ourselves using words like "try," "hope," "busy," "can't," "they," "not in my control," "not my problem," "worry," "should/need/have to," or "sorry" (without making changes or when used as a chronic excuse), we are coming from a place of victim or powerlessness—not ownership. Those words are all contractive and negatively contagious. Try them on now; see how they feel. They're not empowering or expansive, and they shut down possibility. What words would be more powerful? "Try" becomes "will." "Hope" becomes "intend." "Busy" becomes "richly scheduled" or "on purpose." "Can't" becomes "can," "won't," or "choose not to." "They" becomes "we" or "I." "Not in my control" and "not my problem" become some version of "what I can do to contribute to even the littlest thing going well." "Worry" becomes "aware of." "Should/need/have to" becomes "want/will/get to." And "sorry" becomes "I acknowledge my broken agreement and will make it right."

How we state things, and the intention behind them, has significant impact on the energy we bring to a situation.

Matt had some easy wins available to him if he was willing to do the work: clean up his time integrity, be true to his word (with himself first), stop making excuses and own it, clean up his self-care and nourishment, and clean up his language. With those changes, he'd be on his way.

These were our main initial focus areas to shift his presence. Of course, we worked on skills and strategy and presence at other levels, but these formed the foundation for him. Before we knew it, Matt was leading from a place of internal presence and integrity—what I call "personal impeccability"—which set him up to show up better with everyone around him. The members of his team noticed a shift and up-leveled their own presence as well (#contagious). He was more trustworthy and reliable. And he ultimately got his wish for more impact, more connection, and that promotion.

Matt was his own advocate and magic maker. No one did that for him. No one could have.

You—Go Get It

You know what is great about leading you and being in integrity with yourself? No one can take it away from you. Especially if you build it honestly.

Does this mean we're perfect? I hope not (what is perfect anyway?). It simply means we're conscious, we own our stuff, and we are the author and commander of our life.

From a place of personal integrity and impeccability, with that as our main presence and energetic communication—anything we do becomes more powerful.

So . . . back to you now! How much do you want your own goals? *What decisions do you need to make?*

Don't take this question for granted. I've worked with countless people whose main issue was that they'd not *fully* decided to make something happen, whether it was to have that great relationship, get healthy, be successful, make more money, be the captain of their own ship, be a better leader, or something else. Sound funny? Show me a place where you have something you say you want, but you haven't created it yet, and I'll show you a place where there's not a strong enough underlying desire, intention, or clear *why*, a decision that hasn't been made (or has), a place you're making other things more important, or an area you haven't wanted to do the hard work in. (Yet.)

So decide. And let's make that magic happen.

Fieldwork: Make It Real

Ask yourself: Where am I not being my own driver? Where am I waiting for someone else or something to happen to make this situation change? Where am I not clear on my want? Name it and then run yourself through any of the exercises offered in this chapter choosing at least one thing you know you can do to up-level your magic.

Play the *Want Dial Game*. Once you have your "want list," choose three to five areas of focus, and then work each one through the five-step processes below.

The Area or Situation (Name it):_____

"Want It/Love It Up" Five Steps:
See it. _____
Want it._____
Know it. _____
Decide it._____
Love it. _____

"Do the Work" Five Steps:
Own it. _____
Mind it._____
Nourish it. _____
Do it. _____
Be it. _____

Strengthen your personal impeccability. What is the littlest thing I can do now to build my own personal impeccability and integrity?

Here's a list to get you started; just *one* will make a dent.

Time integrity
No excuses
Self-kindness
Ownership
No blaming
Turn complaints into requests
Tell the truth
Say real *yes* and real *no*
Self-care
Direct engagement when there is conflict
Productive language
Decide

CHAPTER 4

Desire, Intention, Impact. Clarify It.

We create our experience in every moment; contract or
expand, repel or invite, fear or love, abdicate or lead . . .
We choose.

Once you've claimed your contagiousness (Chapter 1); have awareness of your current reality, strengths, and blind spots (Chapter 2);
truly own your power to create more credibility and success and are
clearer on your wants and desires (Chapter 3)—you're in the driver's
seat! You are well on your way to creating more impact (and saving a
ton of time, energy, and drama in doing so). This chapter is devoted
to creating intention and opening the "Portal of Purpose" so you can
unlock the next level of your ability to lead, influence, and create the
impact you want. In Part 2 of this book, I'll give you tools to work
from the inside out so that you are set up for sustainable and pleasurable success. And for now, let's open the portal.

I often have people come into our two-day sessions ready to quit
their jobs, ask for a divorce, or make some kind of major radical life
change—decisions coming from a place of scarcity, frustration, and
fear—only to find they have way more power and options than they
realized, and more solutions than they could have imagined. They
go home and re-engage in their roles and with their teams more
effectively. Some redesign their relationships or marriages (if only

internally with themselves in how they commit to showing up), some change their jobs and business models, some change their lives completely, and many decide against other choices they'd been making from the wrong place before they got still and explored their own leadership, presence, and contributions first.

How do people get to the state they are at coming into day one in the first place? Often it's just because they're busy. They've gotten sucked into the swirl and are not in touch with what we've spoken about so far in this book. They're often running so fast and pulled in so many directions that they've lost sight of their desires, intentions, and the impact they truly want to have. This is all shiftable, quickly. But you have to make a minute for it.

Creating an Experience and Designing Impact

"What is the *experience* you want to create with this client and for yourselves? What is the ultimate *impact* you want to have? And what specific *outcomes* would you like to walk out of that meeting with this afternoon?"

After a morning talking about intention, energy, presence, and impact, a team I'd been working with walked out of the meeting space we were in into another space with a client and closed a seven-figure deal. In an hour.

The team texted me after to let me know the outcome, "We got the business! Going for drinks!"

And that was that.

It wasn't until the next day I realized how far off the team members had been from closing that deal until we debriefed what'd happened.

Going into that meeting they knew they wanted the business and they knew they could help the client. They'd had several preliminary meetings and run a couple of experiments. They felt they could do it.

What they didn't know was that they were not aligned in their beliefs about the client (or each other), their intentions for the meeting, or the specific outcomes desired. More so, they were not conscious about the experience they wanted to create or the energy they'd need to bring into the room to close the deal.

Before our session, they were not fully aligned on an "energetic intention" level. After we'd met, they were.

We'd done nothing fancy except go through one of the IEP Method frameworks you're about to learn. They gave themselves the space to be honest within that framework and to take a pause as a team. That was it. It had taken a little less than two hours to cut through the muck and get clear about their desires, what they were going to *do*, and who they were going to *be* in that room. (This process would have taken less time if there'd been more alignment to begin with.) A couple of hours of energetic hygiene and spending time determining a desired impact is worth seven figures, peace within the team, and a client's increased confidence, don't you think?

The lead on the team offered me this: "Anese, I'm not sure if we would have gotten the business or not. I'd like to think so; we'd done some solid prep for it. My sense is, though, that we would have struggled through some critical points, and even if we got it, left the client not as confident. As you saw, we were definitely not jiving as a team—and even scarier, didn't realize how far off we actually were with each other. At best it would have been more effort to close, and for sure not as pleasurable of an experience. Getting clear on our intended impact, our beliefs, our lack of alignment, and how we each needed to show up in that room—and as a team—before we headed in yesterday was essential. I think the project will be better for it too—in fact, the more I sit with this, the more excited I am about all of it and what we'll create."

And then my client asked the magic question, "How do we make this process part of normal business practices, and in the rest of our lives?" And then, in a lower tone, "And how do I use this with my wife?"

The answer I give to his questions, or to anyone asking about how to integrate this work into the rest of their lives? Just use it. Apply it. Get intentional about your desired impact and experience, decide to make it so, and go!

Parenting with Intention and Grace

My girlfriend had an intense conversation she needed to have with her teenage daughter about sex and drugs and a fib she'd caught her in. She was fired up. Angry. Hurt. Scared. And nervous about the conversation. She didn't want to "mess" this up. It was tender, vital, and an important "moment."

She called me.

"I know I'm not in the right space to have this conversation, but it needs to be had. Like yesterday. Can you help me get my head and heart straight?"

Absolutely.

We went through the IEP Method five-step process of creating impact and choosing an experience, stopping where we needed to stop to work through things. At the end of our call, she was ready to go into that conversation present, loving, strong, and clear.

The conversation (worth, in my mind, more than that seven-figure deal) was a success.

What's the price you'd put on building a stronger bridge and giving your teenage daughter a safe space to step into so she might avoid drugs and you might avoid being a grandparent earlier than you'd like?

The entry point into both of these conversations and the results that followed were a blend of the questions, "What is the experience you want to create?" and "What is your intention?"

Clarifying Desires, Intentions, and Impact

Every time I speak, lead a session, facilitate a group, have a conversation with a client, do business development, talk high stakes with my kids, or start a new project, I am putting myself in the frameworks I share here. I've found these useful even if the only person engaging in that experience is me (e.g., doing paperwork or other tedious tasks). I still get to choose my intended impact and how I want to feel. Some circumstances and engagements need a full workup (working the IEP Sheet I'll share later), some need to be jotted down on a Post-it, and some just need to be thought through and intended well.

I have clients who, on every plane ride, go through their five steps for all meetings on the other side. I have colleagues who keep a pad of Post-its or IEP Sheets handy, to use as needed. Some people give themselves five minutes between meetings to run their steps. Some just quickly review them first thing in the morning. Some don't use the framework at all, and instead find that just knowing that their *presence has impact* and that they can be intentional in creating their experience is plenty enough to up-level their game.

You'll find what's true for you.

Does it always work perfectly? No. Are there things absolutely out of our control? Yes, most everything. Stuff happens, life hurts, and impact fails. And we have the choice of what we do with it, how we respond, how intentional we are to begin with, how we talk to ourselves throughout, how we get support, and how we lead ourselves and those we care about amid the mess. It's up to you. Having frameworks, reminders, and guardrails can be helpful "bread crumbs" back to "pulling it together" when everything feels like it's falling apart. Because if you are living a full, rich, risky life, and you are growing—it will. Often!

The Five Steps of Creating Intentional Impact

So what are *these* five steps?

In Part 2, I'll share the formal IEP Method with you. (If you've been doing the work throughout the book so far, you've already started practicing it.) This 5-Step Framework is a core component of the methodology. In *Contagious Culture* (Chapter 5) I shared the five steps in deeper detail, from a different perspective, and with several examples and fieldwork. Here, I'm sharing them *early* so you can start *now*. The framework supports crafting intentional impact, in its simplest form, to create tangible and intangible results in any conversation, project, relationship, or experience.

First, identify the project or discussion you're focused on and why it's important. Note that the following exercise pairs beautifully with the frameworks in Chapter 3; the "Want It/Love It Up" exercise helps you identify what you want, and the "Do the Work" exercise helps determine what you need to do to actually create it. The following 5-Step Framework helps us bring it all together to activate intentions and create the impact we desire.

The Five Steps to Intentional Impact Framework

- **Outcome.** *What is the outcome you want to create?* This should be tangible and something you can see or touch. You would not have created this outcome without the meeting, conversation, project, and so on.
- **Impact.** *What is the emotional impact you want to have? How do you want people to feel? How do you want to feel?* You will create an emotional and energetic experience with your presence and actions either way. Being intentional about it is highly useful.
- **Show up.** *How will you have to show up to create the outcome(s) and emotional impact you desire?* What will your presence be? Your quality of listening? Your body language? Your attire? Anything that impacts how you show up goes here.
- **Believe.** *What will you want and need to believe in order to show up that way?* Make this authentic. If you're having a hard time finding something useful and real to believe, go deeper. What's the truest thing you can believe to help you show up well and congruent?
- **Actions.** *What actions will you need to take to make it all so?* What will you actually have to do? Before, during, after?

You will find that magic happens when you are clear on what you want, have a strong why, put these five steps together, and do the work. You need *all* five steps. Don't skip or take any of them for granted. I've done the legwork, I promise. Every single step is here on purpose. I have countless stories of people redesigning relationships, closing business deals, getting their dream job, changing the energy and effectiveness of their meetings, calling in their spouse/partner, exiting an employee with grace and dignity, completing their marriage, having hard conversations, going through mediation, and on and on using the five steps.

Plug yourself into this framework for your next meeting and see what happens. For fun, as a team, you could even plug the question "What kind of contagious do we want to be?" into the five steps.

When you lay these steps on top of the work we'll be doing throughout the rest of this book, they only become richer.

They can be used for a singular event, but they can also be used in the vision of your life and the overall impact you want to have in business, parenting, relationships, legacy . . . all of it.

Here's something extra special about these five steps—when you use them regularly, they become a habit. They begin to frame thinking, unlock new ways of navigating leadership challenges, and help crystallize themes of what is most important to you. These steps *strengthen* your intention and make it real, which is core to opening the Portal of Purpose for even more powerful and exuberant impact.

The Portal of Purpose and the Power of Intention and Proclamation

The intentions we set create a portal for our reality.

For years I've worked my vision for impact with a full heart. I use my five steps regularly, and I work my Intentional Energetic Presence (IEP) daily. I've had some thrilling wins, and I've also been brought to my knees. What's helped me keep going has been connection to purpose and to my Essential You (more in Part 2). What's also kept things moving is my clarity of intention, my commitment to service, my true presence, my openness to magic, and my willingness to claim it. These together, combined with the factors that support them (that I'm sharing in this book), open what I call the "Portal of Purpose."

The combination is potent.

It was a Tuesday afternoon. I'd just spent an entire day at a client's winery in Napa leading 60 of the client's front-line staff through our IEP Fundamentals session. We'd had a ball, and my car was stocked with good wine. Coming out of the session, I noticed a stream of texts from my manager. I called her back. "Anese," she said, "there's a big conference in education, 600 superintendents representing the State of California and about 4.2 million students in K–12. They have a keynote early Thursday morning in Monterey, 36 hours from now. Their keynoter got sick and they want to know if you can step in. You have literally 15 things on your calendar that we'll need to move, including a 'hot date' tomorrow night, it's your week with the kids, and the dog is going to need boarding. What do you think?"

My task brain said, "Um . . . hell no."

But my heart, spirit, and mouth said, "Hell yes!" before my task brain could take over.

"Tell them yes! We'll figure it out." This was one I definitely wanted to show up for.

Not even 36 hours later I was on stage with some of the biggest decision makers and influencers in education in California, having a chat about showing up for leadership, creating a contagious and courageous culture, and working their own IEP.

After the session one of the superintendents, Dr. Greg Franklin of Tustin Unified School District, asked me to sit down with him in the lobby. He asked me, "How do we get this work into our schools?" Within an hour of the keynote, we'd decided to have me down for another keynote in Southern California in a few months. We'd also decided to do a prototype of our IEP Stewardship Program with eight of his teachers and principals representing 24,000 students. The conversation was easy. It was present, meaningful, and real. Greg and I were aligned—the energy of positive intent, intuition, and "heck *yes*" for both of us was very much alive. I drove home on four tires and magic air.

Within ten weeks the new stewards were trained. Within seven months I was on stage at the district's annual school-year kick-off to speak with more than 1,100 teachers, principals, and others, and then spent the next day witnessing the stewards from the back of their classrooms, as they brought this work to life at the different schools. Within eight months, from "Hello, let's train," to launch, they'd led 1,700 of their fellow teachers, principals, and administrative personnel through the IEP Fundamentals. As I write this, they are still going strong, doing magic with the content in a way that fits for education, and exploring ways to touch the rest of the humans in the district next year.

That's less than eight months for some important contagious impact that's just getting started. Eight months may feel like a little or a lot to you. Trust me: what these folks did in that amount of time is profound. It took some major IEP on all our parts. Because let me tell you, while this story is great, the serendipity of what led up to it is a powerful demonstration of the magic of intention and the Portal of Purpose.

Now . . . here's where it gets extra interesting.

The conference center where I delivered that keynote in Monterey for education was the exact conference center and room and location where I'd spoken as the keynote the *previous* week for a conference in real estate. As part of that talk, the conference leaders had asked me to stay after and be on a Women in Leadership panel. During the panel one of the audience members asked me where I'd like to see this work go. My response? "Everywhere. However, I believe that education and health care are two of the most important industries we can get this work into in order to create a greater, more authentic, and positively leverageable impact on our planet."

I remember the question. I remember the conviction I had while answering it *(clarity of intention)*. And I remember feeling my heart and what felt like goosebumps all over as I sat on that stage and claimed this desire in front of 200+ people *(powerful proclamation)*. Looking back, I can see now that the feeling I had was of absolute truth for me, a grounding in my purpose *(commitment to service)*. The combination of that statement, my internal congruency, and my IEP *(true presence)* was liken to writing a letter to the universe or casting some kind of spell or saying a deep, deep prayer or something else simply powerful and magical *(openness to magic)*. In any case, my "request" was heard. And a week later I was in that *same* conference room, in that *same* center, on that *same* stage, speaking to the audience (of three times the size) I'd claimed the week before *(exuberant impact)* (see Figure 4.1).

CLARITY OF INTENTION
POWERFUL PROCLAMATION
TRUE PRESENCE
COMMITMENT TO SERVICE
OPENNESS TO MAGIC

EXUBERANT
IMPACT

FIGURE 4.1 The Portal of Purpose

This is not an uncommon occurrence. The universe conspires to support us when we are present, clear on our desires, aligned with ourselves, on purpose with our mission, and in service of others. I've witnessed (and experienced) many other stories like this where an intention is set, a proclamation is made, the purpose is strong, and magic unfolds. Stories of serendipitous meetings; people attracting the right business partners, employees, agents, clients, or spouses; colleagues landing serendipitous speaking gigs and book deals; even money or clients "showing up" at the perfect time—all accessed in the Portal of Purpose.

While the portal opens up, things will also clear out. Anything that isn't in service of the greatest good, your soul, your mission, your truth, or your well-being goes "buh-bye." I've noticed that when I'm truly on purpose and clear, anything that isn't in alignment or is dramatic, not truthful, or not serving my energy makes itself painfully obvious that it needs to go. Sometimes this magically takes care of itself, and other times it requires hard and sometimes "trudgerous" but necessary worthwhile work.

Why, oh why, does this all happen? Because when you're in the "portal," it has to. The portal opens up when your IEP is clear, when you *listen*, when you're in service of, when you come from love, when you honor your intuition, and when you're willing to say "yes" to really scary stuff because your soul demands it. The portal opens up when you're willing to be on your edge and to devote to service and creating an impact that is bigger than you.

I believe the portal can only be accessed if we are taking excellent care of ourselves, owning our impact, holding the intention of service, and listening. Add in magic, proclamations, and true presence (which requires great IEP)—the possibilities are limitless.

The more I pay attention to the portal in my life, the more I can feel solid *yeses* or *nos*. I can feel opportunities open and get stronger and wider as I stay in flow. And I notice that when I question the portal, when I second-guess any decision that comes from overthinking, when I get small or try to force something that doesn't feel right—I contract and the portal gets smaller or shuts down all together.

That is the power of intention, of listening, of working our IEP, and of staying true.

It's also the power of saying yes.

Be open to the portal. Say yes. And lead.

Ready? Let's put it together.

Fieldwork: Make It Real

Let's open the Portal of Purpose and create some intentional impact. This can be in any area of your life or overall, it can be for this book (though you likely already did this in Chapter 2), and it can be for any timeline (today, this week, a year, etc.). Do this for as many situations and areas of life you wish.

These two exercises can work together or hold their own separately. I personally like to do the **Portal of Purpose** for overall "big mission" impact, and then use the **Five Steps** to support everything I do in the portal.

The Portal of Purpose Exercise

My intention (what I want to make happen): _____

My commitment to service and purpose (*why* this is important): _____

My proclamation (what I am naming and claiming I want to create here, and *whom* I'm proclaiming it to): _____

My level of openness to magic (trust, faith, serendipity, pixie dust, and the unexplainable): _____

My level of true presence (my breath, presence, self-care, congruency, and being here connected now): _____

Anything I need to do or be to make each of these components even stronger: _____

The Five Steps to Intentional Impact Exercise

Project/conversation/meeting/situation: _____
Why important/What's at stake/Who it impacts: _____

1. Desired outcomes: _____
2. Desired emotional impact: _____
3. How I will show up: _____
4. What I will believe: _____
5. What I will do: _____

With Part 1 of this book digested and applied, the contagious you is now ready to move to Part 2. There we'll work on building your even more positively contagious and healthy presence.

PART 2

CONTAGIOUS PRESENCE: UNLOCK AND NOURISH YOUR SUPERPOWERS

CHAPTER 5

Design Your Intentional Energetic Presence. Be It.

*Does the way you show up help you create the impact
you want and the experience you desire?*

*No? Change it. Yes? Up-level it. This can all be designed.
Let's go . . .*

You are walking into one of the most important meetings of your life.

You care very much about the content and people you are speaking to.

The people matter. What you're going to speak about matters.

It's important that you lead these people effectively, that they know you care, that they listen, that you influence well, and that you have the impact you want.

You must set the tone for all of this to happen.

You feel present, solid, awake, clear. You are prepared. You know what *outcomes* you want to create (and *why*), how you want them to *feel* (and how *you* want to feel). You know how you want to *show up* and what you need to *believe* to do so (authentically). And your *action* plan is in place.

Your intentions are set. Your energy is clean. And your presence is solid and authentic. You are rocking it already, and you're not even in that door.

And now you're there, passionately neutral and ready to serve.

Anything that comes at you, any question, demand, resistance, or responsiveness—you're open to it. Regardless of the energy of *that guy* in the room with his arms crossed, brows furrowed, and face glaring at you when he's not working his phone, you're able to stay present and focused. You hold your energetic state. The more you hold it, the clearer you become, the more the room comes with you. You notice that the energy of resistance and ambiguity you felt from some at the beginning starts to melt away. As different challenges and issues come up, you're able to shift your energetic state to meet them where they are and come up with solutions. "Curiosity" is needed here? Done! The state of "contribution" or "appreciation" here? Zoom! A bit of "rigor and no BS" here? Pow! "Vulnerability" and "truth" now? (Gulp.) Well, alrighty then! You have superpowers, and everybody in the room can sense it.

The meeting ends. It was productive, high vibration, clean energy. People were pumped; they felt seen, connected, served, inspired, and excited for the next step. And you? You were you. One hundred percent powerful, full-grade you.

You feel well-spent *and* energized. You feel on purpose, on point, and of service. You are present.

This meeting might be your annual board meeting or a meeting with a prospective or current client. It could be with your boss, your team, an entire audience, your spouse or partner, or your child who needs your presence as a parent like never before. It could be in person or via a conference call 3,000 miles away. It doesn't matter the venue. What matters is that you *show up.*

And you did. You rocked it.

Why did that go so well?

You and Your Very Powerful Intentional Energetic Presence

Why did it go so well? Because you showed up, you were contagious for good, and you set the tone.

The way you led in that meeting created the container for others to engage without drama, with purpose, and as their better selves.

80

It worked because you did the work—your inner work.

You worked your IEP—got clear on your *intentions*, managed your *energy*, and showed up real with solid and clear *presence*.

And you had positive impact. You were #contagious.

Imagine going from meeting to meeting, and conversation to conversation, creating that every day—no matter how intense the day or how challenging the people. What could you do with your life?

Now of course that meeting could have been a mess, with you coming in late, overwhelmed, guarded, not present, faking it 'til you make it, and just trying to keep up. The people and the agenda may have been exactly the same, but the outcomes would have been totally different.

Why?

You.

You would've been contagious in that scenario too. Just not the helpful kind.

The gifts that come with being positively contagious? Limitless. The return on investment for a bit of internal work on your side? Exponential.

Here's the thing: It's easy to be positively contagious and have a great day when something good happens, but what about when it doesn't? What do you do when your morning or that meeting is disastrous? That's when knowing that your presence *is* your impact is especially important.

And that it can be intended and designed for on purpose.

Our "Vibe," Our IEP, Our Impact

Every interaction we have has a "vibrational energetic" impact. The difference in being successful (or not) in any engagement can be as simple as the impact our vibe creates. We can invite responsiveness—or resistance. We can create inspiration—or obligation. We can evoke doom and gloom—or light up a room. We can inspire authenticity—or fakery. We can open a conversation up—or shut it right down.

All with our energetic presence.

When people come to this work, they often don't know that creating *contributory generative* energy and being *positively* contagious are leadership skills and that the key to unlocking their next level of leadership, presence, and impact is by addressing the things we're discussing here. They don't realize their quickest path to creating the results they want is increasing their self-awareness and tending to their own intentions, energy, and presence. And they also don't realize that there is an "inner game" and an "outer game" of leadership playing at all times. The *inner game* being the intentions, energy, beliefs, mindset, well-being, presence, and who we are. The *outer game* being what we actually *do* in our communication, skills, and interactions with others. The inner game drives the outer game. And no one can play your game but you.

Of course, your skills and tools are important—you can elevate those too. But if your presence is not on point, or you're burnt out or the lowest vibration in the room, or "leaving dead bodies" everywhere you go, and have a weak inner game, your skills and tools will only take you so far, and often even make matters worse.

In other words, it doesn't matter how brilliant people are, how many degrees they have, how much work they do on the "doing," or how great their "outer game" is; if they have bad IEP, they are negatively contagious. They're sunk before they start.

Once people understand this and have claimed their contagiousness (as we did in Part 1), they're on their way. And we begin working in three areas: (1) the skills, strategy, and tangible things that need to happen to move them forward; (2) the nourishment and strengthening of their own IEP so that they're more fully resourced, protected, and set up to succeed; and (3) their ability to intentionally project, "infect," and influence others in a way that will be most positively contagious and helpful to their mission.

As a leader, the most important work we can do is strengthen our IEP. The more we tend to this *proactively*, the stronger it becomes and the easier it is to command our energetic presence at will. This ultimately allows us to respond and lead in the most appropriate, helpful, and effective ways possible.

This is leadership.

We are responsible (and "response-able") for the energy we bring to everything we do and what we do with it.

We are responsible for creating our results, doing meaningful work, and being positively contagious.

We can't do this if we're burnt out, exhausted, depleted, resentful, or simply not fully resourced or present.

So we do the work.

We strengthen, nourish, cultivate, honor, grow, and build a strong *Intentional Energetic Presence.*

States of Being and Your IEP

We walk around our world in states of being in every moment: neutral, calm, angry, anxious, judgmental, or loving. Blissful, fearful, courageous, excited, grateful, or blaming. Apathetic, defeated, present, curious, open, closed, generous, happy, or sad. Amused, accusatory, powerful, vulnerable, kind, cruel, CYA . . . you get it. These energetic states create impact on the field and the person(s) we're with. And they're contagious.

If I'm in a state of blame—when I'm embodying and projecting the energy of blame—and I give you feedback, do you think you'll feel it? Yep. Will you respond well to it and feel inspired to shift? Nope. But if I'm in a genuine state of care, curiosity, or contribution, then what? That leads to a totally different outcome. It won't work if I fake my state; you'll sense it. You won't even need to know exactly what "it" is, only that my vibe is off. You may feel manipulated, condescended to, or resistant, and then your own vibe will shift, perhaps becoming defensive. I, sensing your vibe, will respond to that, feel justified for my blame (or whatever), and off we go into a downward spiral. But . . . what if I could shift my state authentically? What if I didn't have to fake it but could truly up-level my state by being present, setting an intention, and showing up with you fully? Now we're talking.

In the scenario at the beginning of this chapter, I referenced your ability to shift energetic states as needed in order to "meet someone where they're at" and show up in service of the room. This ability is a leadership superpower. The stronger your IEP, the more accessible this superpower is.

"States of being" are our energetic states, the "vibe" we embody and project. When used intentionally (and truthfully), they can help us feel better, get clearer, connect with others more effectively, and shift the tone of any meeting or conversation.

The trick, of course, is authenticity. If you're not genuine, the people around you will feel it. Our energetic presence communicates louder than anything we say. Being aware of it, intentional with it, and able to shift on command is an essential leadership skill. There are a couple of tools in the IEP Method that cultivate this skill. One, the Energetic Xylophone, I'll share with you in Chapter 9. The other, the Presence Reboot (coming next), is a core component of the IEP Method and baseline for the xylophone. To use either of these tools optimally, you must build a strong IEP foundation. So let's do that.

The IEP Method

So how do you work your IEP? And how do you make it work *for* you? And what actually *is* it? In *Contagious Culture,* I introduced the IEP Method—the methodology, the model, and the core components that make it all hum. For this book, I'm reviewing the IEP Method at the highest level and offering some new thinking and resources that have surfaced since *Contagious Culture.* (So please dig into that book as well, as it will support you and your organization in different ways.)

As your Intentional Energetic Presence, your IEP is how you show up in the world (for yourself and for others). It is also your *intentions*—what you want to have happen; your *energy*—the energy and stamina you have to do so and the energy you bring to the table; and your *presence*—how you show up, how present you are, and what you bring to the now.

The stronger and clearer our IEP, the greater our resiliency and resourcefulness, and the stronger, clearer, and more positive our impact can be.

The Three Parts of the IEP Method

1. Reboot your presence.
2. Build a strong, energetic foundation and field.
3. Create intentional impact.

The first part—"the IEP Presence Reboot"—is your ability to reboot your presence *in the moment* and shift state, no matter what. While I talk about this at length using exercises and examples in *Contagious Culture*, the basics are: You check your presence and the energy you're bringing into a room or conversation. If it's not what you want it to be or what will best serve what you're there to do, you *reboot*. You breathe. Intend. Shift. Show up. And go.

We are rebooting thousands of times each day. Anytime we walk into a room, shift gears on a project, get pissed off, or start thinking judgmental thoughts, we're rebooting. Anytime we feel nervous on stage, become overwhelmed, yell at our kid (or get ready to), get ticked off about traffic or life or anything out of our control, have a moment of total joy we want to savor, or have a moment of "ick" we want to move past, we're rebooting. Everything is an opportunity for a reboot. Notice, intend, reboot. Notice, intend, reboot.

The second part of the IEP Method—"the IEP Foundation"—is the ability to build a strong, energetic foundation and field. Building your energetic field is the biggest component of the methodology.

Our first intention is to build your energetic field so you can come fully to your life, feel solid, clear, and energized, and have the capacity and range for even more.

Our second intention is to build your field so well that when others step into it, especially the people who may be more challenging to work with, you can better serve, navigate, and lead them with clarity, grace, and effect—without burning yourself out, getting sucked into their stuff, or giving yourself away.

The stronger the field, the easier it is to hold these two intentions. It also becomes easier to *reboot, shift state,* and *create intentional impact.*

Building a strong energetic field is an inside-out job. We use the *Essential You* and the four quadrants of *Energy and Presence* to get it done (both of which I'll go into deeply later in this chapter). Please note that building the field and having good IEP is a daily practice and life's work. In other words, it's never done.

The final part of the IEP Method (part 3) is about creating intentional impact. I shared this with you in greater depth in Chapter 4 with the "Five Steps to Intentional Impact" framework. (If you did your fieldwork, you've already used this.)

The better you are at rebooting (part 1) and the stronger your energetic foundation and field (part 2), the easier it is to create intentional impact (part 3). The three parts of the method all work together.

So reboot as we go, keep doing your five steps, and now let's build your energetic field and foundation.

The IEP Model: Leading from the Inside Out

The IEP Model has four layers (see Figure 5.1).

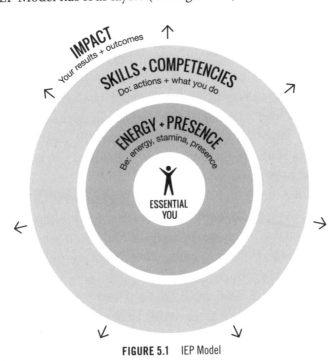

FIGURE 5.1   IEP Model

1. The Essential You (You, grounded, present, real, *here*)
2. Energy and Presence (Your energy, stamina, and presence)
3. Skills and Competencies (Your actions and what you do)
4. Impact (The results and outcomes you create)

Broken down further, you can see there are very specific components of each level (see Figure 5.2).

FIGURE 5.2 IEP Model Breakdown

In this book we're focusing more deeply on levels one and two. Why not three and four? Because when you have one and two right, and in service of four, three (actions) is a piece of cake and four (impact) gets handled. All that said, not to worry! I *will* give you tools and frameworks (and lists!) in Parts 3–5 of this book that will address levels three and four.

Let's dig into layers one and two of the IEP Model.

Layer One: The Essential You and Your Becoming

The relationship we have with ourselves is the most important relationship we will ever have. Therefore, it is best present, nourished, and loved up.

87

Our Essential You is where this happens.

The Essential You is sacred ground. It's you—your space, your "why," what you stand for, who you are, and who you're becoming.

Your Essential You includes your values, vision, purpose, truth; your "bubble" (that surrounds you, holding your space; see Figure 5.3); and your relationship with your authentic self. (You are welcome to call this the Essential *Me* to ground this idea if it helps.)

FIGURE 5.3   The IEP Bubble

The "bubble" is our own personal space, our "command center." We can be intentional with our presence and the state we project out, as well as how we navigate and respond to what is projected at us.

All of this is at the core of your presence and contagiousness.

Throughout my years working with people and organizations on their Essential You, I've distilled the Essential You down to love and purpose—love of ourselves, of each other, of the present moment, of what is and who we are, of what might be and who we're becoming, and of the impact we're working to create—and why.

I've noticed that almost every disconnect, argument, pain, feeling of overwhelm or contraction, unkind act (within ourselves and with others), and even loss of presence can be drilled down to a disconnection from humanness, love, and purpose.

Love creates life, breath, expansion, generosity, curiosity, safety, presence, and space for truth.

Disconnection creates fear, contraction, hatred, burnout, boredom, apathy, and defensiveness.

The antidote to disconnection is presence and love—with and for *ourselves* first.

Then we can pay it forward like crazy.

If I'm not honoring my Essential You, being in right relationship with myself, honoring my values, taking care of myself, loving me, and showing up for me—how in the world can I do that well for others?

The secret to being positively contagious is to be so present and grounded in your Essential You and connected to yourself and love that you can't help but be positively contagious. This means even—especially!—when things are hard.

When we stay connected to ourselves, do our work, give ourselves grace, and act in service of (on purpose), we have a better chance of navigating challenges successfully, being more conscious, and extending that grace to others as well, which is another form of leadership.

This is life's work. We are *becoming* in every moment.

At any moment we can decide to shift, to become something different, to have a better relationship with ourselves, to count on ourselves more . . . to love.

Here are three inquiries you can lean into to support your Essential You:

1. **What is the quality of the relationship I have with myself?**
   Does it make me stronger and happier? Do I listen to myself? Am I my own best friend? Do I "belong" to myself? What is the littlest (or biggest) thing I can do to make this essential relationship with me better?

2. **What do I love about myself? And how do I love myself?** What are the qualities, quirks, and strengths I most love about me? Do I love myself enough to honor my core values and to make space for me? Do I keep my promises to myself? Do I hold my boundaries? Do I take care of myself? Do I give myself permission for authentic emotions? Do I let myself ask for help? How can I love and honor myself even more?

3. **Who am I becoming?** And am I becoming who/what I want to be—or is it by default or a "should" (externally imposed by others)? Is it with love—or with pressure and force? Is it in service of my life and impact—or is it just in survival? Am I making my life happen—or is my life happening to me?

When we have awareness, clarity, and intention around these questions, we can direct our Essential You and our becoming. When we don't, the world directs it.

Want Something Quicker and in the Moment?

There are magic questions I like to ask on the go to ensure I'm staying connected to myself and my Essential You (kind of like an Essential You Reboot).

Here are five of them:

1. Is this thing (I'm about to do or say) honoring and loving (of myself and others)?

2. Am I on purpose? (Or am I off track, in drama, out of my business?)

3. Am I in my space? (Or have I lost it and gotten sucked into someone else's?)

4. Am I belonging to myself and my highest power? (Or am I trying to fit in and belong to someone else?)

5. Am I "bubbled up" and being intentional with my presence and state? (Or have I forgotten *me* and become overwhelmed by it all?)

These questions quickly bring me back when I start veering into a negative mindspace. They provide a simple way to reboot and recommit to the person I want to be, how I want to show up, and what I need to do in the moment.

OK, let's tie this all back into your energetic presence. There is an energy of being in solid relationship with ourselves and actively becoming. An energy of *I am here*. We can feel it in others when we're around it. We can feel it in ourselves. It is awake.

When we claim our relationship with ourselves and our becoming, we claim our energetic field.

The more we stand for and trust ourselves, the better we can serve, lead, and contribute to others.

This is your Essential You.

It is your job to love it, protect, nourish, and fortify it.

How? By owning it *and* strengthening your energy and presence.

Layer Two: The Four Quadrants of Energy and Presence

Our energy and presence support, strengthen, and protect the Essential You.

The Essential You supports our energy and presence. It all works together.

Our energy and presence are how we take care of ourselves and how we show up in the world. This layer of the model is broken into four quadrants and areas of focus that all work together to support each other and the Essential You (see Figure 5.4). When you shift something in one, others tend to shift as well. The littlest things count.

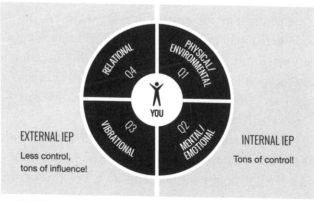

FIGURE 5.4   IEP Model: The Four Quadrants of Energy and Presence

I guarantee there is low-hanging fruit you can pick right this minute to support your IEP. Shall we?

Internal IEP

The IEP Model is broken into *Internal* and *External* IEP. In Internal IEP (which we have a lot of control and influence over), we look at Quadrants 1 and 2. In External IEP, Quadrants 3 and 4, we have influence—however, not so much control. The stronger our internal, the easier to navigate the external, so we want to set ourselves up well here. Let's do that . . .

Quadrant 1: Physical and Environmental Energy

The first quadrant is your *Physical and Environmental Energy*. The physical is all about your physical well-being and how you tend to your body. This can mean your self-care practices, the food you eat, your hydration, gut health, sleep, exercise, and preventative health care. This can also include your overall health, hormones, biochemistry, inflammation factors, allergies, and medical treatment and support. *Anything* that impacts your physical well-being and energy gets TLC in Quadrant 1.

And then there's your environmental energy, which supports your physical and mental well-being. This refers to your actual environment (home, car, pantry, closets, bed, office space, desktop, lighting, clothing, etc.), what you surround yourself with (people and things), how you set yourself up for success in every realm of your life (organization, proactive scheduling, boundaries, bringing healthy food for long meetings, limiting TV and social media hooks, etc.), whatever makes you feel good in your space (flowers, pretty things, your dog, a car organizer), your time/calendar management, anything that impacts your environmental energy.

What you can do for yourself in this quadrant is limitless. The questions we ask ourselves in Quadrant 1 are: "Does the way I take care of myself help me feel and show up at my best?" (Physical) "Does what I surround myself with support me in creating more expansive and life-giving energy in my world (therefore helping me feel and show up at my best)?" (Environmental)

Quadrant 2: Mental and Emotional Energy

The second quadrant is your *Mental and Emotional Energy* (which is very much supported by what you do in Quadrant 1). This quadrant focuses on the thoughts you think, the emotions you have, your mental health, how you take care of yourself mentally and emotionally, and the assumptions you make. It also is about your self-talk, beliefs, judgments, the stories you tell, level of accountability, intentions, language, framing and reframing, self-kindness—all that goes on in that amazing head and heart of yours! The questions we ask ourselves in Quadrant 2 are: "Do the thoughts I think support me in showing up at my best, feeling well, and staying expansive? And do I allow myself to have the authentic emotions I feel, to nourish them, honor them, fully own them, and get support for them as needed so that I can show up at my best, feel well and clear, and stay expansive?"

As you can see, we have the most control in these two quadrants and in how we want to be in relationship with everything in them. And great news, Quadrants 1 and 2 support each other beautifully! In Chapter 6, I will go more deeply into these quadrants and reveal what you can do with them. Right now, I'll bet you can think of one or two things in each quadrant you sense would have immediate impact on your energy if you gave them a bit of tender loving care. Yes? I promise you they are impacting your ability to lead. Write them down on the side of this page, in your journal, or in your fieldwork notes in this chapter and make a commitment to do something about them ASAP (like when you put this book down).

External IEP

So now moving into External IEP, we're going to look at Quadrants 3 and 4. This is the stuff you don't have a lot of control over in terms of how people respond to you. However, if you work your Internal IEP (in Quadrants 1 and 2) and stay intentional with Quadrants 3 and 4, you have a better chance of influencing external factors.

Quadrant 3: Vibrational Energy

Quadrant 3 is all about your *Vibrational Energy.* This is what you "put out there." It's your vibe. It's how people feel when they're with you, when you walk into a room, when they see your name on caller ID. It's how *you* feel when *you're with you.* Does your energy expand or contract, resonate or retaliate, compel or repel, elevate or depress? Is your energy light or heavy, bright or dim, responsive or resistant, positive or negative? Do you project "glass half full" or "glass half empty," "trustworthy" or "run for the hills!," "yummy" or "yuck," "oomph" or "ick," "YES" or "NO"? These are all vibrations we put out and we pick up on. They're impact makers or breakers. They're subtle. They're key. They're contagious.

They're also workable. We can shift our vibe, fast. The trick is to do it authentically and sustainably, which is part of why we're having this conversation right now. The questions we ask in Quadrant 3 are: "What is the energy I'm bringing into the room/this conversation/whatever? And is my vibrational energy contributing to helping things go better or worse?" And on the receiving end . . . "What am I taking on? Is this energy mine? Do I want it? And do I need to bubble up!?"

What you do in the Essential You and in Quadrants 1, 2, and 4 can help fortify your vibrational energy in ways that will have people resonating with you instead of running from you. This work will also help you build such a strong field that "bubbling up" (holding your space) doesn't become something you have to do on demand with effort, because you just are.

Quadrant 4: Relational Energy

By the time we get to Quadrant 4, with our energy humming and our vibes working for us, *Relational Energy* is—ironically—the easiest of all the quads. I've found that the cleaner the first three quadrants are, and the more solid your Essential You is, the easier it is to make real life-giving, sustainable, and even joyful change here—even in the most dire of situations.

Relational energy is about the energetic dynamics happening in your relationships. Let's put it this way—the calls, texts, emails, and invitations you get in your life that make your heart sink, make your energy contract, and have you "swipe left" (or whatever your version of "decline" is), those are relationships where the energetic dynamics are . . . not so hot. They may need a bit of TLC, boundaries, and/or redesign, or you may need to give them the old "heave-ho." The relationships you feel yourself delight and expand in (and you "swipe right")? Those are likely in energetic resonance and great shape and can be nourished in the form of intention, appreciation, and care.

We look first at the awareness of the energy of the relationship. Awareness is 70 percent of the battle. With awareness you have choice. Once you've made the choice in either direction (address or ignore, love or war), I have all sorts of frameworks and tools for you that we'll talk about in Part 3. The questions to ask yourself in Quadrant 4 are: "Do the relationships in my life expand or contract me? Are they life-giving or soul-sucking? Do they make me better or worse? How am I contributing to all of these dynamics? How am I showing up?" Freedom is here, if you want it.

All Together Now

When I put the three components of the IEP Method together (reboot, build the field, create intentional impact), stay present, intend my state, honor my Essential You, tend to my four quadrants and taking care of myself, and use it all in service of good—I design my IEP.

When I design my IEP, I unlock my superpowers for good (not evil). And I become a leadership badass (the good kind).

IEP, it's up to me. Let's design it.

Fieldwork: Make It Real

This entire book is about designing your IEP. Let's start with some basics—the low-hanging fruit that you can apply right now from this chapter.

States of Being

Pick your top three most powerful states of being and embody them. Reboot back to them daily as needed.

_____

_____

_____

Bubble Up

Simply _knowing_ you have a bubble, and your own space, is magic. (Remember, awareness is 70 percent.)

Accessing your bubble:

You can access your bubble at any time (you always have it; you may just forget).

1. Breathe. Notice you in the center of your bubble.
2. Create your own space. Fill it up with YOU. (Release anything that doesn't serve.)
3. Own it.

Nourishing your bubble:

The more you nourish and practice it, the stronger it becomes and the easier it is to "bubble up"! How do you nourish a bubble? Know it, love it, fortify it, hold it, and keep rebooting as needed. The next two exercises will help make your bubble even stronger.

The Four Quads

Write one thing down you'll do for each of the IEP quadrants and tend to it beginning today.

Quadrant 1: _____

Quadrant 2: _____

Quadrant 3: _____

Quadrant 4: _____

Essential You Love

Let's explore (and strengthen) your relationship with yourself. Rate the following on a 0–10 scale (10 = highest) to see where you are with your internal relationship. The stronger this is, the stronger your Essential You. If any of these score lower than you'd wish, no worries. Hop to. What's the littlest thing you can do to shift? This is all by your design. (*Note:* The relationship with self is a never-ending process—the process is the goal.)

- My love for myself
- My love of my purpose and the impact I'm here to create
- My love of the human beings in my life
- My love for and honoring of my core values
- My love of my relationship with myself; I am my own best friend, and I *belong* to me
- My love of my truth and knowing that I can count on myself
- My love for who I am becoming

Extra Credit: Do the fieldwork in Chapter 6 of *Contagious Culture* to dig deeper into your Essential You (i.e., values, vision, purpose).

Strengthen Your Immunity: Self-Care, Self-Kind, Self-Full. Nourish It.

Your self-care is your superpower;
cultivate the heck out of it—love yourself up.

You've claimed; you've intended; you've laid your foundation for good IEP. It's time to strengthen your immunity against negative contagions and create even more space and resiliency to navigate this big life. In *Contagious Culture* I covered some concepts around self-care and continue to receive many questions and requests pointing to some of the biggest cultural stories we make up about self-care and "building our fields." I found this is a topic that people wanted to hear more about. These questions and requests have led to this chapter as well as additional practices to support your Internal IEP.

First things first. Building your immunity and being positively contagious does not mean you are "fake" or "ra, ra, sis boom bah!" or "up" or "positive" or "high vibration" or "happy" all the time. It does mean you have self-awareness and self-efficacy to choose how to respond and show up when you're not feeling "up" or when you need support. It means that you give yourself full permission to be real, have your experience, learn from that experience, and get help where needed. And it means you're "response-able" for working your stuff out (in a safe space with the appropriate people where you aren't vomiting out your issues or taking them out on your team). Building your immunity is essential for all of this.

Building our immunity requires self-care, vulnerability, and courage—it requires we do our work. When we do our work we have greater access to ourselves and a fuller range of emotions. With this access we increase our capacity to hold space for ourselves, for others, and for their range of emotions. Our ability to lead and influence others is highly dependent on the quality of space we can hold. And here's the thing: we can only lead someone as far as we are able to go ourselves. Add to this that it's easy to get clobbered by another's negative energy—and we have unlimited reasons to build our immunity.

You'll notice in this work we're talking about managing *you*—and the energy you bring. We're also talking about managing others—and the energy coming at you from them. Managing other people is where it's especially helpful to build immunity and consciousness. Building our immunity is not about being impenetrable, numb, or fake—it's about being stronger and more resilient so we can help others and do more good. Therefore, self-care is not about being selfish or luxurious—it is generous response-able leadership.

Self-Care Is a Leadership Skill

Every time I lead a session or meet with a new client, I know we will likely be addressing at least two main themes: (1) unlocking new levels of leadership and influence capacity and (2) reframing self-care from being a selfish luxury into a self-full, nonnegotiable necessity and skill.

These two desires—lead well and take care—are often held as mutually exclusive and working against each other when really they need each other. One cannot survive without the other.

Impact needs self-care for power and sustainability. Self-care needs impact for power and inspiration.

If we're keeping score, impact needs self-care more than self-care needs impact because you can't be truly (or sustainably) impactful if you are exhausted or burnt out. As one of our participants put it to me last year after a team member had died of a heart attack, "Forget about us not leading at our best if we're *burnt out*—**we can't lead if we're *dead*.**"

If I'm connected to my intention for the impact I want to have (and why), I'm likely more inspired to take care of myself. I'm less inclined to disregard my well-being or eat junk food or skip my workout or compromise my sleep and personal space if I know that my performance and how I show up for the people I lead depends on me being physically, mentally, and spiritually fully resourced.

Self-care becomes not only essential but one of the most generous things I can do. Not only does it strengthen my immunity and protect me against what I've come to call "leadership depression," but it keeps me physically capable of doing what I'm here to do. Think of the last time you flew. The pilot made the usual announcement that if there is an issue in flight and the oxygen masks drop, you should put your mask on yourself first and then attend to those around you, including your own children. Why? Because if you're passed out or dead, you're of no use to anyone around you. Leadership and self-care are no different.

Self-Care as a Critical Conversation

This past year in almost every room I've been in, there is at least one person who's recently lost someone to an unexpected early death. The majority of causes? Heart attack, cancer, and suicide. I don't think it has to be this way. I do think the way we tend to self-care, preventative health, and mental health does need a big up-leveling. We've come a long way in awareness, disease prevention, stress management solutions, bio-hacking, workplace Employee Assistance Programs (EAPs), the science of well-being, and even having these conversations to begin with. I am wildly optimistic. And we have to keep talking about it, and putting our well-being at the top of the priority list just as we prioritize business and financial results, impact on others, and anything else we want to create.

Fortunately, we're seeing more and more organizations and leaders putting a greater value on mindfulness, self-care, and well-being. Why? Because aside from up-leveling leadership skills and creating a better culture, more importantly, no one wants a burnt-out workforce, an exhausted partner, or another premature death or suicide. No leaders want to have their employees on disability due to depression or illness because people are overwhelmed or not taking care of themselves. Sure, the business results from getting "in front of this" and addressing it proactively are great, the culture optimization is lovely, but we're talking about livelihood and life.

Self-Care Is Not What You Think

I used to think that self-care was a "thing" you did. What I know now is that self-care is something you "be"—it's a mindset that can inform every decision we make. When we *be* self-care, it doesn't matter if we have three weeks for vacation off the grid, two minutes of silence, or no time at all and only a moment of presence with ourselves and a kind thought we can choose—we can access self-care immediately.

The illusion of what "self-care" *is* often deters people from participating in it. It can seem so big and time-consuming, and the idea of doing it often feels overwhelming, impenetrable, and selfish. And then we end up doing nothing. To help demystify the idea of self-care, let's take it down a notch and look at what self-care truly is.

Self-care happens "in the cracks." It doesn't have to mean eight hours of sleep each night, two hours a day in the gym, a nutritionist, a personal trainer, decadent vacations, and a massage therapist following us around. While these may all be lovely (and by all means, go for it), there are more immediately accessible, less expensive, and less time-consuming ways to take care of ourselves.

Self-care is being kind to yourself, taking care of yourself, and being your own best friend and advocate.

It happens when you've had a hard day or moment and, instead of armoring up and forcing your way through, you admit it—and let yourself have a minute.

It happens when you opt out of a toxic conversation or relationship.

It happens when you have to use the bathroom, and instead of holding it, you go. Or when you're thirsty, instead of ignoring it or rushing past the water stop, you drink.

It happens when you bring your "emergency food" with you or a snack in your bag so you don't get stuck without food, or even worse, with bad food.

It happens when instead of being unkind to yourself and beating yourself up for that last "fail" or "dumb thing you just said," you offer yourself grace and even an acknowledgment for being brave.

It happens when you say "no" to a late-night meal or drinks when you're traveling so you can sleep and avoid becoming exhausted.

It happens when you climb into a hot bath and go to bed early as opposed to getting sucked into TV or social media and losing sleep and brain peace.

It happens when you gift yourself a 10-minute time-out for a nap or just a quiet solo moment.

It happens when you set your intentions in the morning as you brush your teeth (bonus points if you say, "Good morning, love, you are fabulous!").

It happens when you guard your morning for your first 10 minutes, only for *you* and stay *quiet.*

It happens when instead of apologizing to the person who keeps interrupting you, you pause and hold your space.

It happens when you ask for what *you* need.

It happens when you look in the mirror and instead of berating the most recent wrinkle, wiggly bit, or gray hair—you love it up and thank it for its service and the wisdom that comes with it.

It happens when your kid gets in the car and is having a bad day, and instead of taking it personally, you breathe and love him or her (and you).

It happens when you say "no" and mean it.

It happens when you say "yes" and mean it.

It happens when you stay present with the dishes you're washing, listen to music, and enjoy the simplicity of that space.

It happens when you enjoy your food, or coffee, or that perfect-sized bite of chocolate.

It happens when we're feeling depressed or sad and instead of brushing it off give ourselves space to get curious, process it, and glean the learning. (There is so much learning in depression and sadness.)

It happens when we get ourselves the professional help and care we need when we need it (therapy, coaching, medical attention, etc.).

It happens when we give ourselves a moment to breathe, get present, and connect with our intention.

It happens when we *pause.*

It happens in the moment.

Presence is self-care.

The examples of self-care, from minuscule to grand, are limitless.

Self-Care as an Act of Generosity

Self-talk and productive language, accessing gratitude, honoring intuition and our deeper voices and emotions, catching the stories and assumptions we're making up before they take us dark—these are all forms of self-care and help us strengthen our immunity. What's more, our self-care is an act of generosity. The more we tend to it, the more we have to give.

One of my very richly scheduled clients, who disliked shopping and whose profession required she look on point all the time, signed up with an online styling and shopping service that sends her clothes each month. (This also enables her to give more to her clients and focus her energy on the right things.)

Another client had a five-minute ritual he did with his wife every morning where for five protected glorious minutes (without their kids and the world pulling on them), they lay in bed (or hid in the closet) and appreciated each other, set their intentions for the day, and just spent time together. (This also enables their marriage to thrive.)

One of our participants from a nonprofit shared that her self-care was in saying her prayers in the morning, setting her intentions on the commute into work, and bringing her favorite tea to the office each day in her "lucky" mug. (This also enables her to be more present for her coworkers and the people she serves.)

One of my favorite forms of self-care is my "no, no thank you" to food that I know may compromise my energetic state or clear thinking. Or "no," when intuitively something feels off or I simply don't want to do something. I've come to love the "no" and find that every time I honor it, I feel more grounded, clear, and trusting of myself, and it frees me up to do better. (This also enables me to give more and be a solid YES for the things I commit to.)

Another form? The self-imposed "time-out" when I feel myself getting jacked or reactive. A simple five-minute time-out (which may consist of me finding a quiet spot to reboot or hitting the bathroom stall to power-pose or dance) brings me back to center, and I'm better able to respond to whatever is happening. (This also spares whomever I'm with from a reactive, and likely not so pleasant or productive, response from me.)

Finally, one of my favorite examples: A friend of mine has a self-care practice that revolves around kindness. Every time she feels overwhelmed by current events, she takes a breath, gets present, feels gratitude for her blessings, and then asks herself, "What is the littlest thing I can do to be kind and help things go better?" This often results in her making a phone call, reaching out to someone in need, making a donation, or doing anything else that feels authentically kind and will do good. She knows it won't solve all the problems of the world, but this little act and intention gives her more internal grace, helps her feel a bit better, and ultimately pays her self-care forward. She's very generous. When I asked her what gives her the energy to contribute again and again, and to not be overwhelmed by it all, she shares that she is able to do this, in part, because she stays conscious with her own self-care first; she allows herself full authentic emotion (which means tears, anger, and even hopelessness sometimes), she gets support from her friends to talk about it, and then she uses her IEP to take care of herself and move through it.

Making Self-Care a Habit Proactively *and* Reactively

The more we practice self-care, self-kindness, presence, intention, and any of the things I've listed here (not to mention your own ways that work for you), the less intimidating self-care is and the more a habit it becomes. Until it's our default and something we can quickly recover to. Have a lot of toxicity in your life? No worries. If you take care of yourself, get present, and stay connected to your intentions, it will become clearer about how you want to navigate and change it (and even how you may be contributing to the toxicity to begin with). Feeling overwhelmed by current events? Take such great care of yourself (while staying connected to your intention for impact) that you are better resourced to rise above the "ick" and ultimately help things go better.

We can build our resiliency and immunity *proactively* and *reactively.* The more we're exposed to negative contagions and react or respond well (by holding our space, taking care of ourselves, bouncing back, and continually learning from it), the more we are able to build our resiliency and immunity reactively. On the flip side, we can build it proactively via self-care, intention, and what I share in this book. Think of it like eating your vegetables, taking your vitamins, and choosing your thoughts—doing these things builds your immunity and resiliency. You might also think of self-care as a "flu shot" (the kind that works and is awesome) that immunizes you against catching others' muck. Whatever metaphor works for you is not important; what's important is that you decide to take care of yourself. This means addressing your kryptonite and building up your superpowers.

Immunity Kryptonite: 31 Things That Weaken Your Field

Just as we build immunity, we can weaken it too! Let's look at some of the things you may be doing that deplete your energetic field (which in turn can hurt your trust and credibility). These are common, they're human, and they pack a subtle and powerful punch. Everything in this chapter (and throughout the rest of this book) can help combat these forms of kryptonite. Look at this list and see if you can slowly knock out a couple of these items. You don't have to do a ton here, and this doesn't have to be hard.

How many of these things do you do?

1. Talking about how busy you are
2. Making excuses
3. Telling your frustrated or dramatic story over and over again
4. Apologizing repeatedly (double points if they're inappropriate or weak apologies with no ownership)
5. Breaking a promise (to self or other)
6. Lying (to self or other)
7. Being late (double points if you make excuses versus own it)
8. Saying "yes" when you mean "no" (and then resenting it)
9. Being a martyr about your time, energy, actions, anything
10. Gossiping
11. Blaming someone/something else
12. Waiting to be rescued
13. Playing your role in the Drama Triangle as Victim, Hero, or Perpetrator (and likely all three at times)
14. Complaining
15. Using weak language
16. Not taking care of yourself
17. Not owning your "stuff"
18. Watching too much TV; watching bad TV
19. Tolerating people/places/things that suck the life out of you
20. Tolerating that *thing* in your environment that bugs you
21. Procrastinating
22. Suffering (pain is inevitable; suffering is optional)
23. Going it alone; not getting help
24. Talking behind people's backs
25. Not engaging issues directly
26. Avoiding . . . anything
27. Giving fluffy "nice" feedback
28. Not deciding but rather being paralyzed in the ambiguity of indecision

29. Not standing for what you need (especially from a self-care standpoint)
30. Not honoring your core values (without consciously *deciding* to *not* honor them for an intentional reason)
31. Overfunctioning, being overly responsible or accountable

What else would you add? In my experience, we've all dabbled in a few of these. The leadership is in owning and shifting them as we wish for stronger impact and influence.

The Mindset of Building Your Immunity (Being)

There is the *being* of building our immunity—our self-awareness, beliefs, thoughts, assumptions, attitudes, intentions, relationship with ourselves, and the way we hold our space.

There is the *doing*—our physical and environmental practices, our rituals, the language we use, what/whom we surround ourselves with, meditation, boundaries, and even travel and "getting in front" of anything coming our way.

They, of course, work together. You need the being and the doing.

Let's start with the being because it will infuse everything you do.

The following are eight principles I've found to be incredibly helpful for shifting mindset, building immunity, and strengthening IEP. Each is immediately applicable, doesn't take a ton of time, and doesn't have to be complicated (unless you wish to make it so).

Own and embody any of these, and you shift the field:

- My presence is my impact. How I show up matters.
- Showing up for myself first is vital to be able to show up for others.
- My relationship with myself is the most important relationship I have. (This includes any spiritual beliefs I hold and my relationship with a higher power.)
- The combination of trust, credibility, and leadership is an inside-out job.
- The clarity of my intention equals the power and quality of my impact (and the ease of doing anything).
- I matter. I have my own space. (I am "response-able" for holding and nourishing it.)

- I create my experience. I author my story. I lead *me*.
- Presence, not perfection.

Which feel most important to you? Whether you are a top-level executive or entry-level administrator, teacher or principal, winemaker or grape picker . . . these principles strengthen the Essential You and build your field. Choose one, embody it for a day, keep rebooting back to it, and see what opens up.

The Practice of Building Your Immunity (Doing)

None of this "showing up" and "setting the tone" stuff is about perfection or doing anything "right." It's about self-awareness, presence, doing the best you can, taking care of yourself, noticing when you're off, owning it, stepping in, and choosing to rise in whatever way will help you hold your space best and serve most.

Only you can know what will work for you.

Here are some of the most valuable practices I've personally found in strengthening IEP and building my immunity. In Part 5, I'll give you a resource that offers some of my favorite thought leaders, services, tools, and publications that address many of these if you wish for more support or information. Consider this a checklist of places to consider that may be strengthening or weakening your IEP.

Sleep. Get your sleep, good-quality sleep. The research on sleep deprivation and what it does to our brains, our decision making, and our ability to be present is staggering. Prioritize sleep. Say "no" to late evenings out; don't get sucked into TV or social media; do whatever you need to—get your *zzzz*'s.

Fuel. Make sure that your food is fuel and that it serves you. Pay attention to how you feel when (and after) you eat certain foods. Notice how food impacts your mood. Food allergies and sensitivities cause all sorts of havoc on the body. It's not just about paying attention to carbs, protein, or fat. We want to look at inflammation, allergies, autoimmunity, and an endless list of other issues that can cause illness, low energy, brain fog, fatigue, grumpiness, impatience, pain, the beer belly/muffin top, and more.

Exercise. The body has to move. Our bodies are our vehicles for change and doing all the amazing things we do. The fact that you are reading or listening to this book right now in whatever way you are is a miracle—thank you, body! My fingers, hands, and arms typed this book, and my heart and brain created it . Thank you, body! Our bodies do so much for us, and yet they're often the last thing paid attention to when time is tight. Physical activity creates essential hormones and processes in the body that are key to our mood, energy, health, decision making, clarity, stress management, and general mental and physical well-being. Find ways to move—if even a quick five minutes here and there.

Meditation. What is your practice? This does not have to be a big formal meditation practice. This can simply be time being present with yourself. My meditation, which means my quiet space in the morning, sets me up for a more solid day. My practice changes. The types of meditation I practice evolve as I do. It may be 10 minutes; it may be an hour. It may be formal; it may be casual. I do what I can, and I'm never sorry I did.

Intentions and gratitude. These are low-hanging fruit state shifters and grounders of ideas and plans. Both set us up for greater success. They work beautifully together. I start every morning with these and tap them throughout the day as needed. My morning process takes under nine minutes and sets the tone for the whole day. I use the IEP Sheet, do my five steps, and access gratitude— not just for the good stuff, but also for the most difficult. (This is the true practice of gratitude; can you find gratitude in the muck?) Remember this: *intention* sets the tone and paves the way to show up well, while *gratitude* creates more joy, space, wisdom, and fuel to make that intention happen. (Bonus: intentionality and gratitude are super-contagious.)

Dancing, music, movement. Some combination of these, even for two minutes, can be absolute state shifters and tone setters for your day, your moment, or that meeting. When you find yourself getting stuck or tunnel-visioned or need a time-out to think, you can recover, get into a more proactive space, and reboot your presence with any of these.

Connection. This one may not always be in your control, as it requires other people (however, connection with self counts too!). I intend to connect meaningfully with at least one person daily I can heart-to-heart it with, if even for two minutes (or via text, video, or voice message) to let people know I love, admire, appreciate, and/or see them. I do my best to be present and connect with any human I come in contact with and find something to enjoy—even if I don't know that person.

Choosing high-vibe thinking. Choosing our thoughts is powerful. My team and I have an agreement around this idea that's so important to us that we've put anchors on our office walls to remind us: *High Vibe, Decide, Show Up, Assume Good, Get Curious, Check Your Intention, Tell the Truth, Honor All, Be in Service Of,* and *Use It for Good.* In essence, this all means that whatever is happening, when we find ourselves going down the drain in low-vibe thinking, or getting snarky in our presence, we're "response-able" to honor and shift it productively. It's not about faking our feelings or bypassing the emotion or situation. It's about having *awareness* and *choice* to create more space and find a higher-vibration thought and pathway that will support what we're up to. These anchors serve as reminders (and bread crumbs) to do this. If we find we keep hitting a low state about the same thing, then it's time to get curious. Find out why it keeps happening: there's gold here; wisdom is waiting. (By the way, there is always a reason for low-vibe repeats. It's either lack of awareness, bad habits, unclear intentions, incomplete communication, or a sign that something needs changing.)

Staying conscious and intentional with your language and state of being. Being aware of and course-correcting our use of language and states is a beautiful immunity builder. Ask these simple questions for powerful outcomes: Does the language you use expand or contract the field? Does your state create expansion or contraction? You can choose different words and states you want to work with as you feel they support your field. For example, let's take "hope," "need," and "sorry"—all weak and often unconsciously used words. Instead, turn "hope" into "intend," "trust," or "expect"; turn "need" into "want," "will," or "prefer"; and use "sorry" only in the most intentional and appropriate of ways. For example, if I've broken an agreement or had an unintended impact, I might say, "I acknowledge my broken agreement or unintended impact, and here's how I'll make it right/clean it up." We're looking for conscious, true, and powerful words. Other examples? I've seen teams replace the word "busy" with "on purpose" or "richly scheduled"; "worried" with "aware of"; "but" with "and"; and the energetic state of "excuses" with "accountability"—all with subtle and powerful positive results. The language and states are nuanced and potent. Pay attention.

Regularly creating chunks of time for silence and unplugging. You *must* create space. (No one will do this for you—*own it.*) This doesn't have to happen daily. Instead, choose a day each week (the whole day or a chunk of hours) and spend it in silence or unplugged. No phones, no texts, no TV, no nada. I do this. It helps a ton. Even if it's an intentional hour. My kids know this, and we've codesigned it with a code for if they really need me and it can't wait because their cute pants are on fire. This has worked beautifully. Quick mini-unplugs and conscious disengagement space are essential and can feel like a lot more time if you are truly present and fully allow yourself space.

Other Ideas for Setting Yourself Up Well

Here are some other things we've had clients and program participants share that they've integrated more intentionally into their lives for nourishment and self-care with great results. Add your own!

- Family dinners and a table setting ritual
- No phones after 6 p.m. (or a time that works for you)
- Only one glass of wine—to enjoy it (not self-medicate with it)
- Intention and appreciation sessions with their partner, family, team
- Intention and appreciation sessions with themselves
- Regular dates and sex with their partner

- Ditching the pressure and quest for "work/life" balance (it's all one life!)
- Love letters, love texts, love emails, and flowers, sent to self ("*yasss*"!)
- An evening bath or soak or walk
- Morning intentions outside for their morning ritual,
- Any ritual that has them be present in the doing (can be anything: coffee making, tea, dishes, making their bed)
- Journaling daily or weekly
- Writing a vision for the future and what they want to create and then reading it daily
- Exercising with friends
- Having a daily check-in call at 5:30 a.m. (or whenever) to ground, set intentions, and address life and learning as it unfolds
- A weekly men's dinner or women's circle

Anything that is "life-giving" counts. Let's acknowledge that it is easy to let "things" slide—travel, time zones, kids, client needs, life demands, deadlines, surprises . . . you name it. Let that be OK. There is *no* pressure here, only an invitation to do what you can—and be the best you can. And when it all falls apart? Be nice. Learn from it. Reboot. And climb back on. If you're building your immunity regularly, your recovery will be swift.

The Morning Ritual: Setting the Tone for the Day

I've had morning rituals for as long as I can remember. They've never let me down. They support me in owning my life and being my best for those in it. When my kids were little, you might have found me hiding in my bathroom, sitting on the floor of the cold tile in Chicago, with a space heater after getting up 30 minutes (or more) earlier while kids and then hubby slept so I could create this space for myself. Now my morning ritual happens in my first 9 to 60 minutes upon waking, whatever I've created space for. Whether it's a minute or many, I find the ritual to be magical and centering. The point? Claim your space; set your tone; own your day; own your life.

Your ritual can be anything you wish—it can be event or activity specific (like making tea or coffee or a meal or doing dishes), and it can be at any time (morning, evening, upon waking, before going to bed, or before or after each meeting). You can create rituals out of anything I've shared in this book, and of course out of your own wisdom and desires. The invitation is to design it in a way that feels amazing and creates a life-giving practice.

Here are two examples of morning rituals that show this can work for you whether you have 15 minutes or a full hour:

1-Hour Ritual

5:30 a.m. Wake up—nine-minute body scan with the questions below (you can use the nine-minute snooze function to time this).

5:40 Capture any thoughts or intentions before shifting state (keep a journal or IEP Sheet next to your bed).

5:50 Coffee/tea/water/let the dog out, etc.

6:00 Meditate for 12–15 minutes.

6:15 Movement/dancing/music/stretching/breathwork (any or all).

6:25 Complete the IEP Sheet with all intentions for the day, the four quadrants complete, and your IEP Practice set.

6:30 Rock your day.

15-Minute Ritual

5:30 a.m. Wake up—five-minute body scan.

5:35 Capture thoughts and intentions; fill out the IEP Sheet stat.

5:40 Dance or intentionally move and breathe your way to the bathroom; brush your teeth; head for the kitchen for coffee; let the dog out. While doing all of the above and getting ready for your day, talk nice to yourself, reflect on your intentions, and love. yourself up.

5:45 Rock your day.

You can do a lot with 15 minutes (or less—make this work for you). The time allotted and components included are up to you. Have fun.

Note: There are no rules. *And* here are two I highly recommend . . . no snooze and no phone in bed! *Do not* go back to sleep (your brain will be grateful). And *do not* check email, texts, voice mail, news, social media, or anything from the outside world that will pull on you and extract your attention and energy before you have completed your ritual and set the tone for your day. I promise you this will magnify the power of your ritual and the container you that create for yourself. (After all, "I find other people's drama, noise, and agendas for my time and energy to be truly life-giving, pleasurable, and productive . . . ," said no one, ever.) If you don't believe me, just do it for seven days and see.

The Morning Questions

Here are some morning questions that can help ground you in your day. Check in with these while doing your morning scan or journaling:

Check in with your **body**: *How am I? What do I need? What feels great? What needs TLC?* Any places you want to give extra care to today will pop up.

Check in with your **mind**: *How is it? What is the quality of my thinking? That thing I was trying to figure out yesterday, does my mind have new information or wisdom for me today? What's the general tone of my mind this morning?*

Check in with your **emotions**: *How am I? Do I feel heard and cared for? What does my intuition "know" about that "thing"? Is there anything tender or joyful that needs extra attention or celebration? Where might my emotions need a little extra honoring today?*

Check in with your **heart**: *How is my heart today? What am I grateful for? What is my desire? Anything you need from me today, heart?*

Check in with your **spirit**: *How are you, spirit? Do you feel honored? Are we on track with our purpose? What intuition do you want me to pay extra attention to today? What do I need to know that I might not see yet?*

115

Check in with your **intention:** *What do I want to create today? What's the impact I want to have? (What's important about this? Whom will it serve?) How do I want to feel? How do I want to make others feel? What kind of contagious do I want to be? How do I want to show up? What kind of contribution would I like to be with this life today?*

Once you've all checked in, huddle up: "We're all in this together, I love you, let's go."

These questions are quiet and gentle. Remember, they're happening while you lie in bed, in meditation, doing your "morning scan." When complete, capture anything that feels important and note any "worries" or "pay attentions!!" that came up during the scan. You don't have to ask them all; use them as you love them. I do find that checking in with each domain helps me pull myself together and create a more solid container and presence for the day, which then of course fuels me up to be more resilient, robust, and intentionally contagious.

Fieldwork: Make It Real

What will serve you most from this chapter? What resonated? What "poked" at you? Where did you feel sad, excited, stressed, relieved? Let's build your Immunity Plan.

Immunity Plan

1. My definition of self-care is: _____
2. Why self-care is important to me. (*How* it supports my intention for impact, *what* it's in *service* of, and those it impacts besides me): _____
3. Circle the things on the Immunity Kryptonite list that you do to weaken your field.

4. Three things you do to weaken your field, which you will take immediate action on, are:

_____

_____

_____

5. Identify three things you will do to build your immunity over the next 30 days. Include mindset (being) _and_ action (doing) in your practice.

_____

_____

_____

6. Create your morning ritual here:

_____

_____

_____

_____

_____

7. Anything else that feels important from this chapter? Name it and claim it.

_____

_____

_____

_____

_____

CHAPTER 7

Your Superpower Toolkit: 21 Practices to Cultivate. Use It.

Our superpowers are ours for the making;
we must grow them and use them well.

With great power comes great response-ability.

"Being kind and talking nice to myself, catching my thoughts, and leading others? It's hard!" At this point you maybe grappling with the time and energy it might take to be kind to yourself, let alone lead others more effectively. It's a lot. Right?

I get it, *and* I invite you to consider how your thinking may be creating resistance before you even get started. (And if not in this scenario, in any scenario you experience the "It's hard!" or "I'm too busy!" inner conversation!) I empathize, *and* an invitation when confronted with "contracted" thinking, to ask yourself three questions:

- "How is my thinking making this harder?"
- "How might this be easy?"
- "What superpowers and resources can I tap to make this more pleasurable?"

These three questions can stop a runaway thought in its tracks. Even better, let's circle back to *intention* and add these: "What is my intention here? What's the impact I want to have? Why is this important?" There now, a bit more space to move forward? Likely so! (If not, breathe, settle into this moment, and run the questions again.)

Is showing up hard sometimes? You bet. Excellent leadership, accomplishments, and things that propel us forward in our lives often are. Creating what we want requires work and grit. However, if we really want it, we'll do what it takes. The trick is to intentionally apply resources and superpowers that will make the necessary work more efficient and pleasurable so we have more energy and are able to do more good. And that's what we're doing in this chapter . . .

Superpowers, Trifectas, and Impact—Oh My!

We've been building superpowers throughout this book. Being intentional and on purpose, strengthening our IEP, choosing our thinking and language, and being in integrity with ourselves—these are all highly contagious superpowers.

There are four things to know about superpowers:

1. They are entirely within your control.
2. No one can give them to you (or take them away).
3. You have to claim and nourish them.
4. Any superpower overdone can become kryptonite.

In the following sections are 21 *additional* superpowers to help unlock your next levels of leadership and influence. These build resiliency, create more space for wisdom and new thinking, and help prevent burnout and what I call "leadership depression" (more on that topic in Chapter 9). The last six are "Superpower Trifectas"—superpowers that stand alone, and when combined are an even more significant force to lead with.

As you go through these, see which resonate most and which you'd like to claim. Also, any superpower can become kryptonite if it is overcalibrated or used unintentionally. For example, the superpower of *behavioral flexibility* overused or used unintentionally becomes wishy-washy and unreliable; *self-awareness* over-calibrated becomes self-centered with a potential side of analysis paralysis; and *forgiveness*, without boundaries and consciousness, can lead to being taken advantage of or being a doormat. Consider what an overly calibrated superpower might look like for you.

Superpower #1: Self-Awareness

Self-awareness is home base for creating any change. I find it's about 70 percent of the necessary work required to create real change. (The other 30 percent being what you actually *do* with this new awareness.) Self-awareness includes recognizing our impact, energetic states, thinking, and emotions, our projections, and how our presence and actions influence our outcomes. Without self-awareness, we have pain, suffering, fatigue, unintended impact, and confusion. With it, we have self-authority, wisdom, and a choice to change, get support, be different, and do differently. Exercising this superpower requires we stop, breathe, notice, get curious, own our impact, and proceed accordingly. It also invites us to ask for feedback on how we're showing up, where our impact may not be what we want it to be, and what our next steps might be.

Superpower #2: Choice Point

The ability to choose our response in any moment is one of our greatest superpowers. Expand or contract; request or complain; be accountable or blame; be positive or negative; be grateful or entitled; be generous or judgmental; be kind or cruel; come from abundance or scarcity; assume good or bad; show up or don't. My choices are limitless; inform future decisions, habits, and ease; and educate my brain on which neural pathways to build to make similar choices easier in the future. (More on this topic in Chapter 8.)

Superpower #3: Conscious Thinking and Beliefs

Ever notice that your thoughts sometimes don't take you to the most fabulous places? Our primal brains are wired for survival, which can cause us to go into worst-case scenario mode and make unhelpful assumptions. The combination of being aware of our thinking and beliefs, witnessing the stories we tell ourselves, and *catching them before they run rogue* is a superpower practice. In addition to impacting our performance and how we show up, research has also shown the significant impact our beliefs have on our biology. Dr. Bruce Lipton's work, specifically in his book *The Biology of Belief,*[1] is a powerful resource for understanding the relationship between our beliefs and our well-being. Yet another reason for activating this superpower. Anytime you notice contraction, unhappiness, or stress, it's likely your thinking has run away with you. Catch it, question it, clarify it, and above all, never believe everything you think. (Byron Katie's "The Work"[2] and her four questions can be a helpful resource for strengthening this superpower as well!)

Superpower #4: Staying in Your Lane and Minding Your Business

One of the greatest energy suckers, leadership killers, time wasters, and credibility busters is getting sucked into another person's energetic drama. Feel yourself getting triggered by what someone else is doing (or *should* do)? Breathe, and mind your own business. This superpower builds our focus, keeps our energetic hygiene clean, strengthens leadership trust and credibility, creates peace in our own space, and therefore helps create more space and grace for others so we can serve more effectively.

Superpower #5: Intuition

Intuition speaks. Do you hear it? And if you hear it, do you honor it? Our intuition—that *quiet, knowing, sixth sense, inner wisdom*—can be cultivated. The more we listen and honor intuition, the louder and more efficient it becomes. Ignoring intuition often results in energetic, financial, and emotional expenses. Honoring it, coupled with discernment and curiosity, will often net priceless outcomes. In my years exploring this personally and with clients, I've found that intuition is always right; however, interpretation may be wrong. So pay attention, honor it, and when not 100 percent clear, pair it with a nice glass of *discernment*, do your due diligence, and make sure you have the information you need. By the way, if you don't think you have intuition—you do. That "gut feeling" you get when something is off, that "Yes!" or "No way!" sense you get in your body when you're first asked to do something is likely your intuition speaking. Listen.

Superpower #6: Decide

Indecision, often at the root of "stuck" and unclear leadership, is exhausting. Being energetically halfway in the middle, with one foot in and one foot out, keeps us stuck and confused. Without a true energetic decision, the people we lead follow us (maybe, if they have the patience) in a fog of indecisive energy, ambiguity, and confusion. If you have things you keep saying you're going to do, or have something you've wanted to make happen that's not (have a great relationship, lose 10 pounds, be successful), or sense your team is not fully with you, it may be because you have not truly *decided* your decision.

To decide is to kill off all other options. A decision is clean; it moves forward and eliminates Plan B. A leader whose decision energy is strong will present with the energy of crispness, knowingness, credibility, and an intentional impactful presence. His or her energy will feel solid, reliable, compelling, and positively contagious. Just as a leader with weak decision energy, who lives on the fence, will likely feel confused, burdened, stuck, and negatively contagious.

So how do you activate the superpower of deciding? First, decide to get good at making decisions. (The stronger your IEP, the easier it will be to intuitively know which decisions are most important and what to do about them.) Next, notice where you feel stuck or where a relationship or result is not shifting. Now be honest and ask yourself: "Have I indeed decided? Do I truly want it? And have I decided to do whatever it takes to make it happen?" (*Or* "Am I getting something out if it not happening? Am I still gathering evidence for all the ways this thing/person sucks? Or do I just not want to do the hard work?") Then decide.

Note: A decision to decide *not* to decide is still a decision. As is naming and owning that you are deciding not to do something that may be unpopular. (For example, "I don't want to change my relationship with George.") Just own it. Clean and simple. A real decision clears energy, builds internal and external trust, and clears the way for new wisdom to come in.

Superpower Accelerator: To counteract decision fatigue and make it easier on yourself and your decision-making muscles, make your bigger decisions earlier in the day when fresh. Reduce repetitive decisions you make every day (e.g., food, wardrobe, routine, the location where you put your keys, criteria for what you say "yes" and "no" to). And simplify daily priorities as much as possible to free up decision-making energy. We have the mental stamina for making only so many decisions a day (which is why at the end of a long day, you're more likely to cave to your kids, say yes to that thing you really didn't want to do, skip that workout, or eat that donut after a perfectly clean eating day). Cultivating this superpower not only supports rigorous and clean leadership but frees us to make the most important decisions unencumbered.

Superpower #7: Acting "As If"

Acting "as if" is a superpower you can have *right now*. Take a deep breath, reboot, intend your presence, bubble up, and act *as if* you already have what you want, are who you want to be, or have the kind of relationship and dynamic you wish possible with that person in your life. Want to be successful and run that meeting beautifully? Embody it, breathe it, appreciate it, and act as if you are. Want to ease the tension in that relationship? Embody, breathe, appreciate, and show up as if the pressure is gone. Want to feel happy and expansive instead of stressed out? Embody, breathe, appreciate, and be. Whatever state you desire, embody it. Breathe it. Appreciate it. Be it. Live into it.

Superpower #8: Intention, Service, and Purpose

Having a clear intention is at the core of creating impact. When we're clear on *what* we want to create, *why* we want to create it, and what or whom it's *in service of,* we eliminate the drama, noise, fear, and unhelpful behaviors and thinking that often sabotage impact. We get braver. Being connected to intention, service, and purpose (our why) is fuel—the blend of the three is a "courage cocktail." When we're connected to what we're in service of and the human being(s) it impacts, we are better armed to get out of our own way and make things happen. Feeling confused, nervous, scared, or resistant about a tricky situation, or about hard feedback or a talk you're going to give, or about a bold move you're about to make that will require courage and vulnerability? Ask yourself any of these simple and powerful questions and see what shifts: "What's my intention? What's my purpose here? What am I in service of? Whom/what will this serve beyond myself? What's the littlest thing I can do to help things go well right now?"

Superpower #9: "Response-Ability"

Try this on: "I am responsible for XYZ. It is my responsibility." Notice what you notice. Contraction or expansion? Heavy or light? Daunted or excited? Soul-sucking or life-giving? Now this: "I am 'response-able' to XYZ. I am able to respond in the best way I can." Different? Similar words, significant energetic differences. Responsibility can feel heavy and drudgerous. Whereas being *able to respond* to whatever is here right now in the best way I can, feels lighter and more expansive, creating possibility and movement. Amplify your "response-ability"; amplify your impact.

Superpower #10: Saying "No"

A solid "no" is a powerful "yes" to something else. The "no" may be a "yes" to yourself, to your self-care, to creating space and time for your team, or to making space for something that is a better use of your energy and time. For example, my saying "no" to going out for dinner and drinks tonight is a "yes" to self-care, personal space, and an early bedtime so I can show up well for tomorrow's meeting. My "no" to traveling this weekend for a business meeting is a "yes" to writing time and self-care. My "no" to a friend or date that feels incongruent is a "yes" to creating space for the right friendship or date later. When we say "no," not only do our "yeses" mean more, but we build trust and credibility, clean up our energy, and ultimately become better at what we say "yes" to.

Superpower #11: Finding the Gift and Reframing

Everything can be reframed as a lesson, a gift, and even an opportunity if we're open to it. We can wade in the bad thing forever. Or we can have our authentic emotion about it and then use the event to make things better moving forward. How? Look for the reframe. "This is terrible," becomes "Interesting, what's the opportunity? What can we learn? What's the littlest thing we can do to help things go better?" The reframe for "I screwed up" or "I failed" becomes "I gave it my best there *and* that didn't go the way I planned," or "I created unintentional impact," and then, "What's the gift? What can I learn? Let's do it again differently." For "I can't believe he did that; he cost us a ton of money!!" the reframe becomes "I'm so grateful that happened now; look at what we've learned and what we can do moving forward to prevent this from happening again and/or make it even better." When we find gratitude, we open the field of possibility and wisdom.

Superpower #12: Forgiveness

Forgiving is a superpower that creates peace, frees the forgiver of carrying toxic energy, and honors the humanity in both parties, and while it is more for the *forgiver* than for the *forgiven*, everyone wins. Forgiving doesn't mean we tolerate it, excuse it, enable it, and let it happen again. It means we have awareness, we let it go, and we don't carry that energy with us.

There is a next-level superpower in forgiveness, which is holding that there is *nothing to forgive*. Consider this: What if there is never anything to forgive because you realize people are doing the best they can, and there is always a gift? (Superpower #11) You *may* find that when you can authentically hold that there is no forgiveness to work through—but rather awareness, honoring of the pain, gratitude for the learning, release, and then moving forward appropriately to make it right (or not)—your energy becomes lighter, you process more quickly, boundaries become clearer, and relationships that aren't right fall away more naturally without stress, contraction, or drama.

Because this superpower can be harder to grok, let me give you an example I witnessed recently. Carol had an assistant who chronically made mistakes and then lied about them. After several opportunities, without success, to change the behavior and level-up, Carol fired her. Carol felt angry, betrayed, disappointed, and taken advantage of. She shared with colleagues that what her assistant had done was unforgivable. She held on to this for a *long* time.

This lack of forgiveness impacted her trust with other team members and colored her hiring process for the next assistant. The energy she exuded was contracted, careful, bitter, and not at all inspiring or compelling. Carol was exhausting herself (and ultimately those around her).

One day it occurred to her that this contracted energy was costing her a lot more than the situation that had actually occurred. Aware that she wasn't feeling so great and was likely prolonging her own misery, she got curious and posed the questions, "What if there is nothing to forgive? What if my assistant was doing the best she could? How might I have contributed to the dynamic? How might this be a gift to both of us? What's here to learn? What if I just let this all go?" These questions gave Carol space to breathe and learn.

In this space, here's what she realized: her assistant *was* doing the best she could—she'd kept doing it, so obviously that *was* her best (this clearly was not OK for that role or for Carol—*and* it *was* her best). Carol realized she'd contributed to the situation by continuing to tolerate the behavior. She also saw that the energy she'd carried and projected at her assistant had likely made her assistant only more afraid to tell the truth. And there was more . . . in the interview process the prospective assistant had told a white lie (the gal really needed the job and was willing to lie to get it and keep it). Carol saw it, and in her urgency to hire and wanting to assume good, she'd let it go. Her gut told her, "Pay attention!!" Her head told her, "Nah, we're good!!" Bam. Right there. Carol had contributed by overlooking it, ignoring her intuition, being lenient when it continued, and instead of naming it and cleaning it up, projecting harsh energy at her.

Here's the thing . . . Carol had done the best *she* could at that time. In her desperation to get an assistant and to avoid conflict, she'd done her best. Now she'd know better. So, really, what was there to forgive? Nothing. They'd both done their best. and this best was not OK or a sustainable match for that partnership. So it didn't work.

There was gold here. Priceless learning gold for Carol: (1) people show you who they are fast (especially in interviews!), (2) don't ignore your intuition, (3) be crystal clear up front about expectations and hold accountability, (4) fire fast when you know it's not right, and (5) don't hang on to anger because anger will only hang on to you (ultimately clouding learning and wisdom and depleting energetic resources).

After Carol worked her way through this, the energetic charge she'd carried was gone. Carol moved on grateful for the experience, for catching it before it netted a more serious impact on the company, and for the learning that would now make her a better leader, human, and boundary holder. She was free.

Note that I'm not saying, "Oh, no big deal, just deal!" with stuff that doesn't work or is downright diabolical. I am saying, allow the authentic emotion, process it, get curious and learn from it, create smart boundaries and agreements with yourself and others, and as needed, get support to heal so you can release and move on.

Don't give your life force away by holding the past hostage.

Superpower #13: Conscious Disengagement (and Play)

Superheroes need their "me time." We've got to unplug and play. Binge that Netflix. Eat that bowl of cereal or popcorn. Stay in your jams all day. Just do it *consciously*. The art of conscious disengagement and active play is an essential leadership skill and superpower that strengthens creativity and resiliency, opens up joy and new perspectives, and builds a more expansive energetic field. Check out and get out! Your leadership and creativity depend on it.

Superpower #14: Behavioral Flexibility

The person with the strongest intention and purpose, the highest vibration, and the greatest behavioral flexibility wins. Oh my. That's a lot to ask, right? Not really. You've got intention and purpose in spades, and you now know how to work your vibration. The mastery comes in being able to hold these two things while being behaviorally flexible—being willing to move, bend, dance, and meet people where they are. Here's the trick: be flexible, go with it, lean in to understand, and be willing to change course as it serves—*all* while holding your stake in the ground for your purpose and beliefs. The more flexible we can be, the better able we can meet people where they are, and the more likely they'll come with us where we want them to go. If we're rigid, the whole thing snaps. It's a dance. Bend, flex, stand, lead. Go for it.

Superpower #15: Holding a Magnificent Container

The size of the container we hold for people has a huge impact on who they—and we—can become. Seeing people as big, capable, amazing, lovely, and good and "holding" them there in your regard— will create that field energetically. They'll feel it and be invited to step in and show up bigger. Just as seeing and holding them as small, a loser, bad, incompetent, and ughhhh will create *that* field for them, inviting them to step in and show up as so. What do you believe is possible for the people you lead? There is a container you're holding for them (and for yourself). How big is it?

The Superpower Trifectas

The following superpowers all work beautifully alone and are even more powerful together. When all three parts are present, their power increases exponentially. If one is missing or weak, work on that one, and the others will elevate as well.

Superpower Trifecta #1

The Presence Trifecta: *Breathing, Accessing Pleasure in the Moment, and Rebooting*

You're experiencing stress or contraction in the moment. It could be for anything, whether you are in a meeting, with your teen, on stage, or in a conversation. You feel yourself get foggy, tight, reactive. What do you do? Activate the Presence Trifecta:

1. **Breathe.** Right here, right now. Full-body breath. (Just noticing breath shifts state.)
2. **Access pleasure.** What will make this moment more pleasurable? It could be moving your body, changing your thinking, remembering your "why" for this situation, getting curious, or simply going to your happy place.
3. **Reboot.** Do the IEP Presence Reboot—notice where you are, envision and intend where you want to be, take care, step in, and voilà, rinse and repeat!

Superpower Accelerator: Say something that anchors this in: "Isn't this lovely?" "I *am* here." "If this isn't awesome, I don't know what is." Anything to ground this feeling in your body and have your brain build neural pathways to lock it in.

Superpower Trifecta #2

The Self-Care Trifecta: *Nourishment, Kindness, and Graceful Rigor*

Keep this one activated at all times for best results. First, *nourishment*: take care of yourself; feed yourself well with food, thinking, and input; surround yourself with things that bring you joy. Second, *kindness*: notice your thoughts; make them work for you, not against you. Love yourself up. Be nice—it's free (and effective!). And finally, *graceful rigor*: call yourself to grow, do more, be bigger, and lead on your edge with tenacity and grace in whatever way is most congruent for you. Make a mistake? Great. Take care of yourself, be kind, learn from it, and get back in there.

Superpower Trifecta #3

The Love Trifecta: *Love, Acknowledgment, and Clear Boundaries*

This trifecta works in relationship with others and with ourselves. All three parts support and amplify each other. Start first with *love*, which in this case we're going to hold as simply "seeing the other person as a human being who matters." Acknowledging this (and feeling it) can create more space and empathy. Your boss, your nemesis, the person who always "one-ups" you at work, these are human beings who have their own challenges, fears, dreams, hard relation-ships, insecurities, bullies, and families just like you do. What can you love (or at least appreciate) about them, this moment, this prob-lem, yourself? Take a deep breath and find the human. Find the love. Find kindness. You don't have to do anything with it, and you don't have to tell anyone; you only have to breathe, access the humanity, and feel it in your body.

Superpower Accelerator: Put your hand on your heart for six seconds to release oxytocin and activate the love more quickly.

An *acknowledgment* is something that says, "I see you." (Have you ever noticed that "intimacy" is IN-TO-ME-SEE?) Seeing someone (and being seen) is one of the most generous and effective ways to connect, understand, and *be* with another. It is also one of our great-est desires as humans. (And ironically, can be terrifying as well!) An acknowledgment is not about what we do—it's about who we are. Do you see people being courageous, kind, thoughtful, wise, vulnerable, genuine, powerful? Tell them so.

The last part of the Love Trifecta, *clear boundaries*, sets all parties up for success by being clear on what our boundaries and desires are. What's OK and what's not? Asking for what we want and being clear is not only powerful and foundational for us personally, but incred-ibly helpful and loving to the people we're in relationship with. "Open heart, clear boundaries" makes space for generous love and self-care.

Superpower Trifecta #4

The Abundant Reciprocity Trifecta: *Generosity, Receiving, and Gratitude*

Abundance is a mindset that means "more than enough." *Reciprocity* is an energetic cycle of giving and receiving. When we put abun-dance and reciprocity together, energy rises.

The spirit of generosity offers time, wisdom, the assumption of positive intent, grace, our presence, and gifts. Asking, "What's the most generous thing I can *be* or *do* here?" creates expansion and opens the field of possibilities and creative thinking.

Receiving is a leadership skill. When we are open to receive and do so with grace, we keep the cycle of abundant reciprocity open and honor the person gifting us. When we don't receive, we shut it down.

Finally, *gratitude*, the magic state shifter, fortifies the trifecta; gratitude for what's been received, for who someone is *being*, for the moment, for breath, for toothpaste. Anything counts. Put these three superpowers together to create an abundance mindset.

Superpower Trifecta #5

The Communication Trifecta: *Naming It, Curiosity, and Assuming Good*

When you have conflict or tension or want to make a shift in relationship and communication and are struggling to do so, the Communication Trifecta moves energy quickly.

First, *name it*. Name and identify what feels off, what you're noticing, and what you would love instead. (You may or may not be "right"—either way, the energy of the situation will shift.)

Next, get *curious* about what is happening without judging it, making it wrong, or assuming you know what's what.

Finally, *assume good*. There is almost always a positive intention underneath what someone says or does—even if you can't fathom what. What is the most generous assumption you can make to create the energy, space, and safety for a productive conversation? All three of these superpowers create space to be in right relationship.

Superpower Trifecta #6

The Solution Trifecta: *Accurate Reporting, Being Senior to Discomfort, and Asking for Help*

The Solution Trifecta helps us identify the facts, be "bigger" than the problem, lean in to discomfort to solve it, and finally ask for help where needed.

Accurate reporting addresses objectively the questions: What happened? What are the facts of the situation? No emotions, judgments, or assumptions. There is only what you'd see if you had a video camera and taped it. For example, George has been late to the last three meetings. *Story:* "George is late because he doesn't care, he's lazy, he doesn't respect our time, and I think he's just bad at managing himself." *Accurate reporting:* "George has walked into the last three meetings late. When he comes in, we stop the conversation to wait for him to settle in." Now you have facts—not story—you can get curious about and design for.

Being senior to discomfort means that you are bigger than your problem, staying conscious with it, versus becoming it or losing your seniority to it. With this comes the courage to lean in to any discomfort you have about addressing the problem directly. With George, for example, his being late is a "problem," but you don't have to enmesh with the problem, get sucked into the story, or have it be bigger than you (where you hide, avoid, and fear confrontation). Instead, stay senior to the issue and partner with the discomfort of having an honest and productive discussion with George.

Asking for help is another leadership skill and superpower, which is essential to the Solution Trifecta. This superpower supports us in tapping additional resources, not going it alone, and modeling that we're all in this together and no one has to know all the answers. In the case of George, you might ask him for help to make meetings better, or ask your colleague for help with the George conversation. Don't let a problem diminish your seniority, and don't let your pride lose the best solution possible.

You now have 21 additional superpowers (33 when you pull the trifectas apart) to use as you wish. Use them well.

Fieldwork: Make It Real

Let's activate your superpowers and at least one trifecta . . .

Easiest Fieldwork Ever

What three superpowers are you committed to practicing this week?

_____

_____

_____

What one trifecta feels most important?

_____

Go get it!
And once you've got it, come back and do it again.

CHAPTER 8

The Science of Showing Up. Explore It.

Your brain and body will back you up.

The majority of this book is devoted to leading with self-awareness. Self-awareness is fundamental to being (positively) contagious. Why? Because when you are contagious, you have a strong presence. And to have a strong positive presence requires internal and interpersonal well-being, cognitive awareness, and command of your internal state (mental and emotional).

I've intentionally placed this chapter in the middle of the book to give you ample space to integrate the principles of *Contagious You* into your life and to build your own self-awareness. Now I'm going to take you into some of the science of contagiousness. If science is not your thing, and your intuitive mind prefers to stay in flow, skip this chapter and go to Chapter 9. Otherwise, let's dig in.

Our Magnificent Brain

The human brain is in a continuous state of change, constantly rewiring itself to be different than it was the moment before. It's always at work, even when we're sleeping. This is *neuroplasticity.* Neuroplasticity is an inherent state of the brain that continuously alters existing neural pathways in order to adapt and accommodate new life experiences, learn new information, and create new memories. One of the most important roles the brain needs to play is "sense making" to perceive and respond to internal or external stimuli according to its interpretation. Like great leaders, we can influence and guide how well our brain performs this task of "sense making" through the process of neuroplasticity by taking excellent care of it.

How? By doing what we've been discussing in this book. Taking care of ourselves, pausing, rebooting, reframing, meditating, sleeping, exercising, and being intentional with what we put into our bodies. Yes, these are all things that make us feel good, but as you'll see in this chapter, there is science that shows these actions also make us better leaders and decision makers, calmer parents, and more powerful positively contagious human beings.

With every tool and idea I've shared with you in this book, your physiology has been at play.

For example . . .

- **Recovery time and resiliency?** This is a critical period when new neural pathways are built and re-establishment of a state of balance and equilibrium of the new pathways is achieved. As a result, our brain's ability to cope with and respond to stressful events expands!
- **Showing up?** That's your brain choosing the courage pathway to "step in" and show up instead of hide out and if you reward it (with a positive result, a good feeling, or even an internal word of kindness), it will do it again even easier and faster next time!
- **The bubble?** Bubble up, because your brain is creating space for you—peaceful, thoughtful, responsive space—that allows you to choose how to feel and interact with your world.
- **Holding your space and not matching the lowest vibe in the room?** (Or not holding your space and getting sucked in?) Your mirror neurons are at work! They are firing and deciding which way to go. You have a lot of control of which mirror neurons win here—"doom and gloom" or "light up the room." Up to you!

- **Feeling inspired and positively contagious?** Well, your brain has learned to look for the good, overcoming its inclination toward bad, and make even the "bad" work for it. It's learned to quickly sort for gifts.
- **Getting over disappointment and anger or contraction quickly?** Yes! Your brain has built new neural pathways that know exactly how to recover faster, find the gifts, and be even better.
- **Feeling disconnected, slow, and depressed—and your main relief is alcohol, TV, social media, or some other form of check-out self-medication?** You're toxifying your neural pathways and killing your cells. While these things are making you feel better for a minute, they're making you slower, lonelier, and less confident.
- **Building your resource state by strengthening your IEP and taking good care of yourself?** Well . . . yes, love. That's because self-care is what heals, builds, and fortifies your ability to think smart, show up well, hold your space, and come to the table peaceful with all cylinders humming.

Yep, every time you choose to pause (versus react), have a positive thought or assumption (versus negative), choose a positive new behavior (versus an old bad habit), or hold your space (versus match the lowest vibe in the room), you override old neural pathways, rewire and build new pathways (that support you in doing this again in the future more quickly), build emotional resiliency, and regulate your stress hormones and immune system and thereby building physical resiliency as well.

All that for a little self-care and presence? Are you in?

Of course, I'm completely simplifying what's happening with all the magical players at this party inside your brain. In this chapter, I'll spend more time fully explaining what I mean. Just know from the start that there are good reasons to do the practices we're talking about in this book. For this chapter, I spent significant time researching the work of several experts in the area of neuroscience and biology, including the HeartMath Institute, Dr. Bruce Lipton's work in

The Biology of Belief, and Masuro Emoto's work with water (although they're not discussed here, I'll talk about them in bonus material).

I also dove deeply into some of the most recent findings on neuroscience, leadership, and trust. And I wanted a live conversation and collaboration with someone who gets the IEP work and could help translate science into something meaningful for all of us. So I worked with Dr. Seonok Lee, a Neuronal Cell Biologist at Neurona Therapeutics (formerly at UCSF) who works on developing stem cell–derived neuronal cell therapeutics to treat chronic refractory neurodegenerative diseases. The science of what is happening in the brain and body in terms of our presence and contagiousness is truly expansive and continually evolving. This chapter distills the scientific discoveries and ideas that I found most helpful in understanding and navigating being contagious and the IEP work.

Contagious Me, Contagious You

Our contagiousness starts with the energy we bring to everything we do. Our energy is generated from the inside out, as is the experience we're creating for ourselves, which can then be felt by those around us. Whatever we're feeling internally is generating an experience externally, and whatever is happening externally influences our experience internally. We proact and react. We project and receive.

The stronger, more present, and more intentional we are, the easier it is to create our experience, to decide what we'll take on, to know when we're projecting our energy on others (and they on us) (more on this in Chapter 11), and to be more intentional about it all. Which means we have great influence on creating a positive and productive experience and on being positively or negatively contagious. When we own this and support it with our well-being, we can more effectively partner with and influence whatever is happening versus be reactive or victim to it.

Everything I've invited you to do in this book plays a part in strengthening your physiology and helping your brain support and manage your presence. For example, physically—being present, pausing, breathing, and taking care of yourself. Mentally—utilizing choice points, reframing, making conscious decisions, using your superpowers, and setting intentions. And energetically rebooting, changing your emotional and energetic states, bubbling up, and being conscious of the energy you bring into the room . . . These things all support you in up-leveling your presence, influence, and impact (*while* feeling good doing so).

Our Operating System: Neuroscience 101

Our brains are the primary operating center managing all of this.

First, it will be helpful to have a shared understanding of key introductory basic concepts in neuroscience to give us a playground to play on. Dr. Lee shared the following points (which can be more fully referenced and learned about in the plentiful research and data available to us in the world right now):[1]

- Our nervous system is largely divided into two systems: the central nervous system (CNS) that consists of the brain and spinal cord and the peripheral nervous system (PNS) that consists of neurons outside of the brain and spinal cord.
- Our brain is three pounds of lipid-rich tissue organized into two hemispheres, right and left wherein reside about 100 billion neurons (only 10 percent of the brain mass). It receives (or gathers) information through sensory neurons that translate external stimuli from the environment into internal electrical impulses. It sends out commands through motor neurons that carry signals to move organs, muscles or vocal cords for language for example.
- Neurons are composed of a cell body that sprouts out dendrites on one side and a single axonal fiber on the other. Axons are insulated with a fatty substance called myelin (white matter) while dendrites are not (therefore gray matter). On average, each neuron receives about 5,000 connections, called synapses, from other neurons.
- Neurons communicate through electrical firing and chemical exchange of neurotransmitters. As it's receiving synapses (via dendrites), a neuron gets signals—usually as a burst of chemicals

called neurotransmitters—from other neurons (via axons). In turn this transfer of neurotransmitters triggers electrical firing of the receiving neuron's axonal fiber.

- A typical neuron fires 5–50 times a second. Neural oscillations, or brain waves, are rhythmic or repetitive patterns of this neuronal firing in the brain. Typically, there are five different brain waves that can be measured by EEG (electroencephalography): alpha, beta, delta, theta, and gamma

- Neural circuits or pathways are generated when a population of neurons are interconnected by synapses that fire and wire together for a specific function.

- The brain is always active no matter what we are doing at the moment, busy processing information and shaping our mind. Therefore, even though it's only 2 percent of the body's weight, it uses up 20–25 percent of its oxygen and glucose.

- Mirror neurons are part of this operating system, a small circuit of cells that reside in the various areas in the brain that modulates both sensory and motor neurons. They are activated when we perform a certain action such as smiling or speaking and when we observe someone else performing that same action, blurring the boundary between seeing and doing. They are known to be one of the most important players that influence our social cognition, empathy, and language.[2-4]

The Power of Presence Comes from a Good Operating System

The operating system is supported and guided through presence, meditation, sleep, and self-care. The stronger our self-care and IEP, the more we tend to our brain nourishment. The more we honor ourselves proactively, the easier it is to build stronger neural pathways that support us in feeling good and clear, shifting our states, balancing our left and right brains, commanding our energetic presence and responses in the most effective ways, and being the best and most influential leaders possible.

This explains why when we're exhausted or not well resourced we're short-tempered and less patient. We also make impulsive and less than awesome decisions. We are also less resilient, take things more personally, make negative assumptions, and are less able to "hold our space" and not get sucked into negativity or drama. This impacts our leadership significantly. As we lead, it's essential to command our state, hold a safe space for the humans we're with, and be thoughtful and intentional with feedback and others' careers.

It's also essential to not take things personally, to operate with care and compassion, and to make the best decisions out of often difficult situations. Just think about the last time you were in a meeting that went horribly, or you lost your patience, or you made a terrible decision on the fly, or you had unintended negative impact because you were tired or moving fast; how did your self-care play into that? Did it help? Might you have been able to have responded or held space differently, or accessed more curiosity and wisdom, if you were more fully resourced? We need our resources to show up well. We can't lead our best from burnout or exhaustion. Presence, self-care, meditation, and sleep are key to helping us strengthen our resources. Is a bit more self-care worth your leadership impact?

It's All About Energy: How's Your ATP?

Everything comes down to energy. Everything about being contagious takes energy. Everything.

- The brain utilizes 20 percent of the body's glucose.[5]
- We maintain and recharge our neuro-system with our energy system called ATP (adenosine triphosphate) that is generated in the mitochondria in neurons.[6]
- ATP is basically the energetic currency of life that every cell in our body uses in all cellular functions, including neurons. Therefore, it is the very source of energy we need for doing the things we do.
- There is an energetic exchange in each moment of being together and being contagious.
- Our shared moments require an energetic exchange through similar neural responses (e.g., brain waves).[7]

- We *need to* exercise and eat good nutrition to clean the body and support the brain in clearing out metabolic waste products.
- We *need to* sleep in delta brain waves for lymphatic drainage to clear out our brain's and body's by-products, create more energy, and support our memory and long-term storage.[8]
- We *need to* support efficient ATP production and efficient consumption of energy to make sure we zoom and are at our best.
- We *need to* focus, be quiet, and be meditative to take in all information, command, and participate in energy-expansive activities.
- We *need to* honor our energy, not waste it, but rather consume and distribute it more efficiently. This comes from managing our state, being intentional about what we take on, showing up in our own space, being conscious of the impact of negativity in our lives, and taking excellent care of ourselves.
- Just like erratic jerky movements take more energy, anger, judgment, blame, and negative states consume energy as well. They're exhausting. They take ATP. And then, even better, they accumulate more by-products of that activity (judgment, anger, etc.) as well as producing the stress hormone cortisol and one of the neurotransmitters called glutamate whose function is to excite neurons. When glutamate accumulates in high levels, it causes uncontrolled neuronal excitation, seizures, and eventual neuronal cell death. In general, our neurotransmitters need to be recycled, cleaned out, and redistributed appropriately. This can be promoted by the calming of the mind through meditation and exercise.

How are you doing on the list above? To elevate the power of these, where I've written *"need to"* replace it with *"want to."* What changes?

The Killers

You're doing all your magic; you're integrating the practices in this book, tending to your beautiful brain, rebooting, showing up, and getting stronger and stronger. You want to keep going, right?

Pro tip: Don't kill your neurons, trigger "dendritic pruning," and lose synaptic connections.

How would you do this?

Alcohol,[9,10] drugs, TV, social media,[11] things that make us feel bad—these create neural cell death and lessen dendrite branching and growth, and therefore "prune away" healthy synaptic connections.

Did you get that? These things change our brains, kill our precious cells, and make our dendrites smooth (without synaptic "docking sites") and wimpy (we want them bushy and exuberant!).

Don't worry; this does not mean you have to cut everything out. This just means be intentional with it.

Now that you know the basics of your operating system, how to fuel it, and how not to kill it, let's look at what's happening in that beautiful system of yours.

The Science of Showing Up

I asked Dr. Lee to walk me through what's happening with our brains when we are "showing up." Here's what she shared:

In order to "show up" we have to empower ourselves with a positive outlook on life. To do that we have to overcome our innate propensity for negativity and the fear-based actions that our brains have acquired as a default protection mechanism to survive environmental threats throughout human evolution.[12] How do we do that? We redirect neural pathways for negativity to those positive pathways, and then rebuild a new neural pathway of showing up. As we experience the reward of reframing whatever that fear was and show up well, we rewrite that old path all together. How does that work? Luckily, our brain is extremely adaptable and malleable to change. Literally, what we do, how we think and where we live will change the anatomical structure, cellular composition and neural wiring of our brain. This is "neuroplasticity"—the ability of the brain to change, rewire and pave new pathways for better (or worse) outcomes.

Furthermore, in order to show up big and go beyond what we think (or thought) was possible, we literally have to expand the threshold of our "neuro-container," or our "brain capacity,"

143

to handle the higher level of challenge (cognitive resilience)! It takes courage to do this. We can do this by overwriting the previous fear neural pathways and rewriting a new path of showing up. This requires self-directed neuroplasticity, being the creator in our lives, and constant enforcement of rewards for any experience of showing up at the end in order to lock it in. The reward is essential to making this all stick!

So How Do You Do Strengthen Your Ability to Show Up and Expand the Field of Possibility?

Here's how. When something happens:

1. Look for positive facts of what's happening and let them become positive experiences.
2. Savor the experience:
   - Sustain it.
   - Have it be emotional and sensate.
   - Intensify it.
3. Sense that the positive experience is soaking into your brain and body—registering deeply in emotional memory. (Breathe and stay present with this.)

Basically, when we "show up," we activate new neural pathways that overwrite the old pathways that kept us small or scared. The more we show up and choose the new pathway and are rewarded for it (meaning we get our result, experience more space, or don't die from doing something scary), that neural pathway is stronger, and it's easier next time we do something positive. The more present we are to the experience, the more it gets locked in and we rebuild our brain!

The Science of Meditation

When we meditate, we build stronger neural pathways, expansive gray matter, exuberant dendrites, robust resiliency, and everything good that makes us show up better and feel better.[13]

With meditation, the area of the brain (prefrontal cortex) interprets all incoming info and communication with clarity and lucidity

144

by calming the area of the brain (amygdala) that activates fear and judgment. This makes us better able to interpret information and decide what to do with it.

Curiosity, presence, mindfulness, compassion, self-care, and sleep develop our dendrites and increase their capacity to make more synaptic connections. This means we are better able to process more information, declutter it, make sense of it, and move forward with clarity to make our next move and decision. Violà, our neuronal capacity gets increased, and therefore, so does our inner threshold!

If we are fear-driven, or in a state of fear (like in a meeting that's going badly), we can't receive all the information present or make our best decisions because we're spending too much energy dealing with fear or judgment or blame or any of the lower-vibration states. In a state of contraction we have a very narrow lens for interpretation and a weak filter. Meditation strengthens our left and right brain connection; helps us relax, breathe, and connect; and allows more information in through the command center. The end result is that we make good decisions.

With the recent advancement of scientific tools, scientists are better able to measure and demonstrate the benefits of meditation. For example, in the brains of people who have been following an 8- to 10-week mindfulness practice, the front part of the left side of the brain is highly activated and gray matter is significantly increased when measured in functional MRIs.[14] This is gold. Why is this so great? Dr. Lee explains, "Gray matter is where the neuronal cell body resides as well as dendrites. [White matter is where the axons are and they are myelinated—insulated—in white lipid matter.] Gray matter is gray, as the dendrites are *not* insulated. Dendrites are like tree branches harboring docking sites for axonal fibers of other neurons to connect and form synapses. The more meditation and mindful presence practice, the more the dendritic branches become exuberant. With more exuberant dendrite branches, we have greater ability to intake and better process sensory inputs and exert motor output."

The Science of Matching and Holding Your Space

Let's say you're in a meeting and Georgette comes at you—she's angry, afraid, contracted, the room feels off, and now you feel off. What should you do? Well first, let's look at what's happening. When we're in a negative or toxic room, the field is filled with fear response. Our mirror neurons are alerting us of the negativity by making us experience it as well. Our amygdala is firing—we're sensing threat. If we have a more developed prefrontal cortex and a more balanced left and right brain, it's easier to modulate and calm the fear, redirect it into confidence, and then turn around and move the energy to something different. We can also override our amygdala with neuroplasticity by taking a pause and choosing a different response.

This is not reactionary. If our left-brain prefrontal cortex is well developed, we don't have to react or respond to threat; we can exude confidence and be contagious for good. Then the other person will match it through his or her mirror neurons. Because now, based on what we're projecting and our own chemistry, that person feels safe. Even in the case of angry Georgette, if you hold your space and stay present, she's more likely to "catch" that and match you than the other way around. And if she doesn't, at least you are not clobbered by her energy.

What Happens During a Reboot?

Here's what happens during a reboot to hold your space, change the field, and get others to match you . . .

1. You override the fear response by focusing on the positive.
2. You activate and reboot the mirror neuron of confidence, projecting inner composure and peace outward (this takes energy by the way).
3. This is contagious and those near you will then mirror it! (They mirror *your* confidence; you are not mirroring *their* fear.)

Overriding your fear response will become easier if you're meditating, thereby developing your prefrontal cortex and attaining left and right brain hemispheric synchronization, so that you can more easily shift from a negative vibe or experience to that of positive. If you're not meditating and strengthening and balancing your brain, this is harder but still doable with practice. A trick in rewriting? We are coming from either fear or love at all times. Fear shuts us down, contracts us, and panics our circuits, activating the negative contagions. Love opens up possibility, creates more space and calm, and activates the positive contagions. Choose love.

The Science of Being Contagious

When it comes down to it, contagiousness is an extreme form of empathy. We see or feel someone, we relate, and we get hooked into them for good or for bad. What's actually happening scientifically though? When I asked Dr. Lee to walk me through the physical process, she shared the *"Neural Substrates of Empathy"* and their three simulating systems: "**Actions** which 'mirror' systems and are in the temporal-parietal lobe of the brain; **feelings**, which resonate emotionally and are in the insula; and **thoughts,** which are the 'theory of the mind' and occur in the prefrontal cortex. These three systems interact with each other through association and active inquiry. They produce an automatic, continual re-creating of aspects of others' experience. This is what is happening scientifically with empathy."

The science of being contagious boils down to this: I am with you, we have brain waves, mirror neurons, group dynamics, energy exchange at play—these simulating systems working together all at the same time. You see and hear and feel me; your mirror neurons respond to mine, matching them, and meeting me at the vibration I'm at (or mine respond to yours).

Basically, one of us is going to catch the other's vibe. It takes energy to maintain one's energy and focus to be contagious, so whoever has the strongest intention, holds his or her space best, and has the healthiest neural pathways and mirror neurons is likely to win. It's hard to be positively contagious (or fight off negative contagions) when we're not present, we're exhausted, and we're not fully resourced or taking care of ourselves.

Let's look at how this plays out in real life.

Story: Mirror Neurons on Stage

We hear about mirror neurons all the time. They're the things that make us mimic another person's facial expression without even realizing it. They're why when someone talks about a painful experience, we wince even though we weren't there. They're why when you meet people, you decide almost instantly if you like them and trust them. They're how we learn new behaviors. They're how a room full of people gets suddenly calm (or chaotic) because of how *one* person shows up. They're magical. Especially if we understand them and know how to nourish and optimize them.

Mirror neurons are composed of sensory and motor neurons working together. They receive input through *sensory* neurons and exert command through *motor* neurons. Our hand movements, facial expressions, mouth movements, and sounds are all part of the circuitry and essential for mirror neurons. Mirror neurons are how we learn and impact how we react and judge.

Here's an example of how this plays out. When I first met with Dr. Lee, I'd given a keynote the day before. It had gone well; the audience was engaged, I felt in flow, and the content came out of me beautifully. Basically, all systems were humming. There was total connection with the audience from the minute I came out on stage. Dr. Lee walked me through what was happening during my event from a neuroscience standpoint.

When I walked out on stage, I was incredibly present and tuned in. I came out standing strong. I was clear about my message, curious about the audience, excited to contribute, full of conviction, and exerting contagiousness. I had the intention of service and being a positively contagious contribution to the room.

My neural state was "cohesive" and "synchronous." This means my left and right brain hemispheres were firing in sync so that I could exert my presence coherently and so that my audience watching me could perceive me as congruent, confident, contagious, curious, clear, and present. When the members of the audience perceived this, and saw and felt me congruent in my state, *their* neurons fired reflecting back mine, mimicking me and experiencing what I was projecting. They saw me and how I stood. They heard my voice and the sound waves it produced. They received and perceived me. This established trust, allowing the audience members to then follow me through their own mirror neurons and the brain waves between us.

We had a brain wave match. The atmosphere was coherent. They matched my vibration.

In other words, because I was congruent and coherent in my energetic state and presence, and I was practicing my seven C's (which I'll reveal later in this chapter), they "believed me" and reflected that back to me. We had a lovely experience. Dr. Lee reinforced for me scientifically what I'd always sensed and noticed about connecting with other human beings: when we are intentional, congruent, present, resourced, coming from love, and in service of—energy flows.

Locking in a Good Experience

That keynote felt great. I felt the audience—I felt expansion and connection. My sensory input came in, and my brain reorganized itself to make that feeling the *new* norm. Note that the brain reorganization and "lock-in" doesn't happen instantly. More neuronal membranes have to be created and neural connections settled. It takes energy and time for the neural connections to settle and become the default/norm. As we do this, we are able to build the neural network and access it more quickly with each situation so it gets easier until we can access that state of being on demand. It ultimately becomes a default. In other words, the more often we do it, the less time it takes; "practice makes presence," and "presence, not perfection."

Turning a Bad Experience into Good

Let's go further to learn how you can use all this science to improve your ability to be positively contagious. Let's go back to my event. Now this event could have gone a couple of other ways. I could have come on stage incongruent, stressed out, nervous, distracted, self-focused, or worrying only about me and whether the audience members liked me. I wouldn't have had to say a word and they would have picked up on those brain waves and vibes and reflected back my negativity. Or they might have ignored me, gotten lost in their phones, or walked out. In either case that experience would be very different.

Another scenario? I could have come out exactly as I was: positive energy, in flow, and totally focused on service, and I could have had a bunch of Georges and Georgettes in the audience in a low state, with arms crossed and nasty facial expressions (or simply on their phones) and disregarding my ideas. When you experience a situation like this, you have two choices: (1) hold your state and stay solid (inviting them to match *you*) or (2) match *them*, in which case you change your state and your presence, feel bad, and ultimately lose the room.

Let's take this one step further. Let's say you have the latter experience; the keynote (or conversation) is crashing. Then what? The good news is tht at any point during any interaction you have a choice to reboot, bring the energy back up, and get command of the room again. This will require courage, a pause, a breath, and getting yourself back to a higher and more congruent state of being.

And this can happen in any conversation or situation—it doesn't matter if it's one-to-one or one-to-a-thousand. While you have zero control over others (however, a ton of potential *influence*), you have total control of *you*. Changing the energy of the conversation—being contagious—is very doable.

Regaining Command of Your State

When you find yourself in a situation where you want to shift the state of challenging energy, try my favorite technique, which is to breathe and acknowledge three core things:

1. I'm still alive.
2. People still love me (even if not in this room right this minute).
3. This is a time to access any pleasurable thought I can. Anything. This might be remembering that you are with other humans and you're all in this together. Or that you are here to serve. You might think about something or someone you love. Or "Presence, *not* perfection!" Or simply reconnecting with your intention. The moment you can take a breath and access a more pleasurable thought, you will be back online.

Each of us has been in a meeting or conversation that was going off the rails, and yet you somehow brought it back. You may have tapped something on this list to pull you through and not even known it.

If you choose *not* to reboot or access a pleasurable experience to shift your state and your quality of contagiousness, then you've likely hardwired in your miserable experience and taught your amygdala to forever fear that situation. The next time you go to do that thing again, it will be scarier. (This can always be rewritten; it's just easier done sooner than later.)

But here's really great news: even if it's a truly bad experience, you have one more chance. If you can catch it and change the story, you can rewrite it. "Recently," Dr. Lee shares, "how the brain assigns emotions to different experiences was revealed when scientists identified two distinct populations of neurons in the amygdala that process positive and negative emotions.[15] In this remarkable study (done by Kim et al., 2016), neuroscientists discovered that how we learned that a particular experience was good or bad depended on where these distinct populations of neurons projected into, even though they initially originated from the same location intermingled acting as a gate for sensory information coming into the amygdala. Most remarkable of all was that shutting down pathways to the fear circuit not only impaired fear learning [negative] but also enhanced reward learning [positive] suggesting that they engage in a push-pull interaction with each other influencing resultant emotional outcomes."

In other words, the experience comes through the same place in the amygdala but homes in on two distinct places dependent on whether it's "perceived" as a negative or a positive experience. The same experience bifurcates into two different outcomes—it's a choice point!

In the case of a bad experience, this process in your brain allows a window of opportunity for us to influence whether we will code this experience as positive or negative. Neuroplasticity enables us to change the outcome of positive or negative based on where we decide to land the experience in our brain.

For example, with the same exact data and situation, I can tell myself the story that I was a complete failure and I'm terrible. Or I can say I was a *success* because I was brave, I tried, I learned, and I'm loved (even though I didn't have my intended impact). I can tell myself that George doesn't like me because he said "no" to my request. Or, I can tell myself that he does like me, he did me a service by being honest, there's something more fitting for him to say "yes" to, or there's someone better I can ask. (Thereby putting myself in a stronger, more positive state to move forward and find the next solution.) I can tell myself that my coworker is horrible and out to get me. Or I can assume good, be grateful for the opportunity to sharpen my collaboration skills, and get curious about the coworker's behavior. (Thereby becoming better resourced to explore what's actually "here" and consciously navigate any issues.) When I get pulled over for speeding, I can be mad that I got stopped. Or I can be grateful that the officer may have just saved my life and maybe the lives of others. (Being grateful likely creates a better experience with the officer, and me being more present and conscious while driving in the future!)

Notice that with each of these choice points there is a different feeling and outcome. The first options feel contracted and negative—narrowing possibility, learning, and the opportunity to create a better outcome or relationship moving forward. The second options feel more positive and expansive, opening the field of possibility for more learning, connection, and solutions. We can strengthen our ability to default to either type of choice point.

Had my keynote been absolutely terrible and I couldn't bring it back up, if I could code the story as positive (honestly), I could rewrite that experience in my brain. This might mean coding it as a "great learning experience," or focusing on the *one* person I saw be positively impacted, or acknowledging my risk taking and courage. Any positive story would help me process that experience (and learn from it), so that the next time, my neural pathways would be ready to rock versus I would never go on stage again.

Mastery Tip #1: The Seven C's of Being Positively Contagious

Want to get into a positively contagious state fast? Access any (or all) of these states:

- Confidence
- Curiosity
- Clarity
- Conviction
- Compassion
- Contribution
- Congruence

Confidence, clarity, and *conviction* communicate that you've got this, you are present, and you can be trusted. *Curiosity, compassion,* and *contribution* communicate that you care, you are present, and you are human. *Congruence* communicates that you are present, aligned, and trustworthy.

To exert contagiousness as a leader, you have to be curious toward others, how they are, and their emotional state. Having an emotional intention toward them strengthens the brain waves between you and them and helps create more coherence.

Having a hard time with feeling confident authentically? Access contribution. Contribution is a gateway to confidence. Why? Because when you're contributing, you're not coming from a self-focused or judgment space, but rather from service and care. Subtract judgment and instead add service and boost confidence.

Finally, compassion releases serotonin and dopamine, which shift our physiological states and make us more compelling and relatable to people around us. Contribution, curiosity, and congruence activate oxytocin (a hormone and neurotransmitter known to be involved in breastfeeding, childbirth, and the experience of being in love), which increases trust, creates safety, and makes people feel good. Ahh . . . the virtual cycle of contagious good!

Mastery Tip #2: Connect with Your Future Self and Create Your Experience

In my work with clients, I've found that when we work with a version of their future self, they have more access to their innate wisdom and are more likely to make better decisions. Why? The brain needs to be able to experience a reality in the future so that it can create it. Imagination and visioning (that can come with meditation) are essential tools for doing this. When you connect with your vision for your future self, seeing yourself being and doing that behavior (e.g., learning a skill or solving a problem) and feeling the experience of it, you have a better chance of creating it.

Writing a vision for what you want to create, and then reading and living it every day, is one of my personal favorites for becoming.

Another way to look at this is to see yourself as contagious externally and internally. Whatever and whomever you see yourself as, you can create it (consciously or unconsciously) by envisioning it and living into it, as if turning on mirror neurons to mimic your own future self. The more you do this, the less effort you need. It becomes a default. The more you show up, create your reality, and even embody it—feeling the way you want to feel—the more contagious you become and the more others respond accordingly. If you mirror what you want to see and be, your internal map of your reality expands, you increase your neural threshold expanding your range for what's possible and how contagious you can become, and you build your neural pathways—making this your new way of being.

Fieldwork: Make It Real

Here are several things you can do to make this chapter real in your life—do one or all and see what shifts.

1. **Digest this chapter as it serves your analytical mind.** Then go take a nap so your brain can process and absorb it.

2. **Experiment with the impact of sleep, meditation, presence, and self-care.** Whatever you're doing right now to take care of yourself, level-up. Do it more and with greater intent. (If you're starting from scratch, that's good too.) Keep a journal to track what you do and the impact of it. You can measure the following:

- Sleep quality and time
- Meditation quality and time
- Self-care, the quality of it, and what you do for it (i.e., food, exercise, rest, etc.)
- Presence awareness, reboots, and time simply being present with yourself

Then measure how it impacts you and your leadership:

- The quality of my presence and focus today
- The quality of my reactions to stress and overwhelm
- My level of intention and thoughtfulness
- My general energy level
- What I learned

3. **Practice choice points for 24 hours**
   - For every situation that comes up today, no matter how aggravating or disappointing, find another frame for it. Remember, this does not mean being "Pollyanna" about it or pretending it didn't happen; this means choosing to find a more expansive thought and frame that will support you in moving forward.
   - Do not complain for 24 hours. Not once. Instead, for every complaint you have, simply consider the request or the suggestion underneath it. (This is another form of "choice pointing.") For extra credit, find the requests under the complaints when others come to you complaining. (You can intuit what the

request is and check it out. You can also just ask and then coach them as needed to explore it.)

4. **Play the Mirror Neuron Game**

- At your next meeting (this could be a one-to-one or with a group), before you even walk in, check yourself—your energy, your state, the vibe you're putting out, your posture and facial expressions, and so on. Set an intention for how you want to show up and for the quality of the experience you want to create. See what happens when you set the tone.

- If it doesn't go so hot, or you notice energy starts to dip or tension is in the room or things are feeling heavy, take a breath, sit back, and practice what you've learned in this chapter.

CHAPTER 9

The Seven P's of Personal Burnout and Transforming "Bad" Things Into "Good." Do It.

Can you find the gift? Find it; create freedom.
Use it; create power. Share it; create magic.

Sam was a "richly scheduled" high-performance leader with a full life. People loved working with him. He'd grown fast in his career hitting the executive track in record time. Consistent and effective, he was known as one of the most influential and reliable leaders in the organization.

He was at the top of his game.

He was also exhausted.

Even with substantial self-care, resilience, and IEP, years of hard work, sacrifice, long hours, great leadership, and showing up again and again had landed him in this moment of his life frustrated, lonely, and unnerved by his current state. He found himself asking, "Is this all there is?" "What's the point?" And "How do I keep this up?"

He had people who reported *to him* and people he reported *to;* being in the middle (with a lot of responsibility to all of them) felt

157

isolating. He'd created a beautiful life, and he had a lovely family he'd built great security for, but now instead of enjoying it, he felt an intense level of pressure to not lose it. Lack of sleep, skipping workouts and meals, nonstop thinking, and trying to please and show up well for everyone and everything had taken its toll.

To make matters worse, he'd noticed a general low vibe among his team recently and suspected he was part of it. He knew that he was contagious and that he set the tone for the people on his team. Yet despite his best efforts to reboot, bubble up, stay high vibe, and show up every day, they felt what he was feeling deep down and were matching his energy. He wanted to do something about it, but no amount of rebooting or IEP-ing seemed to be helping for sustained periods. Sam feared he was burned out and couldn't see a way through.

What to do?

In this chapter, we'll talk about "leadership depression" and personal burnout. I'll share some of the most common reasons I see people get stuck in the grind, offer you powerful reframes to transform bad states and situations into good, and introduce a new way of thinking about the daunting responsibilities that come with leadership. As we navigate through all of this, we'll solve the challenge Sam is experiencing.

Leadership Depression

Sam was not the first high-functioning leader I've witnessed in this situation.

There's a reason for the saying "It's lonely at the top." Leadership *can* be lonely. The further up the ladder we go, the more opportunities and responsibilities we have, the more people look to us for guidance, and the more expectations we have imposed on us or by us. It is all that more essential that we self-manage, show up well, and be responsible for our impact and results. And we have to do this all while being authentic, vulnerable, and a model for the culture we want to create.

Additionally, as we grow in leadership, we may surpass friends, colleagues, team members, and even bosses we've worked with and are now responsible for leading (either formally or informally). Our interests and priorities can change, creating shifts in relationship dynamics that can be disconnecting and jarring. We may worry what our peers think, what this growth and disconnect means, or that we simply no longer fit in.

On top of this, we may find ourselves in the "middle," reporting to a boss and clients while also having others (sometimes people who were just recently our peers) reporting to us. Issues, often sensitive and confidential, need to be handled privately and with care, which can create yet another level of isolation.

And when we've come to terms with all of this—recovering, rebooting, making peace with it, and owning our leadership—there's more pressure with a never-ending list of things to delegate and do. Increasing demands for our attention, technology at every turn, a workload fit for three full-time people, and our family, staff, boss, and company looking to us for those next-level results—while it's a privilege to lead, it can be a lot!

So we reboot. Pull it together. Find our space. Get back in there. Go . . . And then the cycle starts all over again. Over time, this scenario becomes chronic, and while our resiliency may build, the cumulation of tension, fatigue, stress, and go-go-go! can create an energy of what I've come to call "leadership depression." It is a trifecta of constant pulling and internal tension combined with the deeper feelings of "What's the point?" and "How am I supposed to keep this up?"

Not to mention the "Am I enough? Do I even know what I'm doing? And when will they all find out that I'm not and I don't?" internal conversation. It's a conversation that often pervades our day-to-day lives (however quietly) no matter how much we care or how good we are at what we do.

I've noticed that when we have enough leadership depression, isolation, and continuous cycling—without real shifts in the issues that led us into our cycles—we're more susceptible to burnout. These cycles can provide tremendous wisdom, be catalysts for change and expansion, and are often an essential part of the growth and up-leveling processes of leadership. They serve as a "wake-up call," leading to new awareness and shifts in being, boundaries, and goals. And they can ultimately unlock our next levels. So if you find yourself in a funk, lean in. There is growth here *if* you are willing to take a breath, get curious, take care of yourself, get the support you need, and do the work.

Chronic "Not-Getting-It-Done-Itis" and the Hamster Wheel

If you're not creating the results you want, there's a reason. It could be your thinking, wisdom in disguise, or any number of other things. And there *is* a reason. You'll want to pause to consider what that is.

In the busyness of life, instead of taking a step back and assessing what's getting in the way of progress, we often push harder, making the hamster wheel spin faster, as opposed to stepping off for a minute to assess what's happening. The following are seven places I see people get stuck in the grind. Left unchecked, these seven can lead to leadership depression and ultimately burnout. The great news is that even being aware they're at play can clear stuck energy and reveal the next step. Their solutions are embedded in the issue—simply flip it to work *for you* versus *against you.*

1. Not being present to our language, framing, or the accurate reporting of the situation
2. Not having enough information, skill, or support
3. Not being clear on intention, the path forward, the vision, or why we're doing it, or who we're doing it for
4. Simply having a bad habit of automatically assuming things will be hard or work against us (and a bad habit of negative self-talk and assumptions in general)
5. Not truly deciding to do it (100 percent in)
6. Adopting someone else's vision or desire, but not really wanting it
7. Being scared that it will be hard work, *and*, if successful, will create a whole other set of problems and work to be done

Once we've identified what factors are genuinely slowing us down, we can ask new questions, address each issue, explore how it can be easy, sort for the hidden wisdom in our resistance or procrastination, let it go, and use our superpowers to make it so.

The Seven P's of Personal Burnout

I know people who work 60-plus hours a week, have a ton of energy, and feel great. I also know people who work their solid 40 (or less), get their yoga in every day, take vacations, and are burned out. Can you think of a time you had 100 things going on and felt energized, or 10 things going on and felt fried? What was the difference? As you look back, you might see that it wasn't physical, but more related to your mental and emotional states.

In *Contagious Culture*, I wrote about "The Seven Factors of Burnout." The first four, themed as the lack of connection to purpose, people, presence, and appreciation, have become central in many of my talks and client work. The other three, lack of safety for vulnerability and authenticity, lack of recovery time, and lack of accountability and empowerment, have also continued to hold strong, especially in the context of organizational health, teaming, and leadership hygiene.

There are nuances and builds in these that are more personal, which when addressed individually support leadership health on a deeper level. The following seven P's of burnout invite us to tend to our personal nourishment and burnout prevention more rigorously:

1. **Lack of connection to presence and the pause.** *Presence* is about being present in the moment, to our lives, in our bodies, and to our current reality. The *pause* is about taking a time-out (between projects, meetings, wins, fails, and even thoughts) to regroup, reboot, rethink, reassess, and go. Especially when we feel resistance or fatigue and *especially* when we think we don't have time for it. The pause is generative and essential for leadership impact and health. In our opening story, Sam had presence but had stopped pausing. He felt there was *no* space to pause. It seemed the more work he did, the more people expected him to do. It was

unsustainable. Familiar? This is common. So common, that I'm going to *pause* here to go deeper into this one. In Sam's case he realized a few things that helped him significantly, the greatest being that when he didn't pause, he was compromising his well-being, the quality of his work, and his impact on others. (See the "Pause" box for some of the principles that supported him in shifting.)

Sam learned that the more present he was, and the more he paused, the more intentional he could be with his team to codesign workloads and timelines and agreements up front so that things didn't have to fall through the cracks. He also learned with this new level of presence and intention that he and the team became more efficient in their meetings. (It's amazing how much time and energy gets saved when we *stop* the noise and *be* in the moment with what's actually here.)

Life moves fast, and everyone has an agenda. People are not going to let you pause (not because they're evil, but because they're managing their own stuff), so you have to create presence and the pause for yourself. It is a choice. As hard as this can be to believe, especially when we're in the weeds and everyone wants a piece of us, this is when we need these P's the most. Good news, this P is the foundation for the rest of the P's. Get this one rolling and the rest become easier.

Pause

Feel like "pausing" is impossible? You're not alone. Here are some of the best practices I've found to support people in their pause:

Proactively build in your pauses. Plan for your *pauses* in your schedule, put them on the calendar, and communicate them with your team. For example, *after* a big trip, days offsite, a huge project completion, and even a vacation, schedule a "Buffer Day" the first day back. This will allow you the space to get things done, peacefully and presently, without having the external pressure of everyone's demands. Start this day with a solid intention and a clean list of the priorities that *have* to be done. Then chunk them into time blocks with enough pauses built in, to support your energy. You might build a focused time block for email, a block for review of what you missed, a block for previewing the upcoming week and what-ever will be needed of you, and blocks for deeper work. These blocks should be focused, uninterrupted, deep work blocks. (I build blocks of 50–90 minutes, put my phone on "do not disturb," and dig in.) And then do your best. Breathe, pause, stay focused, and knock out as much as you can. (This may not make those 400 emails magically disappear; however, it will help you make a lovely dent in them in a focused way.)

Prepare for performance with a productive pause. This can happen in the moment, right before you "go on," and this can also happen in preparation for a big week. One of my own per-sonal hacks for managing this "P" is to build in a Buffer Day *before* a big trip or event. The "before" day is 100 percent unscheduled with only self-care, prep, acclimating to the new location or time zone, knocking out any loose ends pulling on my brain (responses, emails, etc.), and getting ready for the week/event ahead. This allows me to clear my energetic field, set my intentions, and be my best. If I set myself up well, my biggest job simply becomes to be present in the moment with each thing I do for the week. I do not allow myself to stress out about the following week, or even the *next* event that is not in the *present* moment. I trust that if I am prepared, am well-resourced (my IEP), and show up fully, each event will have exactly what it needs from me. (After all, if I'm stressing about the *next,* I'm not present for the *current.*)

Knowing I have the Buffer Day on the back end (as above) helps ease my mental energy as well as does the fact that I'll have a 100 percent unscheduled (and also intentional) day when I return. This day will give me space and grace for self-care, taking care of my kids, tending to the little things I may have missed while gone (in the time chunks), setting the tone for re-entry, getting caught up on email (or whatever), getting myself organized and grounded for the next week, or even being totally lazy if that's what I need.

While proactively pausing takes practice, discipline, and a bit of extra effort at first, the return on investment in time and boundaries is immeasurable and highly appreciated by my team, my performance, my output, the people I serve, and my own energetic system. This is another case of an "ounce of proactiveness is worth cleaning up two tons of mess-up later."

Note: Despite all planning and intentions, these proactive pauses will fall apart. All the time. No problem. Breathe. Reboot. Get back in there. And do your best.

Protect your pause. Whether your pause is 1–5 minutes, 60 minutes, a day, or a week, protect it. Hold this time as the most important "appointment" ever. (It is; we're talking about your well-being, presence, and performance.) Research has shown that we need an average of 25 minutes to return to an original task after an interruption, and that a typical office worker only gets 11 minutes between each interruption.[1] This doesn't support productive work. I know you don't need this stat to know how frayed our attention is, so protect it. Pause quietly for your shorter breaks (be unavailable for five minutes—it's OK). And for the longer pauses, let the people on your team know you'll be out and not available during this time. Direct them to cluster their requests or needs into one document you'll review when you're "back." (You can also have your assistant organize this for you.) My team and I have found ToDoIst, Google Docs, and Trello very helpful for this process. Not only will this give you more space; this will help people get better and more efficient at managing their own thinking, requests, and demands of you.

Watch for overcommitting, be realistic about your workload and saying "yes," and be conscious of how you're training people to work with you. Have you designed a life, and a way of being

164

and responding (*"yes!"*), that has trained people to expect things back right away, putting yourself on the hamster wheel, creating an insane amount of internal pressure, and eliminating any space for pausing? If yes, yay! Retrain. We train people how to treat us and ask of us; sometimes we just need to redesign and retrain.

Be nice to yourself; give yourself (and your thinking and perfection) a pause. What stories do you make up about other people's expectations? Are all things urgent? How much time do your truly hold for focused work? How does your self-talk support you (or not) in managing your workload? What is "perfection" anyway? (Blech!) Pay attention to the mental cycles you spend shifting gears with multiple demands and tasks, worrying about being behind, letting people down, feeling bad, stressing out about stuff you can't control, trying to do it all "right," and letting yourself be distracted by the multitude of interruptions (social media, texts, email, and all) that pull on us daily and devour conscious pausing.

Pause, breathe, reboot. This may be the easiest to integrate immediately, and you're already doing it in this book. Pause, breathe, and reboot every time you feel *dis-ease, overwhelm,* or *contraction*. This will increase awareness each time you do it and create a new default response (as I discussed in Chapter 8). In this moment of pausing, just be. Then question your thinking: Am I present? (Or am I fixating on past and future events, cycling on made-up stories and issues, and getting lost in self-talk and worry?) What's here right now? What's the next best next thing I can do to create more pleasure and internal space? (Hint: Breathe and be here *now*. Handled!) Pausing is a leadership muscle; build it.

2. **Lack of connection to purpose and the portal.** It's essential that we stay connected to *why* we're doing what we're doing to create impact (for the sake of what and for whom?),

and also that our "why" grows with us (becoming bigger and more compelling as we lead it). Whether we're running a big project, leading our team, navigating tricky relationship waters, addressing world hunger, or doing the dishes—purpose is valuable fuel. When we're connected with purpose, service, and the humans we impact, our mission becomes clearer and stronger. From here, we're not alone but rather in the portal of purpose *together*. Part of Sam's challenge was that he'd disconnected from purpose, forgetting (and even outgrowing) his "why."

3. **Lack of connection to people.** In Sam's busyness and focus on the work, he'd disconnected from the people he was leading. He'd also let his circle of friends go untapped. Not feeling seen or cared for, not seeing or caring for others, being separate and inferior or superior to others, or forgetting we're in relationship with the people we are with, creates separation and resistance, disconnects us from love, and violates a core human need to be a part of tribe. We have to "see" each other. Our humanity frees us.

4. **Lack of connection to pleasure and pain.** Sam hadn't played in a long time, and it was only when he came to speak with me that he allowed himself to share how much pain he was actually in. Up until that point he'd been forging through. This just created more pressure and fatigue for him. Accessing pleasure—playing, acknowledging delight, appreciating the moment, celebrating wins and failures, and taking time-outs for fun—is essential for regeneration. Accessing pain and authentic emotion is just as important. In order to have our full range of experience, more of our authentic selves, and clean energetic hygiene—permission for pain and true emotion is vital. Not honoring pain and pushing through contributes to armoring up, resisting our humanity, and ultimately tiring ourselves out. Not to mention potentially hurting others (hurt people hurt people). We must make room for all of ourselves. Sometimes this gets done by simply acknowledging, caring for, and being witnessed by a

good friend, and sometimes this needs more care in the form of therapy or other professional support.

5. **Lack of personal power.** Sam had gotten so sucked into everything that'd happened, he'd diluted his power. This was almost instantly shifted with awareness and then action. Owning your power and being responsible for creating your outcomes and results puts you in your own driver's seat and clears things up fast: your life, your accountability, your knowingness, your busyness, your priorities, your power. With a lack of personal power or accountability, energy gets heavy and mucky and tends to spiral, creating more of the same. Owning our power is contagious. Holding clear boundaries and taking accountability clears energy and empowers and supports others in doing the same as well.

6. **Lack of partnership with myself.** Sam's internal partnership and relationship needed a bit of tender loving care (TLC). He'd broken some of his core agreements with himself. Awareness of the broken agreements, with action to reinstate them, got him back on track almost immediately. The most important relationship we'll ever have is the one with ourselves. My relationship with myself requires nourishment and partnership throughout my day. This means instead of making myself wrong, judging and blaming, beating myself up, being unkind, or compromising myself—I get curious, care, and tend to whatever I need. When I am present to my needs, honor my internal agreements with myself, and trust I have my own back, I am stronger for everything else.

7. **An overabundance of pleasing (others) at the compromise of oneself.** Sam was quite rooted in being in service of versus pleasing the people around him; however, this one needed TLC too. In his quest to show up well *everywhere*, and with many of these "P's" compromised, he'd diminished his well-being. Trying to please everyone will wipe you out fast. (Newsflash: You can't anyway.) "Pleasing" may show up like this: putting yourself last, "sleeping when you're dead," compromising your desires or beliefs because

they're unpopular, giving up time for someone else's repetitive drama, being a ragdoll for others' demands, or being a scapegoat for another's blame. Do not compromise your well-being or beliefs to please others. Do be in service of, support, or even help others—but let go of pleasing. (Bonus tip: Notice the difference in the energetic intention of these five things: *contribute, serve, support, help, please.* Which feels weakest? Strongest? Yep, embody that.) When we are operating authentically, doing our work, taking care of ourselves, and showing up clear and in ways that we are in service of what we stand for, we're likely to disappoint at least 30 percent of the population—maybe more, maybe less. Do what's right; honor your senses; let it go.

Not taking care of yourself, pulling all-nighters, and having poor self-care will contribute to burnout. However, when these factors are nourished, physical issues are less likely to occur because when we're present to these seven, we're more in tune with what we need physically and emotionally. These seven work beautifully with the organizational seven and the rest of the IEP work to combat leadership depression, exhaustion, and burnout, and to strengthen organizational and collaborative health.

Transforming "Bad" Things into "Good"

Another factor that contributes to burnout is our thinking. Any state or situation can be made into a productive gift, *if* we learn how to reframe, use, and partner with "bad" things for "good." When something happens, ticks us off, or hurts, we can get stuck in dwelling on it, gathering evidence for more suffering, and spiraling down. Alternatively, we can have our authentic emotion and experience—process it, learn from it, and then find the most genuine way we can flip it to support us, create more space for wisdom and next steps, and spiral up.

For example, we might feel jealous of someone—which can cause great angst and resistance in our system. However, if we use that jealousy productively, we can transform it into a *calling* or a *desire*, learn from it, and let it grow us. We can take judgment and transform it into *curiosity* or *discernment* that helps us unearth new information and wisdom we'd have missed otherwise. We can convert the contracted state of "busy" to *richly scheduled, on purpose*, and even *powerful* if we're conscious of our "busy," own it, are response-able to it, and *use it* to help us see where we're not managing our lives well, honoring our priorities, and tending to what we say is most important to us. (*P.S.:* This one is huge. Get busy with your busy. #gamechanger). What other states would you transform? Below are some of the most common I see (Figure 9.1).

FIGURE 9.1   The Spectrum of Transforming "Bad" Things into "Good"

Jealousy becomes an indicator that I desire something someone has (or has done). So whom do I need to become and what work do I need to do to create that for myself? When partnered with consciously and productively, jealousy becomes a calling or desire.

Apathy becomes an indicator that I'm not connected to this "thing" or idea. So where do I need to get curious? Where is this wisdom that this plan is a dud or that I'm not the right person to be involved? When engaged intentionally, apathy transforms into passionate unattachment or neutrality.

169

Anger tells me a boundary has been breached. I'm out of alignment with myself, I'm scared, or I'm hurt about something. Anger can be the push I need to stand up for myself or something I believe in. I can use it for good. Anger transformed becomes wisdom and catalyst.

Failure gives me an opportunity to see that I've had an impact—just not the impact I wanted. It gives me precious learning and insight into ways to do it better. Failure becomes resiliency, wisdom, and future success for something different, better, and more sound moving forward.

Burnout gives me the opportunity to pause, take stock, be honest, ask for help, connect with others, and/or hide out for a bit so I can figure out what's truly true. It gives me the opportunity to revisit purpose, regroup, and come back stronger. Burnout becomes the next chapter.

Depression offers me a moment to lean back, get curious, be loving with myself, and see where I may be out of alignment, where my needs aren't being met, and where I need a bit more TLC and support. Depression can become nourishment, expansion, and elevation when honored and cared for.

Grief offers me space for true emotional authenticity without timelines or expectations. It provides a space to honor what was, what's lost, the disconnection from something meaningful, or the disappointment of betrayal. All necessary experiences to be acknowledged and cared for so they can process through and heal. On the other side of grief is strength, more of me, and joy.

Judgment gets a bad rap and yet is so essential to our survival. Judgment gifts me the opportunity to decide yes and no, to know when something is safe or not, to discern if a person is a right fit for me or my team, to make that call on my kid's requests for doing something I don't feel great about. Judgment partnered with productively becomes curiosity and discernment.

Procrastination is often wisdom in disguise or a sign that something is off, but our relationship with it culturally is to judge it and make it wrong. What if procrastination is wisdom? What if it's a sign you don't really want to do something, that you don't have enough information, or that it's a bad move? Or perhaps you do have a bad habit of procrastinating, and it's time to hop to. Procrastination leaves clues. Getting curious about it turns it into a diagnostic tool for next steps. Procrastination used intentionally becomes wisdom.

And finally, in its simplest form, a **no** is just a "yes" to something better or more congruent.

The moment I have an awareness that there is contraction in my system and trust there is a gift to be found, I'm halfway there. If I allow myself the authentic experience, identify the state or thought I am having, and then get curious and explore, I'll find new information.

The Energetic Xylophone

The IEP Energetic Xylophone can be handy here (Figure 9.2). The xylophone, which I wrote more about in *Contagious Culture,* and which I refer to in Chapter 5 of this book when discussing shifting energetic states, is one of our participants' favorite IEP tools. Just like

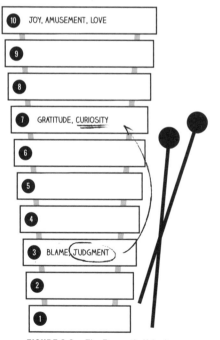

FIGURE 9.2 The Energetic Xylophone

a musical xylophone where the vibration and quality of the sound will shift as you move up or down the instrument, the Energetic Xylophone does the same thing for shifting our energetic vibe. For example, if my energy is negative or detracting, and I'm about to lead a meeting, I will want to shift it to be positive and contributory. This has to be honest, or people will feel my incongruency. The xylophone helps us shift to the highest energetic state possible, authentically, without doing a "spiritual bypass" or "faking it till we make it"—so we can operate in a better resource state and think more productively and positively.

For example, whatever state we're in (say, a "3," feeling "judgmental" and contracted) can be shifted upward to something with a higher vibration and more productive (like a "7" at "curiosity") if we can access the energy of "curiosity" in our body (or any higher state on the xylophone). In this case, the energy of *judgment* shifts to the energy of *curiosity*, which is a more informative, expansive, enrolling, and productive place to think and engage from. From a more expansive energetic state, we also now have more access to discernment and thinking differently about the situation.

Note: Everyone's xylophone is different. It's your work as leader to notice what emotional and energetic states bring you to a higher, more expansive and *helpful* vibration (i.e., love, gratitude, curiosity, contribution, etc.) and what states create contraction and a lower vibration (i.e., blame, judgment, anger, entitlement, etc.). Learn what your states are and work with them intentionally.

Being "Response-Able" and Making a "Dent"

Responsibility can be another energy sucker that makes us feel like we have the weight of the world on our shoulders. I've noticed when we get caught up in being responsible for all the challenges of our life, the world, and our organization, we can become so exhausted, or even paralyzed about what to do next, that little or nothing happens. We then make it worse by stressing about it and ultimately feeling guilty about failing it. It's a no-win.

So . . . let's dump it.

Instead a reminder to replace "responsible" with "response-able" (being *able to respond* in your most present and best way possible to whatever shows up, that you can best serve, in this moment), and then make a nice "dent":

- **Do** what you can.
- **Engage** with heart and honest intent.
- **Now**, right now—do what feels right and is the best use of you today and in this moment.
- **Trust** that it is enough. (And that by being clean here, you'll have more energy to contribute in other ways.)

No matter how big or little the "dent" is, if your energy is clear and you're coming from an expansive, honest, and loving place, you're contagious. People feel it. And they'll catch it. If your energy is not clear and you're coming from a contracted, fearful, complaining, hopeless, scarce, manipulative, or resentful place, you're contagious there too.

Of course, it is much easier to discern what to take responsibility for, what to respond to, and where to make the most meaningful "dents" when our intentions, energy, and presence are clear—so keep on IEP-ing.

Back to Sam . . .

In our work together, Sam addressed many of the things we've talked about in this chapter. None of them were complicated—most were about awareness, presence, support, and making a few changes. That being said, Sam also realized that a lot of his drive and internal stress and pressure were being created by issues that were beyond the scope of our work together. So Sam did one of the greatest things a leader can do—he got additional professional support and engaged in therapy with a highly qualified therapist to do the deeper work.

Today, I'm happy to report that Sam is still a thriving rock star (brighter than ever), and now with much more access to himself, command of his leadership, a stronger presence, and more impact to boot.

When You Need More—Get It

If you find yourself doing this work, rebooting, and all of the good stuff that goes with it, and you still sense (or know) there are deeper stressors that need attention, get support. Getting help is a leadership skill and an act of human grace.

"What if 'bubbling up,' eating well, exercising, reframing, finding the P's, and all of these great tools are not enough for real true mental and emotional health? What if I can do these things, but I need more?"

This question was posed by a participant in one of our sessions. I was grateful for it. This organization had just lost someone to suicide. I knew that three of the people in the room were navigating divorces, and a few people had mentioned major life changes and losing loved ones in the past year.

So when this question came, we let out a collective breath as if to say, "OK, this just got really real."

My response?

This work offers powerful and effective frameworks and principles to guide and support you, *and* not any one modality, tool, or resource is the be-all and end-all for growth, healing, behavior change, or support. The IEP Method is a framework for helping us be more intentional, create stronger leadership and accountability, have better energy and impact, and show up even more effectively in our lives.

Part of showing up well and being accountable for our leadership impact is making sure we get *whatever* support is necessary to heal, mend, nourish, and strengthen ourselves. This may include engaging in other bodies of work, psychological therapy, counseling, medication, and additional forms of support with professionals who specialize in the areas we need help in. Asking for help, getting support, and allowing ourselves to receive it *is* showing up for ourselves.

Throughout the IEP Model (as discussed in Chapter 5), there are additional resources and bodies of work that can help people go deeper and further into what they need. For example, in Quadrant 1 of Figure 9.3 (if this looks familiar, it should—it was first presented

174

as Figure 5.4 in Chapter 5), this may mean engaging with nutrition or physical training professionals, a bodyworker, physical therapist, chiropractor, professional organizer, or physician. Or it may mean having your hormones and blood work checked—anything to make sure you are physically and environmentally well.

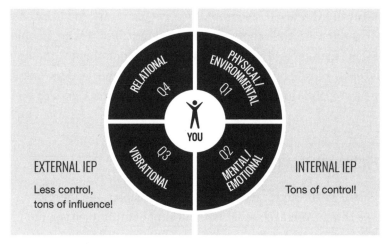

FIGURE 9.3   Internal and External IEP: The Four Quadrants

In Quadrant 2, in addition to the skills, superpowers, and frameworks offered in the IEP work, this may mean asking for help from friends, from a therapist or counselor, or from your Employee Assistance Program (EAP) at work. It may mean working with a coach, somatic work, Neuro-linguistic Programming (NLP), PSYCH-K®, Eye Movement Desensitization and Reprocessing therapy (EMDR), trauma therapy—anything to support your mental and emotional well-being.

Your Internal IEP (Quadrants 1 and 2) is the most essential to attend to in supporting your presence, impact, and well-being from the inside out. For External IEP (Quadrants 3 and 4), you might work with a presence coach, a mediator or couple's therapist, a team facilitator, or many others. There are so many fantastic bodies of work and professionals in the world to support us whatever our needs.

We have many people that use the IEP work *and* also see a therapist or coach or participate in other programs to support their needs.

The intention is to use the IEP framework and tools to support you in showing up for yourself and others and to create the leadership and self-care plan that works beautifully for you. Only you will know what that is because you know you best.

How can we more effectively support individual and cultural health? As leaders—and organizations as a whole—we can make it culturally OK (even celebrated) for people to ask for help. Model it. Champion it. Talk about it. Pay attention. Point your people to EAP and therapy and other modalities to honor them in being the healthiest, most connected, and most supported leaders possible. Our future, and the well-being of your organization, depends on it.

Fieldwork: Make It Real

Please go through each section of this chapter and identify *one* thing from each area that will support you in either navigating "leadership depression," fatigue, and burnout or preventing it altogether. An ounce of prevention is worth a ton of cleanup. Wherever you are in every moment starts the next now. Let's go.

PART 3

CONTAGIOUS RELATING: BUILD, HEAL, AND OPTIMIZE YOUR RELATIONSHIPS

CHAPTER 10

But What About "That Guy/Gal"? Understand Them.

There will always be "that guy" or "that gal" or the infamous "they"—mind your business, hold your space, do your thing, and if you really want to lead, love them up.

"So what about George?" Remember him from Chapter 1?

You're doing your work. Your IEP is strong, and you're IEP-ing along, clear on impact and purpose, minding your own business, using your superpowers, and serving as you go. And then comes "George" (or "Georgette" or "G"). No matter how much personal work you do, that extremely negative person seems to show up in every room, at every annual family event, and every time you want to engage people in a different initiative.

You know better now than to make that person wrong, get hooked, or lose your power. You also know to check yourself before you wreck yourself because the best way to work with G is to work with yourself first. But still, what's the best way to deal with these personality types?

In Chapters 1 and 2, when it was all about you, I gave you some indicators and an assessment to know if and how you might be

George. Now that we're in the navigating relationships part of the book, this chapter gives you four common types of George, and some frameworks to guide, learn from, contribute, and even complete altogether with G when it's just not meant to be.

"George" Is Everywhere

We've all worked with, hired, avoided, been burned by, and/or learned from George. We have also likely been George at some point in our lives, and not even known it. It's possible *you* may be someone's George right now.

George is in your meeting sucking the life out of the room with his very presence.

Georgette is at the planning session complaining about everything and naysaying every idea you come up with.

George is hosting cultural training and leadership development programs, but not attending them.

Georgette is at your dinner table "Debbie Downer-ing" all the good ideas you bring up.

George is taking all the credit for the good stuff, no accountability for the bad stuff, and leading in a "Do as I say, not as I do" kind of way.

Georgette may even be *in your head* as your biggest bully offering the voice of judgment, blame, and self-doubt.

They are in your meetings, in your audience, at your annual events, rolling their eyes, crossing their arms, being negatively contagious, gathering allies, and—if you let them—exhausting you before you've even started.

And it's OK. You've got this. And you're closer than you think to working through it.

While you can't control or change the Georges in your life, you can definitely influence them. Remember, you are contagious. I've worked with many Georges, and I've seen others navigate their own, and what I know is that G can shift with the right leadership, space, timing, and invitation.

One of the ultimate acts of leadership is to hold your space with grace, be you, lead, love, help things go well, *and* be an invitation in service of another's greatness. Georges make us better leaders. George may be your greatest teacher right now, and if you stay intentional, present, and energetically clear, you may find yourself becoming the invitation for George to shift.

That's leadership.

So Who Is George?

There are many types of Georges. The descriptions in this section are extreme versions. Your George may fit perfectly in one of these, have tendencies for one or two, or be a fine blend of all on the George spectrum.

Data George is numbers-driven, is highly analytical, and scoffs at anything that can't be measured, proved, or put in a concrete box. You may experience his energy as sharp, intimidating, negative, buzz-killing, and even cold. He means no ill will; it is simply how he's wired. He wants the facts. The "soft stuff" may be intimidating to him; it is unknown, is hard to quantify, requires vulnerability, and is a new way of thinking about outcomes. This is not a "bad" George. This George can become your greatest advocate and partner if you show up, do the work, and listen to where he's coming from. His leadership style may be very different from yours. Great, learn to influence him and you can influence others like him. This George can be a tremendous gift in stretching perspective and thinking if we stay conscious and curious and look for the good.

Note: When this George adds in a bit of curiosity and space for the soft stuff, he becomes even more brilliant and relatable.

Gloomy Georgette brings doom, gloom, and heavy energy wherever she goes. Hanging out with her is like wading through energetic mud. There's always a crisis, a complaint, a story to be told in which she is the victim, something hard has happened, some reason why things aren't going to work. She may find you on your kid's playground, at the grocery store, or in your office. Even a phone call with her can wipe you out if you let it. You find yourself bubbling up and doing extra IEP work in preparation for any encounter with her. She means no harm; the struggle is real but . . . she is exhausting to be with. She may say she wants things to change, but the mileage and attention she gets out of the "drain train," the coziness and familiarity of the status quo, and the habit of her negative thinking, make her *think* she can't make the changes. (But she can.) The gift of this Georgette? She makes us appreciate the light, bounce back from the dark, ground ourselves in higher-vibration states, get clear on necessary boundaries, *and* learn compassionate leadership in new ways.

Note: When this Georgette is given space to be heard, seen, and cared about *while* being held and championed as a powerful human who is the author of her life and responsible for her outcomes, she can experience an invitation to step up, and often will. (Tip: Hear, see, care, champion, invite, and make sure your IEP is genuinely right.)

King George is the George who has no idea he's George but rather seems to *think* he is *the* boss, *King Boss.* He struts around, walks in late to meetings, talks a big game, passes the buck, and takes the credit. He also speaks badly about others, obliterates trust and safety, leaves "dead bodies" everywhere he goes, laughs at things like "vulnerability" and "feelings in business," looks for gossip, is condescending and inconsiderate, and gives people what I call "the ick." While he may be wildly talented, seem confident, and say that things like "authenticity and safety" are important—he's usually the most feared, least respected, "falsely followed," and most insecure of them all. The possible gifts of this George for you? Resilience, boundary clarification, seeing the humanity in everyone, and building greater skills in holding your space and meeting people where they are without compromising your energy or values.

Note: King George can be one of the people most positively impacted by this work, and your contagiousness, if you can find a genuine space to meet him where he is, give him productive *direct* feedback, and tap into his intended legacy and long-term impact.

Georgy Georgette knows she's Georgette, and . . . doesn't really care. She got here by being who she is, and if people don't like it, too bad. She has no interest in changing. She's terrifying to be in a room with. She'll throw you under the bus faster than you can say "contagious." If she's forced into any kind of leadership development, she is likely doing it because a bonus or a bigger move in her career is at stake. Here's the thing. Georgy Georgette may be one of the most successful people in the company. She may be making your organization a ton of money and be adored by clients, so the company will not be exiting her anytime soon. (The company doesn't think it can't afford to, but doesn't realize, yet, that it can't afford to keep tolerating her behavior either.) The gift of Georgy Georgette? She gets stuff done, but often at the expense of the humans around her. Your job is to learn to navigate this Georgette more effectively, be aware of what you can count on from her, and ask for what you want clearly. You'll also need to notice even the littlest moments of impact and opportunity, hold her accountable for toxic behavior by naming it (and even reporting it to your HR or compliance department), and, as necessary, guard your loins.

Note: This is the trickiest Georgette, *and* she can shift if she finds a compelling enough reason to. Sometimes the shift is surface-level, and oftentimes if sustainable genuine shifts don't occur, a company will exit this Georgette when the cost on the culture and other players on the team becomes too great.

These are all extreme examples of four common types of Georges and interacting with them personally. In some cases simply being the change you wish to see will shift a George, sometimes it's feedback, and sometimes it's more extreme measures.

Why Is George, "George"?

I've sat in many rooms with Georges, and I can tell you three things:

1. Rarely does anyone set out to be George. People generally do not wake up and say, "I'm going to make everyone's life harder today" or "I'm going to be a terrible leader" or "I'm going to be the lowest vibration in the room."

2. George is a human being, and when people are showing up like George, there is usually a very human reason, including:
    *   They may be feeling insecure or vulnerable.
    *   Something bad has happened to them.
    *   They don't feel safe or valued.

- They feel they need to prove something.
- Their feelings are hurt.
- They feel irrelevant or unseen.
- They want to be important.
- They need support or healing.
- They just aren't aware of their impact.
- They're busy or overwhelmed.
- They're exhausted and not managing themselves well.
- They just don't know how to shift. (Yet.)

3. Georgette often doesn't even know she's Georgette. She actually desires to do good, to show up beautifully, and to be helpful.

So how does someone become George? I believe that question is best answered by asking ourselves how we've become George at times. Things happen. Life experience, bad behavior that isn't given honest and direct feedback, unconscious impact, bad modeling, bad habits, assumptions, fatigue—all these things play a role in our Georgeness. We can also become George due to history, insecurities, hurt feelings, misunderstandings, childhood stuff, and self-protection. These are all part of the human experience. And instead of being vulnerable, getting curious, asking for support, or taking a pause, we may armor up, act out, and fortify bad habits that have worked for us and even been rewarded in the past. Done over time chronically, we become George.

To "George" is human.

Working with George

In the scenarios shared in this book, there have been core practices, intentions, and ways of being to support your dance with George/Georgette. Before I give you more, are we all in agreement that we must check ourselves first and do our own work before we get huffy about them? Do you get that you holding your space, staying clear, taking care of yourself, being positively contagious, leading with love, and being the change you wish to see is your best bet for creating change around you?

Good.

So now when you run into George and you've done your own work, you have three basic options:

1. Appreciate and navigate.
2. Serve and lead.
3. Honor, codesign, and complete the relationship as necessary.

For best results, to avoid #3 all together, use a blend of #1 and #2.

To make this more real, at the end of this chapter I'll share one of the trickiest situations I've ever witnessed with one person who wanted to lean in and make things right and one who didn't. This work doesn't always have a happy ending. In fact, it can be messy. How you navigate the mess will determine your ability to lead, influence, and create the impact you desire.

Appreciate and Navigate

Appreciation makes the world go round, and intentional navigation can move mountains. So let's put this to use with George and see what magic we can create.

Navigating George

You may notice at this point in the book that George is becoming less challenging to work with and that solutions for working with him are becoming more obvious. You might also notice that navigating issues isn't as difficult as it was, and people aren't irritating or affecting you as much as they used to. You may feel clearer, tuned in, energized, on purpose, and in alignment. One of the coolest things about owning our space and doing our work is that when we change ourselves, take care of ourselves, and feel solid from within—everything, including George, looks and feels different.

So celebrate that. And let's get you a few more more tools for navigating and leading George.

Bubble Up

The "bubble" is a tool I've spoken about throughout this book (especially in Chapter 5) and write about more deeply in *Contagious*

Culture. It's your energetic space—100 percent yours. Imagine it is about 18 inches around you on all sides: above, below, front, back, side to side (Figure 10.1). It's made out of whatever you wish (glass, steel, bubbly material), and it's filled with your energy. It is a protective, nourishing, energetic boundary.

FIGURE 10.1   The IEP Bubble

The bubble creates more space for our pause, gives us a moment to decide how to respond, and helps us interact with the world and people around us more effectively. We get to decide what gets in, what we let out, what we hold, what we clear and release, and ultimately how we respond.

Our bubble is always present, *and* we can forget it and lose our space when we're moving fast, feeling overwhelmed, or not present ourselves.

A confrontation or simple interaction with George is a great place to activate the bubble. Take a deep breath and remember you have your space. Then, own your bubble (it can help to visualize it all around you), and set an intention that this bubble is a safe space and no one's negativity is getting in it.

The bubble doesn't make George, our problems, or chaos go away. It creates a boundary, giving us our own clear space to decide how to interact with George and navigate the situation versus overreacting and becoming energetically overwhelmed.

Use Your Superpowers

The superpowers I put in your toolkit in Chapter 7 work beautifully when it comes to navigating George. The more you use them, the more they become habits, and the less you'll need them.

Here's what I've found over the years: the stronger my IEP, the cleaner my energetic hygiene, and the clearer I am on my intention, the more I trust myself not to get hooked into George or drama, the less stuff bugs me, and the less I find issues with George. I can see things clearer, influence more effectively, be kinder, know what superpowers to use as necessary, and walk away easier when I need to. My clients report similar results with the Georges in their lives, too. (*Note:* The more you do this work, the more you'll likely find that anytime you're *really* triggered by George is an indication of the next level of personal work you get to do to expand your leadership ranges and edges. #growth)

Love Your "Nemesis"

Our biggest challengers can be our greatest teachers and a gift if we let them be.

In working with Georgette, especially if there is specific tension, you'll want to take the energetic and emotional "charge" out so you can see and be more clearly. These questions can help increase awareness and loosen up tension to create space for different perspectives:

1. What *is* the issue? What's *really* triggering me?
2. What can I appreciate about him/her?
3. What does he/she have that I want?
4. How am I like him/her?

5. What's it like for him/her to be in relationship with me? (How am *I* showing up?)
6. Where are my feelings hurt? (And is he/she even aware there is an issue?)
7. What am I not saying that needs to be said? (And what do I actually want?)

For a fuller version of this exercise, see the *Contagious You Resources Toolkit* offered in Chapter 16.

Appreciate George and the Present State

Can you appreciate George? Can you appreciate the moment? Can you appreciate the tension? Here are three questions to set you free:

- **What can I appreciate about George?** (He asks for what he wants. He's stubborn. She's demanding. She's making me a better leader as I figure out how to navigate this situation with her. This person is a human being.)
- **What can I appreciate about this moment?** (I'm alive. I am in touch with my emotions. I know I'll grow from this. I'm wise and present enough to ask this question right now!)
- **What can I appreciate about the tension?** (It's a sign that something needs to change. It means I care. On the other side of this will be growth.)

When we can find appreciation, we open space and create access to better solutions.

Give George a Chance: Ask for What You Want and Need

Sometimes George doesn't even know there's a problem. He may sense your resistance and tension and have no idea why. (And then respond with his own resistance and tension. And now, bam, you have a bigger problem!)

Does George know there's a problem? Don't expect anyone to read your mind.

Name the issue or challenge; make the request; share the story you are making up. Get curious about George's experience.

Ask for what you want (and need) and be prepared to negotiate the difference.

Give George a chance.

Serve and Lead

You have an opportunity to contribute to George. You see the issue (he still might not). You have the superpowers and awareness and heart. (He might not know how yet.)

If you wish to, you can be in service of George if you are able to:

- Hear his tender agenda.
- Get into shared reality and intent.
- Give productive feedback.

Listening Below and Beyond

A complaint is simply an uncommunicated request. When George complains or gives you a hard time, there's a request in there somewhere. For example, "You don't respond to my emails or calls" becomes "Please respond." Find the request.

Underneath that request is a dream. He wants something. He desires something (e.g., to have a better working relationship, create a better outcome, stay on track with a timeline, or be a good partner). Find the dream.

Underneath that dream is likely a tender agenda. He's afraid or feeling vulnerable about something. It's usually something to the effect of: *Do you like me? Am I good enough? Do you care? Do I belong? Do I matter to you? Do you believe in me? Am I going to be fired? Will I get that promotion? Am I safe?* Make yourself aware of the tender agenda (we all have one—it's human).

Find the thread and be free.

By the way, this works for you too. What's your request, your dream, and your tender agenda? The more fired up you are about George, the more important it is to get clear on what's going on for you below and beyond as well.

Get into Shared Reality

If you want to influence George, you're going to have to meet him where he is. What is George's experience? What's yours? Get together and name what you both sense is going on, and then connect the dots. This is a good place to name assumptions; share intentions; talk purpose, fears, and dreams; and then clarify next steps where everyone wins. If you get into trouble here and truly can't find alignment, or there's a conflict that is just too big for a simple shared reality discussion, refer to the IEP Conflict Navigation Model in Chapter 12.

Give Feedback

Giving feedback is consistently one of the trickiest challenges I see people in leadership have. Recently I met with someone who'd just had a $500,000 project go off the rails because none of the team members wanted to give the leader honest, direct, hard feedback in the early stages when they saw the project going down a bad path. They all hoped it would work itself out (or that someone else would speak up). It didn't. (And they didn't.)

This is not uncommon. Feedback is hard. It challenges harmony and connection. We take it personally and make it mean more than it does. It's easy to soften it, withhold it, hope someone else will give it, or pray that the issue will just go away—all to avoid discomfort, confrontation, or hurting someone's feelings. When we get into this dynamic, no one wins. George is still doing his thing, thinking everything is fine. You are still frustrated and wishing George would shape up. And the people around you witnessing this dynamic are learning not to trust you because if you won't give George direct, clean feedback, then you won't give it to them either. So no one has anyone's back, and your team or company is not going to have a good result. Bummer.

A lack of honest, direct feedback is one of the greatest toxins in an organization (or any relationship); it creates a lack of safety and a "culture of careful." So, while it's hard, it's also one of our greatest opportunities for building trust, changing behavior, supporting each other's rock stardom, and doing good work. It's also kind.

Real feedback is kind (as are acknowledgments of what someone is doing well).

In Chapter 13 we'll talk about specific formulas, tips, and mindsets to give the most productive feedback (even when it's about the intangible stuff). For now just know you must give George feedback. Have you?

Honor, Codesign, and Complete the Relationship as Necessary

Sometimes, no matter what you do, it's a no go. You've done your work. You've done all you can, and you know in your heart you're clean.

George keeps breaking agreements and promises, putting you in a bad spot, not following through, and disregarding feedback and support.

For whatever reason, it's not the right fit, you're not the right leader (or person) for him, he doesn't want to play, or the whole thing is just complete.

Cut it loose—in whatever way is appropriate for you and your circumstances. This may mean terminating a relationship, getting him a new leader, exiting him from your company, or simply disengaging from the cycle of drama. (As always when exiting someone from your team or company, check with your organization's guidelines and rules for compliance and legalities.)

Relationships have arcs. People come in and out of our lives for all kinds of reasons.

Honor George, find gratitude for the experience, send him love and light, and gear up to move forward.

If you work with George and are related to him or her, this may all be easier said than done. In that case, move to the next step.

Name, Release, Shift, and Protect

Here's some potential language for when you've truly done all you can, you know you are clean, and it's at the point of no return. As always, use your own language. Here are some talking points:

191

George, I care about you and care very much that we have a good relationship [or create great results together, or you do well, or whatever]. And I can't care about it more than you do. And I'm noticing that I feel like we're rolling uphill. My experience of you and this situation is that we've tried several different ways of moving through this, and it's not working. I'm not sure how else to shift it on my end, or how else to be more useful, and I know that I've done all I can to this point until you want to lean in with me differently. If and when you'd like that to change, please come to me with a proposal for how. In the meantime, I am going to extract myself from the situation or exit you from the team [or whatever]. I wish you all the best and am grateful for your contributions to the team, my life, and the learning.

Breathe and release.

Sometimes, this naming will shift the energy enough to create a new level of authenticity in the relationship. And sometimes not. Either way, name what's true for you. Be clean about it, and let it go.

That's one option.

The other, especially in the case where it's toxic or dangerous to your spirit or well-being, or George is simply not in for a collaborative experience, is to take care of yourself first, cut yourself free, find the gifts and the learning, and move forward.

But What if George Is My Mother?!

If for some reason you still have to work with George, live with George, or be related to George, then you'll want to bubble up and work around it, act "as if" it is how you want it to be (and just show up that way—you'd be shocked how many times this can change a dynamic), and/or name the dilemma and codesign with George how you'll be in relationship together most effectively given the circumstances.

It's Not Always Pretty: Casey and Georgette

Casey had a Georgette on her team. In meetings Georgette cut her off, took credit for results, passed blame, and invalidated Casey's ideas in front of the room. Outside meetings, Georgette talked smack about Casey, withheld information that could help her, baited other team members to collude with her (Georgette), and passive-aggressively diminished Casey's contributions while gathering evidence for any shortcomings she could find.

While Casey's peers stayed out of the drama for the most part, this dynamic created negative impact and tension on the team.

Casey knew enough to know that Georgette's behaviors and responses were not about her, but it still hurt, created an energy suck, was a waste of time, and distracted her (and others) from focusing on results.

After several rounds of assuming good, getting curious, naming what she noticed with Georgette (only to be told she didn't know what she was talking about), finding what she could appreciate about her, and acting "as if" all was good, Casey decided to simply bubble up, stay focused, and work around Georgette.

Having created more space for herself to decide how to interact with her leadership bully and stay high vibe, the dynamics get easier, in some cases. But Georgette, still committed, only gets more creative with her energetic whacks.

Casey is baffled, frustrated, hurt, confused, and concerned about the effect on the team and the ultimate impact on the work.

She approaches Georgette again with a request to explore the tension between them and redesign their working relationship. She asks a third party to help them navigate the conversation. Georgette wants no part, saying that her style works for her, that Casey is "just being dramatic," and that she prefers to move forward and focus on her job. Ouch!

Casey knows she's done her best and all she can. She decides to make peace with it, let it go, take care of herself, mind her own business, stay focused on the work, and create a positive impact with the team. She lets HR and Georgette know it doesn't feel good, it's affecting the work and the team, *and* that if anyone wants to fix it at any point, she'd like to. Otherwise she'll be a professional and work around it.

The organization values both players, decides to let it be, and with the situation and implications named and documented, agrees to support them in working around each other. Eight months later, Casey is promoted to a new position and also as team lead. Thirteen months later, Georgette is still in the same spot continuing to create similar dynamics with other members of the organization.

I purposely share this story because navigating George does not always have a great ending. In the best-case scenarios, not only does Casey succeed, but Georgette catches her vibe and becomes a better performer and contributor; they end up solid colleagues. In the worst case, Georgette won't budge, the organization won't do anything, and Casey leaves. After all, Casey is a rock star (especially if she was able to navigate this scene) and doesn't need the hassle, and if the organization is going to tolerate toxic employees, she's not playing.

More commonly the Casey/Georgette scenario nets out in one or a combination of these fives outcomes:

1. It eventually works itself out.
2. Georgette leaves on her own (or Casey does, often taking people with her).
3. The organization is forced into a decision to let Georgette go when it realizes it's losing trust, credibility, and top performers by keeping the negatively contagious toxic ones.
4. Some form of legal action is taken against the organization for tolerating a hostile work environment.
5. Casey will "match" Georgette, lower her vibe and performance, and they all stay unhappy.

Let me just say, when Casey catches Georgette's energetic stance, no one wins.

Number five is perhaps the most dangerous situation of them all. When Casey matches Georgette, compromising her own energy, attitude, and performance (because she's exhausted from trying her best and the organization has demonstrated that low-vibe behaviors and performance are tolerated), she is now a contagious Georgette, the rest of the team is at risk, and the organization has lost an A player. Again.

Hold your space, have grace, and do your work. Do all you can to help things go right. Stay connected to your purpose. Keep your intentions clear. Pay attention to what you (and your organization) tolerate. Be thoughtful about what you take on and the boundaries you hold. And lead.

In Chapter 11, we'll dig into other people's problems, projections, and expectations (OPPPE), which will further support you in this topic.

And first, fieldwork.

Fieldwork: Make It Real

This is a super-important chapter. All of us have Georges (are Georges), and we're also our best way forward in navigating or shifting the dynamic. So please make this chapter count, now. Consider the following. (Journal as you please.)

- What have you learned about George?
- How has your perspective of him/her shifted since Chapter 1?
- Who is your George/Georgette/G now? By chance, are you someone's George/Georgette/G? How so?
- Using the content in this chapter, what are your next steps?
- What's at least one acknowledgment you want to give you about what you've created for yourself with this book? (Even reading to this point and staying engaged is to be celebrated.)

CHAPTER 11

Other People's Problems, Projections, and Expectations. Rise Above Them.

*They may ask a lot of you; they may tell you
what to do . . . But why?*

Other people's problems, projections, and (contagious) expectations (OPPPE!) are things we deal with every day—on both the sending and receiving end. They are easy to get hooked into and one of the greatest causes of resentment, confusion, exhaustion, blame, judgment, and lost time and energy. We're often so close to them, we don't realize they're happening. Yet with awareness, we can start to discern what's ours, what's not, and what energy we choose to expend appropriately. Nourishing our IEP and using the tools offered in this book help us get better at navigating OPPPE. The frameworks and stories in this chapter will take you deeper into awareness of where and when OPPPE maybe at play that you may not even realize.

This chapter deepens superpowers #2 (choice point), #4 (stay in your lane), and #5 (intuition) from Chapter 7 and will support you in further noticing and managing energy killers and toxic contagions (in Chapters 8 and 10), so you don't take on the negative but rather hold your space and even shift the situation to the positive.

Human Elixir

First, can we agree that, generally, we're doing the very best we can? Me, you, George, Georgette, Mary, Marvin, Max, Clyde, Doris? All of us humans—even when it doesn't look like it or feel like it?

This belief can be magic elixir in leadership especially when we're feeling contracted or self-righteous about something or someone and ready to jump into hard-core judgment, blame, and fury. It can provide space and grace to look at situations from different perspectives so we can find a more productive way forward.

Can we raise the bar, get over ourselves, and show up a bit better (or even a lot better) on those really bad days especially when we *know* we're not doing our best and are showing up badly but can't seem to help ourselves? Sure. And generally speaking, even then, are we doing the best we can? Probably.

People don't show up badly, disappoint, or fail each other because they're trying to. People just are. And sometimes we just don't know how.

Yesterday when I was edgy with the parents of one of my kids' friends, it wasn't because I wanted to be a jerk or am a jerk. I was scared, feeling protective, and doing my best.

When your friend gets upset at you for declining a request to connect or because you've been too "busy" or "richly scheduled," it's not because that person is bad or selfish. Your friend may just miss you, be afraid of losing you, or be struggling with his or her own busyness.

When your colleagues get frustrated with you for not showing up how *they* want you to, it's not because they're terrible people. They may be disappointed, feeling tremendous pressure, or even working through their own stuff.

When your kid or partner blames you for a bad day at school or work, it's not because you did anything wrong or aren't doing enough as a parent or partner. You are safe space to lose it and let it all hang out.

When George gives you a hard time, projects all his stuff on you, or blames you for being a bad or flaky coworker or leader, it's not because George sucks. George is managing his own challenges, pain, and discomfort (and may not even know it).

We're all doing the best we can.

And yet at times it may not feel like enough for ourselves and others in our lives.

When expectations and projections collide—whether on the receiving or sending end—the path can be tricky to navigate. Throw in tender agendas as well as doing our best and still not feeling like it's enough for other people's (or our own) problems and expectations, and it can be a catastrophe. So we need awareness and presence to figure out what's what, who's who, and what the heck we even stand for.

Of course we don't know what a George, Georgette, Mary, or Marvin is going through or what's behind the emotions or actions projected toward us. Still, we can assume good, meet things with grace, and take care of ourselves with intention and boundaries so as to not clobber or get clobbered by OPPPE.

Other People's Problems

You're heading out the door (or off to a meeting, to the gym, or even to the sofa with a good book for some much needed me time), and your phone rings. You see the Caller ID and your heart drops . . . it's *that person* again. You know if you answer, you're likely in for a long conversation about problems, drama, or that thing she's (or he's) been complaining about for months (and not fixing). You decide not to answer the phone and instead stay focused, honor your space, and keep your energy clean for whatever you were about to do. You'll call her (or him) later. (Ah, that feels good.)

But that person calls again, or maybe texts, and despite your best knowing, you pick up.

As you sensed, it's go time. And now his or her problem is your problem. You're sucked in. Thirty minutes later, you're exhausted. Your energy is lower, and you're not your best self for your next commitment (or you've missed it all together). You also know you weren't your best for him or her. Why? Because your own energy was off. You knew not to have that conversation. You overrode your intuition and your agreement with yourself to be more intentional about these kinds of pickups.

Now nobody has won. You're depleted. The person feels let down. The whole thing is a bummer.

And now *you're* mad.

But are you mad at the person? No. Look closer . . . you knew what to expect. You picked up. And you got sucked in to the first "P" of OPPPE: someone else's problems.

Here's the thing. The person had you at "hello." Before you even said a word, your energetic state was compromised. Why? Because you broke your agreement with yourself to hold your space and not get hooked. And this made you more susceptible to any negative contagions you'd meet on the other side of that conversation.

This could have happened on the phone, in person, at the office, at the grocery store—anywhere. It could be personal, business, family—anything. The scenario is the same: someone has a problem and wants you to commiserate in the problem (and *maybe* fix it), and the time or topic is not right for you to serve or have the conversation. But you override this knowing, relinquish your space, and bam . . . you're into OPPPE!

You might be irritated with him or her, but really if you look deeper, you're likely frustrated with yourself.

Great news! You have the power to shift this dynamic.

First, breathe. Notice where you got hooked. Envision how you would do this differently next time (pause time, response, and any boundaries or agreements that would support this situation in the future), let that land and rewire your future process, and let it go.

HELP: A Formula for Navigating the "Problem P" of OPPPE

Most of us have had some version of this experience: the guy who wants you to stop everything to brainstorm or fix his problems, your neighbor who stops you at the corner to complain, your kid's friend's parent who grabs you in the grocery store to gab about her issues, your colleague who keeps dropping the ball or repeating the same problem over and over again.

I'm not saying don't help. I'm saying don't take on the person's problem, and make sure you're in the right space to support as you are best able so as not to compromise your own well-being. (Oxygen masks, remember?)

Being helpful and contributing are human needs; we want to show up for each other, and we can do so in a way that sets us up for success. We can value being a good friend and being available, while at the same time holding boundaries for protecting our time and mental and emotional energy in order to be the best and most present coworker or friend possible.

In order to do this, you can pause, be conscious of your triggers, and design boundaries to support how you show up.

The next time someone comes at you with the first P in OPPPE, asks you for support or to "have a chat," or anything in this domain that feels "off" or heavy, HELP.

HELP

The following is a formula I've created to help me create intentional space for myself in order to be as helpful and supportive to others in the best ways possible. I've personally found this to be wildly useful (as have those I've shared it with). Modify this to make it congruent for you.

1. **Hold/Honor.** Don't respond instantly to everything. Take a pause. Ask yourself, "Can I serve best in this moment? Am I in the right space to contribute?" Hold the energetic state and boundary of service and intention. Be willing to decline calls, requests, and conversations that don't allow you to be fully present or bubbled up so you can serve well.

2. **Engage/Enroll.** When you do respond, ask the other person to be specific. What's the topic? How much time would he or she like? How can you be most helpful? And what are some potential times to talk so you can both be present? Asking what is wanted or needed from you (to just listen and be

present, give advice, solve the problem, etc.) reduces ambiguity, saves mental energy, and is crucial for how you'll show up for that conversation. Getting clear here allows you (and the person) to plan and to be more fully present and in the right headspace to contribute.

3. **Love/Lean in.** When you do talk, give the person 100 percent of your presence and care—100 percent. Contribute as best you can. Love the heck out of the person. Be generous. Be there.

4. **Plan/Parameters.** Be clean about the conversation and your role. Is it something you are qualified for and the best person to support him or her in? If yes, great. If not (because it needs specific expertise from another team member, professional, or even a therapist), communicate that. And . . . if the person wants to just chronically complain and not resolve anything, acknowledge that reality too. The superpowers of curiosity, contribution, and naming it are helpful here. If you know you are incapable of hosting a long "complaint session," then name it and perhaps offer to be the person's Responsible Venting Partner, or RVP. (See "When They Really Just Want to Complain and Be Heard.") But be clean about what you will and won't hold for the person.

Just as we teach people how to treat us, we train them how to come to us with problems. If you don't hold boundaries and stay honest and clean, but instead get hooked by OPPPE when it doesn't feel good, you can't HELP. And if this is a recurring event that frustrates you, it's not their fault; it's on you. You've trained that.

Train differently.

When They Really Just Want to Complain and Be Heard

This happens. Sometimes we just need to let out feelings that are bottled up inside. This is where Responsible Venting Partners (RVPs) come in handy. The job of an RVP is to witness, hold space, and also hold the other person accountable to do something about his or her frustrations. The job of the RVP is not to complain with the person, make it worse, collude, rescue, or foster a chronic complaining relationship.

Here's how it works: with agreements for "safety, confidentiality, and no judgment" in place, give the person a three- to five-minute "whining window" or "clearing container." The person has full permission to go at it and "clear his or her space." (You simply hold sacred space in silence.) At minute three or five, stop the person and ask, "OK, now what would you like to do about it? How can I help?"

What if the person is more committed to the continual complaining than to creating a solution? Then name it (with care), and let the person know when he or she is ready to do something about it, you're happy to support. In the meantime, a few more conscious and intentionally contained RVP sessions may be needed. (I find that once I've given people *full permission* and space for this, they often don't need it anymore and instead get into productive action to shift or are clearer on the kind of support they do need.)

Other People's Projections

Projection is a tricky beast.

We project our experiences, feelings, thoughts, and judgments—good and bad—on each other all the time consciously and more often unconsciously.

Projection is energy and a form of communication through presence and a way of being that is usually communicated nonverbally.

Projection is the mechanism of a contagion, either positive or negative. To project is human, to be aware of it and in command of it, divine. The leadership practice is in being aware of our state, being responsible for our experience, and exercising our "choice points" (as discussed in Chapters 7 and 8). This enables us to choose what energy we will project, what we will say, and what we will take on. You can only do this if you're aware and conscious of what's happening. (Hence the point of this book.)

And it's contagious. The more I project on you, and you take it, the more you project on me with your own triggers, and I take it. Before you know it, we're infecting anyone around us who's open to a little projection.

Have you ever been in a meeting where it's going beautifully and then someone comes in who has just come from a stressful meeting (or conversation) that he or she is irritated about, and then that person leads the room through that energy? Before you know it, the rest of the people in the room start to "catch it" and now they're tense as well. When people leave that meeting (now infected), they head to another meeting, bringing that energy with them, only to infect the next people they come in contact with. (This can happen in a one-on-one conversation or with a big group.) If you've experienced this, you've experienced contagious projection.

Have you ever had someone hurt you and then you took it out on someone else? Have you ever had a bad day and then gone and spewed toxins on social media? Have you ever been ticked off about something, perhaps feeling unheard, unseen, or unvalued, and then jumped in your car only to rage at the traffic or other drivers? (They did nothing; you're just projecting your frustration at them.) Or perhaps you went home to see your darling family and lost your temper because someone forgot to do something as promised? (It was small, not a big deal, but your projection of what just happened earlier makes it a big deal.) Yes? You've experience contagious projection.

If you've ever had someone tell you how you *should feel*, and *then* you started to feel that way—congrats, you've been projected upon, you caught the vibe, and you became it.

Of course, it works *both ways*: we are projected upon, and we project upon each other—and we do this in negative ways and also positive ways.

The trick is not to never do it, but rather to be conscious of it, to catch it, to breathe, to be responsible for it, to get curious, and to get into right relationship with ourselves and others as quickly and consciously as possible. This is a practice—it is a leadership muscle.

204

Max and OPPPE

So what does projection look like?

We started this book with Max in Chapter 1. Let's break down what happened, with the idea of projection in mind.

As you'll recall, Max was having a day. He came at me (and the woman talking with me at the time) with his "stuff." I felt his negative energy, and because I was present and clear, I recognized it quickly as a projection. At that moment, I had a choice point: (1) get sucked in, match him, catch his negatively contagious energy, feel bad, doubt myself, and lose my space; or (2) take a breath, stay present, recognize the negative contagion bait, hold my space, know this was not mine, get curious, and engage with grace.

Ultimately, I chose option two. I didn't match his energy. Doing so would have meant letting his energy enter me and then me reacting back at him. This would have created a negative contagion feedback loop that I would now have been a part of. This loop would have fed the fire, created more resistance, and ultimately had us spiraling together. We'd have ended up going back and forth, building up our negative contagions (like an out-of-control snowball), and dropping the energy even more, until it became a full-blown argument, one of us walked away, or ultimately we just both felt revved up and crappy. No matter which way, had I chosen option one and gotten hooked into OPPPE, the negative energy would now be in me and then I'd likely go out and project it onto others. (Unless, I was aware of this and able to reboot back into clean and clear presence using my IEP!)

Reception and Projection

Does the scenario in the last section sound familiar? You may have been so close to it, you couldn't see it (until later).

Here are more real-life examples, on both sides (being projected upon and projecting out). Because we're all in this together, and these are common, I'm using the collective *you*.

Perhaps you have made business decisions based on projections from others' advice. Only to find later, when you got quiet and looked inside yourself, that you'd just taken a left turn (taking your team with you) that was not yours, but rather guided by what someone else was struggling with.

And . . . you've likely given advice grounded in your own experience and unconscious projections.

You may have ended friendships that were laced with assumptions, projections, and soul-sucking expectations.

And . . . you may have had unreasonable expectations of people in your own life that were based on your own unconsciousness, pain, and challenges.

You may have second-guessed yourself on other people's projections, doubting your own feelings or desires.

And . . . you may have told others how they should feel based upon your interpretation of their situation.

You may have dumbed yourself down to match other people's problems, wanting to fit in and not seem too happy or great.

And . . . you may have judged people for being so happy and great and "rah-rah!" when you were struggling or not feeling like enough.

You may have made a decision about a client or colleague based upon someone else's filter and guidance, and later you found out your experience of that person was completely different.

And . . . you may have polluted someone else's experience with your own filter.

You may have shrunk your power to match a lower vibe because to break connection or leave someone behind would be too painful and you wanted to belong.

And . . . you may have hoped others would be small with you—or even said or did things to keep them small—when you were feeling small.

You know you are dealing with a projection from others when what they say is not at all what you are experiencing—it feels off.

For example, you get a divorce, get laid off, or have some big life event happen. Some will say "Omg, I'm sorry, how terrible, you must be wrecked," when in truth you're doing really well. Or some will treat it like no big thing, "a gift(!)," sing "everything happens for a reason," or growl "get over it already!" when actually you're not there at all and need extra tender loving care.

Sometimes our own assumptions about, and projections onto, others are really things going on with ourselves, for example:

- You think someone's mad at you or avoiding you, but really you're mad at or avoiding that person (or yourself).
- You don't trust anyone . . . because you're not trustable.
- You think everyone judges you . . . because you judge.
- You think everyone is lying . . . because you lie.
- You think people think you suck at your job . . . because you think you suck at it.
- You think your partner is cheating on you . . . because you have thoughts of cheating or you have a history of being cheated on, so you look for it (even unconsciously).
- You think your spouse has lost the magic for you . . . because in truth, you're a little bored yourself.
- You think someone is too busy and not showing up for you . . . because actually you're too busy and not showing up for you (or that person).
- You don't tell someone the truth . . . because you think he or she can't handle the truth (you'd be terrified to hear *that* truth!).
- You avoid giving direct feedback . . . because you're afraid to get it. (This is extra toxic if you then judge people harshly when they fail.)
- You give someone feedback or advice that is actually for you.

Projection is everywhere. It's created through past experiences, forecasted experiences, and our own internal landscaping, emotions, fears, desires, and judgments. We lovely human beings walk through our worlds working our stuff, with our own backgrounds, wounds, and tender agendas, filtering life through our lens, and reflecting and projecting it upon each other.

To project is human. To have awareness and to be responsible for what we put out there in service of other humans, is leadership.

Note: Heads up! Even in this book, as I share these ideas and stories, I have to be very careful not to project my own beliefs upon you. This is where we need caring feedback from others. For this book, in places where I wanted to "check myself" and be extra responsible for content, I've pulled in subject-matter experts. For this chapter in particular, I consulted with Dr. Victoria Stevens, a Clinical Psychologist and Psychoanalyst on the power and nuances of OPPPE.

Propelling Your Projection Prowess

Want to strengthen your projection awareness muscles?

Here are five steps:

1. **Be present.** You've got this one. That's what this book has taught you so far.
2. **Notice.** Notice what happens in your body when you are judging, giving someone advice, being self-righteous, attacking, or feeling attacked. Most often, when we're *projecting,* or experiencing *being projected upon,* there's a feeling in our body. This may show up as contraction or feeling dirty or crooked. The minute we have this sense, we're at choice to own it and proceed accordingly.
3. **Get curious.** The trick is not to make ourselves feel wrong for projecting or being projected upon. Instead, the mastery is in noticing it and getting curious about what's here? What's mine? What's theirs? Where might I need support because something tender is getting triggered? What's next?
4. **Receiving it? Course-correct.** If you are on the receiving end, take what resonates (or serves), find the gift (or the boundary), and move forward. Don't take someone else's stuff on as your own.
5. **Sending it? Course-correct.** If you're on the sending end—and you're aware of it—stop. Take back your projection before you act or say anything. If it's too late and you've already spoken or acted, you can clean it up. This is called a "repair." Acknowledge that you were making an assumption or that you had expectations that were not spoken or agreed to by the other person. Own it, apologize as you feel right, and

move forward clean. Naming it is being responsible for it. The repair heals, connects, builds trust and credibility, and is an act of leadership.

When we clarify projections, we can keep the container clean, stay in grace and appreciation, thank people for their input, take what serves and resonates, and move forward true to ourselves.

Other People's (Contagious) Expectations

Expectations of how people should show up for you, or how you think they should be, are the building blocks, rebar, and foundation for a big old "house of resentment."

Assumptions take us many places, most often wrong, leading to even more broken expectations.

We have expectations of how people should show up for us, how they should perform, what they should hold as important, and what they should do for us. We have assumptions about what people agree to, how they feel about us (or anything), how busy they are, what's going on in their lives, and why they did something.

Both expectations and assumptions are a form of projection. (Assumptions *inform* expectations, which *become* projections; the whole process is almost always done unconsciously.*)

Neither work out so great.

Trying to live up to someone else's expectations and assumptions (especially when they're from that person's own projections and are not in service of us—or vice versa) sets the tone for burnout, takes us out of presence, and diminishes trust and credibility on both sides. For example, your spouse, colleague, friend, or parent thinks you should show up a certain way, take on a particular profession, think like that person does about life, or share a core value (e.g., fitness)—and you don't. However, you keep trying to live up to it and

---

* I'm referring to projection in this chapter as "unconscious." While I understand that "unconscious," "subconscious," and "nonconscious" are often used interchangeably, for the sake of simplicity I am using "unconscious." I've found this terminology, along with the ideas offered in this chapter, useful for the purpose of navigating and optimizing our IEP. For more resources on the topic of projection, please see the *Contagious You Resource Toolkit* in Chapter 16.

make that person happy by trying to meet his or her expectations and assumptions. You'll likely get quite tired. Not only that, but your focus then becomes more on external validation and striving than on internal presence and congruency. This will have an impact on your energetic presence. People will sense something is off.

So how do we navigate expectations and assumptions (those of others and our own)? We stay present and clear. We stay tuned in. And we remember. We remember we all have unconscious expectations and assumptions; we all have our preferences for how things should look and be, and we all want what we want. So then we stay in our lane, show up in a way that is true for us, check ourselves, and name our expectations and assumptions as clearly, cleanly, and proactively as possible.

Our First Priority in OPPPE

When it comes to other people's problems, our first priority is to honor our own self-care and space, to hold appropriate boundaries, to ask for what we need to be most helpful, and then to support and serve as best we can in the cleanest manner possible. Does this mean we don't care or don't help when others have problems? No, not even a little. Actually, when done with intention and consciousness, it's the opposite. Staying conscious, holding boundaries, and honoring our space means we can help others more because we didn't get sucked into OPPPE where we are of no help to anyone.

This means we work our IEP. Big time.

Remember, 70 percent of this work is in the awareness; the other 30 percent is what you do with it. As you become more aware of OPPPE and your hooks, it may feel daunting at first, and hang with it. Before you know it, noticing and navigating it will become the new norm.

This is a lifelong practice. I still get sucked into people's stuff. I still get triggered. I still make stuff up. I project and get projected upon. I get hooked into OPPPE more often than I'd like, especially when I'm close to someone or care a lot. And I'm way faster at catching it, rebooting, and getting myself to a healthier space to decide next steps.

Remember, presence, not perfection.

Not Everyone Will Love Your OPPPE Management Style

When you start to get clear on how you want to navigate OPPPE, not everyone will like it. As your awareness, boundaries, leadership style, and way of relating get bolder and cleaner, you may find your relationships change. People push back. They may get angry. You may even lose friends. This may sound terrifying, and I agree, it doesn't always feel great. However, trust that being true to yourself and honoring your space makes you better for everyone. And trust that at the end of the day, you being clean, congruent, and in right relationship with yourself means more peace, authenticity, trust, and credibility with those you *are* in relationship with.

I think we all struggle with the notion of letting someone down, being kicked out of community, or losing someone because we don't show up the way the person wants us to. (By the way, these are all assumptions that include fears. When we're aware of these, it's a great time to move to curiosity and ask if our assumptions are really true.)

I've found that 97 percent of the time people are grateful for boundaries, clarity, and the understanding of what they can count on us for. And what we can be counted on for and what they want are not always a match—in which case this clarity becomes even more valuable. Clarity creates safety, clears assumptions and false expectations, and sets us up to be present with each other in an authentic way. Why would you want a relationship any different?

Your best friends, colleagues, family members, and the people you want to surround yourself with will be grateful for, inspired by, and supportive of your clarity and becoming. I've learned that this level of truth, clarity, and clean lines only leaves our truest relationships stronger, more intimate, and more powerful. And if truth and clean lines don't work, it's not always bad. You may just be dealing with a relationship whose arc is complete or that needs to be redefined. It's all good. Stay true, because being designed by each other's OPPPE does not serve any of us, our energy, or our leadership in the world.

Creating Boundaries That Serve

One of the most frequent questions I get in this work is "How do I create healthy boundaries? How do I say 'yes' to me without my 'no' totally letting someone down?"

I have two answers for this. The first is a three-step formula I'll share in a minute.

The second, is this . . . if you are present, holding your space, clear on what you stand for, taking care of yourself, and coming from love, and you have positive intentions, then boundaries become less daunting. I could even say boundaries become less necessary, because when we're clear, we naturally hold a clean container and energetically communicate what our boundaries are.

That being said, it's useful to get in the practice of identifying and naming them. Awareness, clarity, and action make this easier.

Step 1: Awareness

When you catch yourself feeling that "pull" or "hook" to get sucked into someone's stuff, take on his or her projections, or feel bad because you're not showing up how that person might want you to—*stop*. Notice and get present to what's happening in your body. What's the feeling that has you aware something's off? Where does it live in your body? The more you pay attention to this, the faster you'll catch when OPPPE is happening. Get present, breathe, bubble up, and . . . get clear.

Step 2: Clarity

Ask yourself these questions:

1. What is the current situation? (No drama, no making stuff up. Just the facts: What do I know and what do I not know?)
2. What about this situation *is* my business? (In other words, if I respond, if it works for me to talk, what requests I make so I can be available, and how I show up in that conversation.)
3. What about this situation is *not* my business? (In other words, how the person responds, what the person thinks of me, and why he or she keeps creating this situation over and over again.)

212

4. What are my criteria for "yes," "no," and "not now, later"? (This relates to your priorities on time, energy, your team's needs, your well-being, and other obligations. It also relates to "Am I the best person to help? Can I? And do I *want* to?")
5. What will work for me now so I can show up clean and in service? (What requests do I have? What communication or information is needed?)

Step 3: Action

Now you have better awareness and information to respond with so you can show up well, support whatever is happening in the most helpful way possible, and also honor your own well-being and space.

Note: If this is hard, or it is a chronic issue, or you notice you feel fuzzy or have a hard time creating or holding a boundary with a particular person (or area), get support. Ask a friend, coach, advisor, or therapist to work through it with you.

Fieldwork: Make It Real

Let's make this content even more conscious in your life. An invitation for you to apply what you've learned in this chapter as it resonates most and to play with the additional following 20 ways to work with OPPPE as they serve you best.

20 (More) Ways to Work with OPPPE

Use these together, pick one (or more), lean in for what you need most right now, and change your game:

1. **Be aware.** Just know it exists. No need to blame, feel victim to it, or run for cover—it just is. You know you best; stand in for you.
2. **Stay in the right business.** Your business is your business. Nobody else's business is your business. Stay awake to what your business is and is not.

3. **Honor the right monkeys.** "Not my circus, not my monkeys"—in other words, stay in your space. Now if their monkeys mess with your monkeys, you may want to do something about their circus. But other than that, let's all honor our own monkeys.

4. **Beware of your physical cues and language.** Contraction, feeling like you're not clean about something, extra-strong emotion, self-righteousness, judgment, and blame are all signs of projection and unreasonable expectations.

5. **Get clear on your own Essential You.** Your values, purpose, vision, and authenticity create solid ground to stand on.

6. **Take really good care of yourself; nourish your resource state**. Stay connected to intuition, catch when things are off and correct as needed, get sleep, eat well, move your body, meditate, create space (turn off your phone, social media, and TV as needed), and do whatever you need to do to be the best, clearest instrument of change.

7. **Intend.** Remember that the strongest intention wins. If you have no intention, the default (or other people's agendas for you) will win. So again, tap into your IEP. Level-up!

8. **Keep your priorities straight.** Be so clear about what's most important that you are unwilling to compromise your energy and bandwidth. Are you up for drama if it sucks the life out of you? Where do you prioritize self-care, other people's expectations, and showing up for you and showing up for them, and what is it all in service of? Step back. Make your priorities clear (for you first), and then design criteria and boundaries to support those priorities.

9. **Be clear about your boundaries.** The clearer we are about who we are and what our boundaries are, and the more we can trust ourselves to honor both, the less

we need to worry about losing our space, being judgmental, or getting hooked into another's drama.

10. **Have clear criteria** for what you say "yes," "no," and "not now, later" to; those you share tender information with; and what kinds of things you can be most helpful in with your expertise and bandwidth.

11. **"No" is a complete sentence.** If something doesn't feel right, a full clean "no" is way better than an incongruent "yes." Just say "no." You do not have to justify it . Your gut is fine.

12. **Have clear expectations about what you expect and what you can be counted on for.** Speak to it with friends and colleagues, have an active dialogue, and don't leave that conversation without agreement of not only what this looks like, but how you want to navigate it when it falls apart.

13. **Know that your definition of how you want others to show up and their definition of how they want to show up may be very different.** Be aware of this. Look for where you're imposing your "stuff" on them. And find the gifts. Where something is really important, make requests and also work with them in the codesign of what success might look like for each of you.

14. **Be clear on what you want, ask for what you want, be prepared to negotiate the difference, and be ready even to be told "no." Let it be OK.** This goes for anything, but especially in managing expectations.

15. **Own your projection.** If you know you are, or even sense it, name it. Naming it cleans it up, clears the energetic field, and enables the person to receive your contribution (or reaction) in a way that he or she has all the information. The person can decide accordingly what to do with it.

16. **Don't rescue! Don't rob!** When we bail others out, fix them, take their issues on as our own, or come to the

rescue so they don't have to deal with their own lack of planning, thinking, accountability, action, and so on, we rob them of the experience of learning how to navigate their own challenges. Serve and support—help even—but don't rescue. Let them do their work.

17. **Opt out of the relational Drama Triangle**. Watch yourself falling into *victim* (I'm helpless! Nothing is my fault!), *hero* (I'll save you; you can't do it!), or *perpetrator* (I'll blame you, punish you, and take your opportunities away!) roles. None work. Instead, be accountable. With accountability, the *victim* becomes author and creator, the *hero* becomes coach and champion, and the *perpetrator* becomes provocateur and advocate.

18. **Make sure it's yours.** If you're feeling pressured about something and it feels off, check in. Is it *your* dream, *your* value system being honored, *your* desire? Or is it someone else's being projected upon you? Don't make the person wrong; he or she likely means no harm. Just be aware and do what makes sense for you.

19. **Love them big *and* hold your space.** Holding your space *is* love.

20. **Don't *worry* about any of this.** Just live. Enjoy. Serve. Show up. Work your IEP. It will all work itself out.

System Wellness: Navigate Conflict and Design Life-Giving Relationships. Create Them.

Conflict is inevitable; suffering is optional.

Design your systems to support you.

Let's talk system wellness.

A "system" is any container that holds a relationship. Family, organizational and cultural, personal and professional, and team systems are at play every day and can make or break authentic connection, peace, and results. Systems are also contagious. In this chapter we'll dive into ideas, tools, frameworks, and practices designed to support you in creating the healthiest systems possible, maintaining them once they're created, and healing them when they break.

Of course, before you step into any of the tools offered in this chapter, you'll want to work your own IEP and come into the system clear. The stronger and cleaner your IEP, the easier the system work becomes.

Components of System Wellness

There are seven components I've found helpful in creating system health. They all work together:

1. A name and definition for the system
2. A desire and decision to have a healthy system
3. Commitment for all parties to show up and do the work
4. Proactive design and agreements to support the relationship system
5. Clear roles and accountabilities
6. Safety for maintaining, expanding, and challenging the system as needed
7. Willingness and frameworks to fix the system when it breaks

#1. A Name and Definition for the System

As obvious as this may seem, it's worth taking a moment to get clear about what the actual system is, the purpose of it, who's part of it, and whom it impacts.

For example, your organizational team is a system. The purpose of that system is to create a container to do your best work together; to create meaning, safety, and connection; and to fulfill your collective purpose. Your system consists of the people on the immediate team. It also affects people beyond the immediate team, including your team members' direct reports, their clients, their leadership, other departments in the organization, and possibly outside vendors or partners. We can go even further and see that your immediate team's system also impacts the team members' families and personal relationship systems, as they'll bring the energy of stress or joy from this original system home with them. We could play this all the way out to see the ripple effects of the system and its contagiousness on even more people (e.g., the people your company's products or services impact).

Once we're clear on who's in the system, and we all know we're in it together, we can move to the next step.

#2 and #3. Desire and Decide. Commit, Show Up, and Do the Work.

I put #2 (a desire and decision to have a healthy system) and #3 (commitment for all parties to show up and do the work) together here because they need each other. A decision is a commitment; a commitment is a decision. Both need desire. So we'll address them together.

What's the quality of the system you desire? What's important about that to you? Are you willing to do the work to have it?

To establish a durable system (and to get in front of conflict and mess later), there must be an expressed desire for a healthy system, clarity of why it's important, and a decision to do the work, both as individuals and as a collective team. This can be as simple as naming the issue/opportunity with your team, partner, or whoever is in the system with you; declaring your desire for a healthy system; sharing your why; and committing to being fully committed to make it happen.

What does being committed look like? Ideally, this is codesigned between you and the others in the system. This conversation can be rich in itself, building trust, awareness, and authentic connection. What you're looking for at the end of this conversation is a shared desire and commitment, clarity of what success looks like if you're all doing (and being) it well, and agreements to support you in doing so.

What Agreements May Look Like

We commit to:

- Doing our work (managing ourselves and our IEP)
- Being responsible for the projections, impact, and energy we bring to each other
- Staying at the table when uncomfortable (and coming back if we need a minute)
- Naming discomfort and speaking up—even when we're scared
- Asking for what we want and need
- Assuming good (and gathering positive evidence)
- Making it easy to be in relationship with

- Giving each other honest feedback in service of growth and connection
- Taking ownership and cleaning up our messes (and giving each other grace to do so as well)
- Doing all we can to help things go better
- Staying curious and finding the gifts
- Cocreating and honoring agreements to support us
- Staying awake to the needs of the system, the individuals in it, and the purpose of it
- Being willing to revisit and re-create agreements as we grow
- Being willing to intentionally complete when the system needs to change or an arc of relationship has come to a close

These are all forms of agreements we can make to support ourselves in showing up well together and getting our needs met. In *Contagious Culture,* I wrote an entire chapter on creating life-giving agreements and engagements. People have been shocked at how powerful (and easy) getting in front of their systems' health with agreements and clear intentions has been for them. They've reported significant reductions in lost time, lost energy, ambiguity and confusion, pain, and chaos by integrating this conversation into their life. What I've become more deeply aware of since that book is the power of *explicitly* naming the desire to be a part of the system and the *decision* required on each person's part to *live* the agreements.

The leadership skill and superpower of "decide" holds here as well: until you truly decide to be in a healthy system and do the work required, the energy and intention of making great progress will not be in full force. It doesn't matter if we're talking team, partnership, friendship, marriage, or devotion in a project. When someone is not fully in, it is felt by the other(s) in the system. This is contagious, exhausts individual and team resources, and hinders the energy and progress of the collective system. Most of us have experienced this, on either the giving or receiving end. Just think of a relationship where you cannot fully feel the presence, devotion, and decision of "in," of the person in it with you. Or where *you* are not entirely in. Awareness is power here. This scenario is an opportunity to get clean; get curious; and name, honor, and decide what decision can be made next.

Everything is an opportunity for the next level of conversation and the next version of a clean system. Don't avoid; head right in.

When the Decision Is a No or Not Clear

The strength of the system depends upon the congruency and purpose of the people in it. If it's not the right system for you, it's of service to name that, be clean about it, and codesign next steps for moving forward. It serves no one to have you in a system you don't want to be a part of or can't fully stand behind.

That said, in some cases it may be important that you're a part of the system, either for professional reasons (they need you on the team for another three months) or for personal reasons (it's family), or it's something you don't want to do anymore (and you want to finish that last 7 percent so it's set up well). Here are some places to look to support you in being able to decide to stay a part of the system congruently until it is complete:

- What *is* important about this to me?
- What's to gain by making this work? What's to lose if I don't?
- What are my alternatives?
- What opportunity am I missing with the way I'm thinking of this? How can we all win?
- What if I do decide no? What if I dismount and get out; Then what?
- Where might I want to get out of this because I'm uncomfortable?
- Where might I want to get out of this because I have conflict or am not naming a truth with someone in the system?
- Where am I just exhausted and need a "minute" or a day off?
- What's the littlest thing I can decide upon that feels good to me?
- What core value would I honor by staying with this for now?
- What if I decide to decide *not* to decide right now and simply pause?

You don't have to force a decision. Sometimes part of creating a healthy relationship system requires you to ask new questions, decide on a time-out, break the relationship, or do nothing (but do nothing *consciously*). These decisions all shift energy, giving us a new reality, new choices, and new places to step into with further information. Sometimes our most challenging relationships and situations, which we may work on for years and years—contorting, pushing, and grappling—only get healthy when we decide to tell the hard truth, walk away for a bit, or let them go altogether.

#4. Proactive Design and Agreements to Support the Relationship System

You've named the system and decided to be in it; you're here. Let's proactively design it. I have a tool for codesigning agreements and partnerships. The intention of this tool is to get in front of your relationships with clear questions and honest dialogue to support you both. I use these questions and structures with new team members, with vendors, and even in my personal relationships. Here are some core talking points and questions you can ask each other either one-to-one or with your whole team. Choose one or all as they serve.

IEP Relationship Design Model Questions

Here are 10 conversation starters, talking points, and questions to help you design your relationships proactively. (**Note:** It's never too early or late to do this exercise.)

- What I appreciate and admire about you is _____. What I'm most excited about in working with you is _____.
- My ultimate dream for this relationship/partnership is _____. What's yours?
- My concerns (or what I see might get in the way, if applicable) are _____. What are yours?
- I'm wonderful to work with in this way: _____. I'm difficult in this way: _____. (Be honest!)
- My intentions for this relationship are _____.
- I need _____ to be most successful in this collaboration. Here are some specific requests. (Great place to share pet peeves and quirks too!)

- What do you need from me? (Requests? Peeves? Quirks?)
- What agreements do we want in place to have a healthy relationship?
- How will we handle conflict or misunderstandings?
- How will we give each other feedback?

Designing for Messy

It's going to get messy. Any good relationship system will. The mess is where you create intimacy and realness. So be ready for the mess, celebrate it, and have a plan so that when you're in the mess, you have a rope.

This can be handled in the codesign of your relationship from the start in the previous section. Anytime in a relationship is a fine time for a new design—whether you've been married 20 years, worked with your business partner for 8, or had your friendship for 2.

It might look like this:

Hey, our relationship means a lot to me. I want us to be able to be honest and real and amazing together. To do this, it may get messy. We may disagree, we may fight . . . and I want that to be OK. Before we get to that point, can we design for messy? Can we put agreements in place to support us both in showing up honestly, coming back to the table, and feeling safe when we hit the ick?

No one is going to say "no" to that (if the person does, he or she may not be your person).

And then you design.

Here's what I'd put in that design:

- How do we want to handle conflict? (Name the tension; get curious about it; check ourselves before we wreck ourselves.)
- Do we want to have a code word for when we're upset or something feels off? ("Marshmallow!")
- Can we have an agreement that we can "name it" without getting it right or judging it? (Yes, please. If we do our IEP work and stay in our space, this will be easier.)

- Do we both agree to come back to, and stay at, the table until we resolve it? (Knowing that taking a "time-out" is OK—we just need to let the other know we're taking it.)
- What is the thing that is bigger than we are that we will always be in service of no matter what? (This is an anchor and could be "in service of our kids," "in service of the health of the team/company," "in service of our lasting partnership," "in service of our shared vision," etc.)

#5. Clear Roles and Accountabilities

Setting up clear roles and accountabilities is magic sauce for system health. This is beautifully done proactively, and sometimes you don't know until you know—so anytime is a good time to engage this component.

Yours, Mine, Ours

In creating a system, maintaining it, or even fixing it, there are conversations and explorations that will support enhanced perspectives, points of view, and reframes; clarify feelings; and create shared accountability—all at the same time.

The Yours, Mine, Ours Framework provides a structure for having honest conversations to clarify roles and accountability in creating the healthiest system possible.

Determining Accountability and Clarifying Roles Up Front

Yours: What are you responsible for?

Mine: What am I responsible for?

Ours: What are we both responsible for (and who owns what in that)?

Exploring Individual and Shared Dreams and Tender Agendas

Yours: What is your dream for this? Your greatest fear?

Mine: What is my dream for this? My greatest fear?

Ours: When we're looking at our ultimate impact, what's our dream together? Our greatest fear?

Clarifying Emotions and Deepening Understanding and Empathy

Yours: What are your feelings about this?

Mine: What are my feelings about this?

Ours: When we're in service of the ultimate outcome we want to create and whom we're serving, what are our feelings about this?

Owning Accountability and Finding a Way Forward

Yours: What issue have you created here?

Mine: What issue have I created here?

Ours: What issue have we created together? What are our next steps to making it right?

Proactively Nourishing and Serving the Relationship

Yours: What will you do to make sure the relationship works?

Mine: What will I do to make sure the relationship works?

Ours: What will we do together to make sure the relationship is nourished and works?

All of these questions and frameworks are valuable launch points for these conversations. Used as they authentically resonate, any of these questions can clear relational clutter, clean up energetic hygiene, and create a higher-quality container for your system to thrive.

Note: More on role accountability, three types of reciprocity, and the Super 7 of Cultural Health in *Contagious Culture.*

#6. Safety for Maintaining, Expanding, and Challenging the System as Needed

One of the most significant agreements you can create in a system is making it safe to relate to each other and speak honestly.

Do you make it safe? How? Everything I've shared in this book has been in some way related to making it safe to show up, to being positively contagious, and to bringing our best independently and collectively. Besides having positive intent and solid IEP, there are seven areas I see as both some of the greatest sticking points and also some of the greatest places of opportunity we can home in on to create safety in systems (or not):

- Receiving feedback
- Giving feedback
- Taking and supporting risks
- Being clear on expectations
- Being trustworthy
- Trusting
- Asking for help

To support you in exploring this, I've created a table of some of the most common wins and fails in each of these areas. If you adopt any on the left side of the table, you'll find that the others are affected as well.

RELATIONAL SYSTEM SAFETY

Area of Energized Collaboration and System Growth	Creates Safety	Creates Fear
Be an invitation for *receiving* feedback. *Feedback is a gift; do not get in the way of your own growth by making the giver wrong.*	You ask for feedback, recognize it as a gift, listen, receive, say "thank you"—acknowledging the giver for his or her care, courage, and time in crafting productive feedback. You ask for clarity if you need more understanding (from an intentional energetic state of curiosity and desire to learn), and you do everything you can to help the giver be successful in giving you the feedback. You follow up with how you're integrating, ask for support as needed, and again say thank you. You receive feedback with love and gratitude.	You avoid feedback, punish the giver by making the person wrong, giving the person the silent treatment, or disparaging the person with others. You scowl through the whole conversation, demand an explanation, get defensive, make excuses, and tell the giver he or she is wrong. If the feedback is not clear, you don't help the giver be successful in clarifying it—instead you have their lack of feedback mastery justify how wrong he or she is.

Area of Energized Collaboration and System Growth	Creates Safety	Creates Fear
Be an invitation for *giving* feedback. *Giving clean, productive feedback is an act of kindness. To not give honest feedback is cruel.*	You ask for permission to give someone feedback. You give it to the person directly (as opposed to telling everyone else instead). You provide feedback in service of the human you're giving it to. You consider what his or her experience of the situation and feedback is. You do your energetic hygiene work first so your intentions are clear, your energy is clean, and you are fully present. You give the hard feedback because you know it will serve the person most even though it may be challenging to say. You give feedback that is productive and actionable—not personal and vague. If you don't know the exact feedback or "how/next step," you offer to work through it with the person. You stay and be responsible for your impact, making sure that it landed and that it feels clean and useful. You give feedback with love and care. You give positive feedback too, frequently and authentically, acknowledging awesomeness.	You don't ask—you tell. You sock it to them. You don't do your energetic prep but rather go in fast with no clear intention, scrambled energy, "busy," and "let's just get this thing done." (You may even be annoyed.) You don't work through the feedback so it's clean and in service of; rather it ends up being personal, projections on your part, unproductive, and even mean. You don't pay attention to your IEP or how the other is receiving you. And you leave the person in the fetal position not knowing what to do with it. Even better, you tell everyone, except that person, what you "really think." You don't give the real feedback that would actually serve that person most because either you haven't thought it through, it's not worth the trouble, it will require a hard conversation, or it's just easier to see if he or she will figure it out. Finally, you give zero positive feedback or acknowledgments for what the person does well.

Area of Energized Collaboration and System Growth	Creates Safety	Creates Fear
Be an invitation for risk taking. *Our success as a leader is dependent on whom the people around us can become. Making mistakes and learning are part of this.*	You invite risks (and take them). You encourage growth and learning with each risk. You model healthy "failure." You invite the conversation of risk and explore how you can support the person in being successful. When their effort succeeds, you celebrate, honor the courage, capture the learning, give the person big credit, and plan the next. When it fails, you celebrate, honor the courage, capture the learning, share in the aftermath, and plan the next. You model the same in your own risks. Succeed? You share the win. Fail? You own the loss, thank people for their support, and rock the learning. You build trust in spades. "Win" or "fail"—it's movement, courage, and growth. The system is stronger, more creative, more connected, and set up for success.	You *say* that risk taking is great and that you support it—but only when it works well. You play it safe yourself because you don't want to be judged by others the same way you judge them. You talk a lot, but it's talk. When someone goes out on a limb, you don't support that person to make it work and have his or her back; rather you see if the person can swim, and then watch from the side. If the person succeeds, you join in the glory—he or she is "the best!" When the person fails, you stay on the sidelines, keep your distance, and may even pretend not to know the person. You don't back the person up, you collude with others in discussions behind his or her back, and you ultimately wait for more failures. You create a system of fear, judgment, stagnation, and playing it safe.

Area of Energized Collaboration and System Growth	Creates Safety	Creates Fear
Be an invitation for clear expectations. *Unconscious, unclear, or uncommunicated expectations are future resentments.*	You let people know what you want and expect. You're clear about what you can and cannot be counted on for. You clarify and honor agreements. You confirm that all parties are on the same page with expectations. You're explicit about timelines, what "good" looks like, and what the ambiguous stuff is and where it's OK to let it unfold. You name where expectations aren't clear. When you have an unmet expectation, you get curious about where you didn't communicate it clearly, and if you did, where it fell off. You hold people accountable for doing what they say they'll do. (And you hold yourself accountable as well.)	You assume people can read your mind, you avoid the expectation conversation altogether because it's uncomfortable (or you're not clear yourself), and you hold expectations for people that they're not aware of—or sometimes even capable of. When they don't meet your expectations, you judge and resent them. You're hazy on what you want to be counted on for and soft on creating, clarifying, and honoring agreements (if you have them at all). You're not clear on timelines or directions, and you don't hold people accountable. You hope the whole thing will just work itself out, and when it doesn't, you're disappointed and angry, and you blame everyone but yourself.

229

Area of Energized Collaboration and System Growth	Creates Safety	Creates Fear
Be trustworthy. *We can only trust as far as we are trustworthy.*	Everything on this table has brought us here. If you're giving and receiving clean feedback, managing risk taking well, being clear about expectations, and asking for help, you're building trust. What else are you doing if you're building trust? You do what you say and say what you do. You tell the truth, especially when it's hard. You know that your truth is your truth, and you don't make theirs wrong. You have clear boundaries. You honor others' boundaries (and if you're not clear on them, you ask). You trust yourself and listen to yourself. You own your mistakes. You give credit where credit is due. You stay present. You get curious. You hold confidentiality and honor what Brené Brown[1] calls "the vault." You honor people. You do the right thing—even if no one knows. You trust. All of these things build your energetic trust field. The most important person here to be trustworthy with? Yep, you. (The more we trust ourselves, the more we can be trusted, and the more we know whom and when to trust. This quiets lots of noise.)	Well . . . pretty much the opposite of the "safe" column. When you break an agreement, talk behind someone's back, or don't follow through, you diminish trust. Even more nuanced, you don't give people *real* feedback (extra bad points if you tell others though). You talk behind people's backs, and even if *they* don't know, the people you're talking to do, and now they don't trust you because, surely, you'll do it to them too. (Even if your intention in sharing was to benefit them or to bond.) You avoid difficult direct conversations. You gossip. You get sucked into drama. You bask in drama. You're the lowest vibration in the room, you know it, and you do nothing to change it. You're not present, but you pretend to be. You make excuses, using *busy, overwhelmed, tired,* and *forgetfulness* as your main "go-tos" when you don't follow through. You're late. You don't own mistakes or account for broken agreements. You complain but don't request or give direct feedback. You act out of alignment with what you say is most important to you. And you don't trust others.

Area of Energized Collaboration and System Growth	Creates Safety	Creates Fear
Trust others. *Trust grows us. Boundaries show us. Presence is the key to both.*	You trust others. Let them lead. Assume good. Gather evidence for their trustworthiness. You ask for help and give them opportunities to shine. You make it safe to come to you with mistakes. And ask for clarity when not clear. If it's off or trust is broken, you name it, claim it, and help things go right. If someone continually breaks trust and doesn't honor you or your agreements, you hold your space, clarify your boundaries, and move forward accordingly, present and clear. You create more trust because your assumption of trust and your own trustworthiness inspires the same in others.	You trust no one. You second-guess everyone. You micromanage the shizzle out of your people. You do it all yourself. You swoop in to "hero" and "rescue" mode to save the day, holding others as small and incompetent. You "pretend trust," meaning you trust but energetically and logistically stay in their grill. You gather evidence to show you can't trust them. Mistakes are etched in stone forever. You make people nervous and ultimately create the exact outcomes you *say* you don't want, with no one feeling safe, inspired to work with you, or at their best. The energy of "careful" is palpable.
Ask for help. *We cannot do it alone. We must help each other.*	You ask for help. You show vulnerability. You don't have to know it all. And you trust people enough to let them in. When people ask for help, you celebrate their brilliance for doing so. You clarify what help you want/need, you communicate it effectively (and get help doing so if you're not clear), you make it easy for others to help you, and you receive with gratitude. This creates more safety, more connection, more trust, and ultimately a better experience and result for all.	You do it all yourself. You are tough. You know it all. And you don't let people in. When people ask you (or others) for help, you feel superior and judge them for being weak. If you do ask for help, you may not be clear on what you need help on—or are willing to receive—so you make it hard for them to help you. Ack! You feel alone, gather evidence to prove it, and may not know how to break this cycle. It's OK; start *anywhere* on the left side of this table and you break the cycle.

Maintenance and Healing

Once you've created the container for a healthy system, it becomes about maintaining it and then healing it when things break. Maintenance is as simple as regular check-ins, ongoing feedback, open dialogue, culture checks, using any of the assessments in Chapter 2 or questions in the fieldwork sections of this book.

Ask for what you want, celebrate the good, and let messy be OK. You are always growing.

Inevitably you will hit conflict. Any healthy system does.

#7. Willingness and Frameworks to Fix the System When It "Breaks"

The system is broken; there's been a breach; it's falling apart. Now what?

Use it, learn from it, fix it, and make it better. This is all so much easier with the first part of this book under your wing.

Ready?

Clarifying Conflict: The IEP Conflict Navigation Model

When I work with people in conflict, whether it's two people or a whole team, it's always interesting to see how often they're not clear on what the actual conflict is. This is so common that I use an exercise called "The Purple Pen" to help people see how far off they may be in what their different perspectives on the problem are—or *if* there is even conflict. More often than not, the "purple pen" is not purple; it's "green" or "blue"—and this opens up a whole new area of wisdom for the people, the project, and the system.

Conflict is human. It can also be scary—sometimes so scary we forget to clarify what it is.

In Parts 1 and 2 of this book, I gave you tools to stay present, stand strong, and stay clear in yourself to hold your space. In Chapter 7, I shared IEP superpowers with you, and in Chapter 9 I shared the Energetic Xylophone and turning "bad" things into "good." In Chapter 10, we went all in on George, loved our nemesis, and learned other tools and frameworks for navigating the tricky stuff. Then in Chapter 11 we looked at OPPPE, and, now, in this chapter we've created a healthy system and explored ways to grow it. Here we'll put everything together and end with a framework for navigating conflict.

Conflict? Or so you think? Let's see.

The IEP Conflict Navigation Model

There are two parts to conflict navigation: the individual work each person must do and explore (part 1 below) and then the collaborative work you'll do together (part 2). It's important that the individual work is done first, independently. This can help each person own his or her own space, lay the foundation, set the tone, and create more clarity and ease for the collaborative work together. Sometimes, after doing part 1, part 2 becomes unnecessary. See what's true for you.

Part 1: Individual Work

1. Identify the conflict? What is it? (Name it.)
2. Who is it with? (Beware the "they.")
3. Is this issue "worthy" of conflict? (Or can you find another perspective, and/or let it go?) Yes, conflict worthy? Continue . . .

Check yourself before you wreck yourself:

1. How's your IEP? Is it in service of, or not?
2. What's your regard for the other people?
3. What assumptions are you making?
4. What might *their* experience of *you* be?
5. What truth are you not speaking?
6. Where are you in defense—proving it or attached to being right?
7. What's your request?
8. Is there a boundary breached or a new boundary that needs creating?
9. Are you "assuming good"? Curious?
10. Have you *truly* "decided" to resolve this/have a good relationship/etc.? How might this be "serving" you?

Once you've done your own work and you're clean, if there is still conflict, ask your person/team (whom you have "conflict" with) to get

233

together, get curious, and explore the talking points in part 2. (**Note:** If you are really stuck here, or the situation is extra charged, it may be useful to do the "Love Your Nemesis" exercise I offer in Chapter 10.)

Part 2: Collaborative Work

With part 1 complete, if you've found there is still conflict and tension, it's time to move to part 2. Get your IEP clean and right, and then together, you'll explore the following . . .

1. Name (with curiosity and care) that there is conflict or misalignment. ("I'm noticing something feels 'off' here. Do you feel it?")

2. Create a statement of intent ("I want to resolve this because I care about our relationship/I want you to succeed/I want our team to rock it.")

3. Agree on what's bigger than both of you; what is this conflict navigation in service of? What is the ultimate thing you are serving? ("We are in service of our kids, this team, our client, our employees, or this invention that will cure cancer . . . ")

4. Name what you believe the conflict or misalignment is. Does the other person agree? What's the other person's experience? ("I sense it's this _____. /I'm making up that it's this _____. What is your experience?")

5. Get curious together and *listen*. Hear each other out.

6. Ask for support from an unbiased party if needed to help work through the issue. (Do *not* preload the person with details on either side; keep it clean.)

7. Work it back and forth, keeping the bigger thing you are both in service of as the third entity you are creating alignment around. Keep breathing and staying present.

8. Create new agreements, including next steps, any communication needed, and new ways of working or being together.

9. Apologize, own, honor, commit, champion, and acknowledge each other for coming to the table to work this out.

10. Revisit the first exercises in this chapter to now up-level your new relationship and design for the future.

Now that you've got *you* handled, your presence humming, and your relationships zooming, let's move to Part 4 as we step into leadership, bringing people with us, accelerating team magic, and growing more positively contagious leaders.

Fieldwork: Make It Real

Let's get to work and make your relationships more pleasurable and life-giving! I've addressed seven components of system wellness in this chapter. You may have found that these apply to all kinds of relationships (personal, professional, private, team, etc.). Here are four things you can do now to address any and all of your systems, up-level your leadership in them, and create more positively contagious outcomes:

1. Address anything that "pulled" (or "pushed") you as you read this chapter. Unclear about your system? Name and define it. Need agreements as a team? Create them. Not clear on a decision? Dig in. Roles and accountabilities tripping you up? Engage. Use the structures, questions, and exercises in each section to support you here. And then go deeper . . .

2. Choose three relationships you want to up-level and do the exercises offered in component #4 (the IEP Relationship Design Model Questions and the Designing for Messy exercise).

3. Review the Relational System Safety table. How are you doing? Give yourself an honest assessment on both sides of the grid in all seven areas. Choose one area this week to improve. Next week, choose another.

4. Choose one relationship you have conflict with and work your way through the IEP Conflict Navigation Model Questions offered in component #7.

CONTAGIOUS LEADERSHIP: INSPIRE AND GROW OTHERS

CHAPTER 13

Bring People with You. Enroll and Serve Them.

Our greatest opportunity as leader is to nourish, champion, and grow other leaders.

Masterful leadership inspires, enables, and creates more positively contagious leaders, who inspire, enable, and create more positively contagious leaders, and on and on and on—all in service of creating positive impact.

So how do you grow other leaders? How do you inspire, enable, and enroll them not only in being more positively contagious, purpose-driven leaders, but in paying it forward?

Welcome to Part 4: "Contagious Leadership" where we'll discuss making this work even more contagious through creating other leaders, using this work with your team and organization, and ultimately up-leveling your impact all together.

In this chapter we'll discuss five core components of creating other leaders. These complement the work we've done thus far in this book:

1. The powerful intention of service.
2. Don't "empower" them: hold a big container and set them up to win.

239

3. Give productive feedback (especially on the "soft stuff").
4. Enroll, recognize, honor, value, trust, and see the humans you lead.
5. Let them lead.

Once you have these, elevating team magic in Chapter 14 will be a piece of cake. Ready? Let's go!

#1. The Powerful Intention of Service

What is the point of your leadership? Your business? The products or services you offer?

What is your intention behind it all? Why do you lead, give people feedback, take risks, step out of your comfort zone, make things? What's important about these things? What fuels your desire to create impact?

If you're on purpose, driven, and feeling in flow, it's probably not just because your leadership is directing you to be or because you're supposed to for your job.

It's something way bigger than yourself or your desire for comfort. Underneath it all is likely the intention of service.

If you're exhausted, not leading well, stagnating in business results, or being negatively contagious, you may be missing (or have forgotten) the powerful intention of service.

Being in service of another human's well-being, care, and humanity, and being in service of the success and growth of something (or someone) you care about, is the core of effective and productive leadership.

It's easy to disconnect from our purpose when we've lost presence or are in the weeds of our life. The intention of service can help us focus on what matters most, get out of our own way, and unleash the most potent version of ourselves in service of others. From here, our leadership is no longer about surviving or looking good or being right or careful—it's about people:

- Having a challenging conversation with a colleague? What's it in service of (e.g., the health of your relationship, your colleague's well-being, or the success of the project or team)?
- Need to give difficult feedback to someone you care about? What's it in service of (e.g., the person's growth, the project's success, the person's credibility in the company, or the ability for that person to achieve his or her best)?
- Asked to take on a project that is out of your comfort zone or inconvenient—and it's big stakes with significant impact? What's it in service of?
- Is your business feeling stuck? Are sales slow and your prospective clients not engaging as you'd like? What's your product in service of? Yep, find that.

Connect with what you're in service of and you're free.

Any conversation, feedback, or act of leadership when tied to the intention of service becomes easier, clearer, and more compelling to whomever you're doing it for.

When I facilitate a group or speak on stage, I know that if I'm focused on "doing it right" or "looking good"—it will not go as well. I also know that if I'm all about my audience and hold service as my intention, it will thrive. In the moments I feel stuck, nervous, or on my leadership edge, it's choice point time. All I need to remember is that I'm there to contribute my best and focus on the people I'm with. The moment I become present to this, I'm good. The internal noise and nerves go away, I'm connected to impact and the human(s) in front of me, and we're ready to rock.

I see this with clients as well; their most difficult conversations, scariest leadership moves, and even sluggish sales results are often related to losing sight of the person in front of them and staying connected to purpose and service. When they remember, and reconnect with the intention of service, things flow again; the conversation is less painful, the leadership move becomes powerful and effective, and their enrollment results improve.

Putting "Service" in Customer Service: What Is Your Intention?

Jack was having a hard time closing a sale and was feeling tremendous pressure.

"What's important about this sale?" I asked.

"We have bills to pay, this would help us make our goals, and we've been working really hard on this for a long time."

I instantly felt the problem. (Can you?) The focus was on *himself*—not on serving his customer.

"What's important to you about serving this customer? What will your service do for your customer?" Ahhh, right! This would help the customer's company do "X, Y, and Z" and make the company better at its craft, which would help a lot of people. Jackpot.

Embodying this energetic intention, my client went back to his customer, had another conversation, and closed the deal by the end of the day.

What is your intention, and where is your attention? If you're not getting the result you want or you're feeling stuck in your leadership, ask yourself this question and rework it until you feel "the click of clean."

#2. Don't Empower Them: Hold a Big Container and Set Them Up to Win

I've never been a big fan of the word "empowerment" or this notion that we empower others. In truth, it bugs the heck out of me. I think it's way more important, interesting, and useful if we empower ourselves. Your people are on their own paths. A core part of the leadership journey is to learn how to stand and unlock one's power from the inside out. They already have the power. It's not yours to give them; it's yours to evoke and support.

Our role as leaders is to serve, nourish, and clear the way however we can to help others access more of themselves and use their power authentically and in service of others. Support your people, remove obstacles, give them excellent feedback, serve as a thinking partner and guide, lead them in the ways they need it, be clear, and be an advocate and champion for them. Hold a humongous container of belief for them to step into, own, and expand.

But empower them? No.

In *Contagious Culture* I talked about the "container." The container is the energetic space you hold for someone to grow, do the best work in, and show up as powerfully as possible. The size of the container we hold for another can impact who that person becomes. If we don't believe in someone and hold a small container, he or she will likely sense it—and show up accordingly. If we believe in the person and hold a large container, he or she will sense that too—and show up accordingly.

One of your greatest duties as leader is to hold space for the people you lead. If you cannot hold a large container for them, you shouldn't be leading them. By the way, this doesn't mean you tolerate bad behavior and performance and just hold a big container. Sometimes holding a big container includes letting someone go.

"But What if I Don't Like Them?"

"What if I just don't like them? They annoy me. *But* I'm responsible for leading them. Then what?"

I get asked these questions a lot when I coach others. It happens. Here's the thing. If you've signed on to lead them and have the prestigious and precious honor of that role in their lives, you do not have the luxury to not show up for them because you don't like them.

If you're going to lead them, work your stuff out.

There is a difference between liking people and being able to hold a container for them. It's way more pleasurable when these things work together, and if they don't, you can still hold a big container and believe in them without them being your favorite person or someone you want to hang out with all the time.

That said, if you don't believe in them, can't hold the container, and truly can't work your personal feelings out, find someone who can. This does not make you a bad leader—it makes you honest and accountable. Being honest about our ability to lead someone is an act of leadership in itself.

The Contagious Container Game

In *Contagious Culture* I gave you the Container Game. I've altered that game for this book to bring in more of the principles we've been discussing including beliefs, desire, value, feedback, and contagiousness.

Think about the people you currently lead and consider the following:

- **Belief.** Do you believe in them? Who do you believe they can become? What's possible for them in their career?
- **Desire.** What do you want for them? What's your greatest dream for each person?
- **Value.** What value do these people bring to your team, the organization, the work, you? What is it they are magically gifted at?
- **Contagiousness.** How do they infect you, the team, the people they work with? Are they positively or negatively contagious? What's one thing they could do to amplify their contagiousness?
- **Leadership strengths and opportunities.** What are their leadership strengths? Their biggest opportunities for growth?
- **Obstacles.** What's getting in their way right now?
- **Feedback.** What feedback and acknowledgments do you have for them? What can they do now that will propel them forward?
- **Support.** What support can you give them? What support might they need from others? How can you serve more?

Once you've worked through the Container Game, and know where you stand and how you can support them, you're on your way. The energy is already shifting. The next step is either to communicate anything you sense will serve them, to get into action in supporting them (you don't even need to tell them—just do it), or to do nothing and simply hold a bigger energetic space for them to step into.

I've found this exercise to be clarifying for myself, team, and clients in exploring growth opportunities. It's also useful to do when you feel stuck and are unable to discern why (especially in identifying obstacles and support needed). This can be done alone or with the person and even as a team. One of my favorite points to work with is contagiousness. If there's a place I sense people can be more powerfully contagious or show up even better, I'll intentionally model that skill or way of being when I'm with them. (Remember, presence begets presence.) Often just the modeling is enough for them to "catch it" and up-level.

Set People Up to Win

We can contribute to others by doing big and little things. Sometimes the littlest things help the most in setting the tone for another. The way we introduce or talk about people, the way we hold space, give feedback, respond, speak to them about possibilities, support them when they're "failing," stay present with them, all of these things are moments that influence the game.

Here are some quick, powerful, and important wins:

- **The way you introduce and/or talk about people.** Are you present, truly present, when you introduce people to each other or speak to someone about another person? Do you speak to people's character, how they show up, what they've done, and who they are to you? Do you speak in a manner that truly sets them up for success, communicating that they're amazing, invaluable, and that the person meeting them (or working with them) is wildly fortunate? (Or do you play down the introduction, give it a half-hearted hello, diminish their contributions, and show up flip about the whole thing?)
- **The way you speak to their challenge or growth opportunities.** Is it with the energy of excitement for what's next, honoring that they're growing, and "You've got this!"? (Or with the energy that they're "broken," and it's the end of the world?)
- **The way you give feedback.** Is it in service of their best interest? Is it in celebration of who they're becoming? Are you present

with them, honoring the tenderness that feedback can provoke? Do you set them up with next steps and make sure it all landed? Do you offer them support for integration? (Or do you drop the feedback bomb without thinking it through, move fast, and leave them in the fetal position not knowing what to do with it?)

- **The way you help people get back on track.** When you see someone on your team falling down or making a mistake (especially in front of a client or group of people), do you stay present and hold space for that person, maybe even asking a question he or she knows the answer to just to give the person a quick foothold and reboot? (Or do you look the other way, let the person tank, and avoid contact after?)

- **The way you hold space for them.** When you are with them, do you hold absolutely present space, put your phone down, give them your undivided attention, listen deeply (to what is and is not being said), and make it so they are the only person in the world on your mind right during that moment? (Or do you multitask, watch over their shoulders, check your phone, pretend to be present, and surface-listen?)

- **The way you elicit more wisdom and creativity from them.** When they offer ideas you think won't work, do you "create from" the idea; *"yes, and"* them; find something you can like about it (if only their courage to bring it up); and give them something to build upon? (Or do you shut it down, even energetically, making them feel small for taking the risk?)

- **The way you give or take directions and set expectations with them.** When giving or receiving directions or setting expectations, do you clarify, make sure they understand, stay present, and leave the conversation with agreement on timelines, next steps, and appreciation for each other? (Or do you go fast, assume everyone gets it, and bolt quickly to the next thing?)

These are all acts of humble and helpful leadership. They help others thrive. They are contagious. And bonus, when we're generous here, not only is the person we're serving set up for success, but we look (and feel!) good too.

#3. Give Productive Feedback

In Chapter 10 when we discussed George, I shared that not giving honest and direct feedback is one of the top cultural toxins. It is also a leadership and trust killer. To lead well, you must get good at feedback. This includes giving it and receiving it. In *Contagious Culture* I provide a framework for feedback and ways to think about it. Here are some general guardrails and beliefs to support you in making your feedback as honest, loving, productive, rigorous, and effective as possible.

Feedback Guardrails

Ready to make your feedback count? Done well, the feedback you give someone can propel the person to the next level of becoming (and beyond), build a more solid relationship between the two of you, and even set the person free from struggling with whatever has been getting in his or her way. Here are some guardrails to support you in gifting it well:

1. Make sure the feedback is in service of your person, clean, clear, and specific. (I like the COINS model: Context, Observation, Impact perceived, Next, Stay—which I'll go into in a minute.)
2. If you are struggling with giving feedback, check yourself. Are there any hidden agendas? Is it personal? Is it a projection? If there is fear, what are you afraid of?
3. See the humans you are giving the feedback to—they are just like you with hopes, dreams, fears, heart, and a desire to do well. Love them.
4. Remember that their growth (and your honesty) is more important than your comfort.
5. Feedback is a gift—for them, you, your relationship, and the organization or outcome as a whole.
6. You do not have to be right or brilliant in your feedback. But you do have to prepare, be honest, be in service of, and also be *unattached* to if they take it or not.

247

7. Not giving people feedback and letting them continue to fail (and even worse eventually terminating them because they didn't get it) is an act of cruelty.

8. Give positive feedback too! Acknowledging how they're doing, what they're doing well, what you appreciate, where they shine—anything, big or small—is of major service. Do not take it for granted that they know you think this. See their shine and tell them.

With these in mind, let's move to something a bit trickier.

How Do You Give People Feedback When Their Energy Is Not Great?

It's intangible. It feels personal. And sometimes there's not a lot they can do about it. It's just the way they show up.

And it makes a huge difference.

This can be coached if they're willing to work it. (And you're willing to lead here.)

Our first step is to tune in and see what's here.

First . . . Notice *Them*

Get clear, for yourself, on what you're actually noticing before you give any feedback:

- What *is* it they're doing? Who are they *being*? (They're scowling, being negative in the room with their face and presence, complaining, grunting, rolling their eyes, or sighing, or they just seem off.)
- What is the *energy* you feel from them? (Is it negative, disdainful, superior, disinterested, sad, arrogant, insecure?)
- What is it you *make up* about it? (There's something wrong; they don't like you or their job; they're just "George"; something happened . . .)

The goal here is awareness to find an entry point.

Now Notice *You*

Before you give feedback, ask yourself:

- Am I bubbling up, holding my own space? (Yes or no.) How am *I* showing up? (Ah! Actually, I'm hooked and fixated on them right

248

now.) How am I contributing to it? (They may be feeling me judging or analyzing them.)

- What might I be projecting at them? (That there's something wrong, or that I think they don't like me, or that I don't like them.)
- What am I making up? (Everything.) What's the accurate reporting? (They keep sighing; they are rolling their eyes; they've grunted three times in five minutes; I am curious.)

Depending on where this all lands you—now you can have a clean conversation and get curious.

Now . . . *Together*

Name it (with curiosity):

- I notice this happens . . .
- I'm curious about . . .
- The story I'm making up . . .
- What do you notice?

Stay present with them and converse.

Giving Them Feedback

If after doing the groundwork there is clean feedback to be given, you can use COINS to give them a place to go:

- **Context/When it happened, what we're talking about.** "In our meetings . . ."
- **Observation/What I *noticed*.** "Your body language and facial expressions communicate displeasure, and your comments are generally negative."
- **Impact perceived/What I *sense* happens.** "The energy of the room drops; people stop contributing because they feel shut down; things feel sluggish; people leave drained; we're not as productive as we could be."
- **Next/What I'd love to see instead/what will make you more effective.** "Pay attention to body language, tone, facial expressions, and your vibe. Make statements from a place of curiosity, 'yes, and,' and requesting or suggesting versus complaining or

making people wrong. Get present and set your intentions before you come into the room."

- **Stay/Identify support needed/desired:** "How can I best support you here? I can walk you through the 5-Step; we can check in weekly; we can have a signal for when I see it happening again; etc."

Coaching Their IEP and Creating Space for a Rich Authentic and Productive Conversation

Here are some additional talking points to support the feedback conversation and help people up-level their IEP, impact, and overall *positive* contagiousness.

In the coaching conversation, ask:

- How do you think you show up? How do you want to show up?
- What do you think your energetic presence is? What do you want it to be? What's one shift you can make to up-level it?
- How do you think you impact others? What is their experience of you? How do you want to impact them? How do you want people to feel around you?
- How engaged do you feel in this project/team/conversation/ situation?
- What are you most excited about creating? How do you think you need to show up to create that?
- What is the legacy you want to leave? How do you want people to remember you in your role and leadership?
- How do you feel about our team? Our presence? Our meetings?
- What agreements do you think would help us as a team show up better together?

Point, Request, and Support

Now you can direct and support them even more effectively:

- My experience of you is . . .
- What I'd love more of is . . .
- I'd love to support you in this by . . .
- How can I help?

A Couple of Things to Know Here

Your feedback will be much more useful, and the process more pleasurable, if you remember these two things:

- This is all an active two-way conversation. These prompts are talking points to open up new levels and lanes for this discussion.
- Just because you give feedback doesn't mean it's right. So be open, honest, and unattached. When you get feedback, same thing. Get curious. And if you find yourself getting upset, look deeper. There's gold there.

When It Gets Tough

If they're resistant and the way they show up is having a negative impact on the team, then that behavior truly needs to shift. You can then move into a more serious conversation about performance, requirements, and outcomes and even put them on a plan.

When you handle feedback *honestly, directly, swiftly,* and *with care* using the frameworks I've offered above, getting to the point of a performance plan is rare. Remember, people *want* to show up well, be great to work with, and be successful. And we all need support sometimes.

#4. Enroll, Recognize, Honor, Value, Trust, and See the Humans You Lead

In the midst of going fast and doing and being all we have to do and be, it is easy to forget why we're leading, whom we're leading, and what we're leading for. Leadership is not an act of pushing and forcing; it is an act of enrolling, inspiring, and serving. When you come from the intention of service, with the right energetic presence, you create enrollment and inspiration.

I've found the following to be helpful reminders when we lose sight, get fuzzy on what all this leadership stuff is about, or find ourselves pushing and forcing leadership:

1. **You are leading human beings.** They have hopes, dreams, fears, families, lives to juggle, things to prove, pressure to

251

manage, and, of course, their own drama, trauma, and magic. They are you, and you are them. We're all in this together. Remember the human.

2. **You must see them: their values *and* their value.** We are walking billboards for what we value in our lives. As discussed in Chapter 5, when I'm honoring my values in my Essential You, I'm congruent. When I'm not, I stop. I'm out of alignment with myself. People show us what their core values are by what they talk about, what they do, how they spend their time and money, what delights them, and what ticks them off. Pay attention. If you understand their core values, you understand and can meet and serve them better.

On the other side of this is seeing, honoring, and speaking to the value they bring to the company, the team, and your life. What is special about them? What are they super-duper good at? How is their unique contribution essential to what you're all up to? What do they bring to the team? Naming someone's value as a member of a team, and telling that person how much he or she matters and why, taps core human needs demonstrating that we're seen, valued, honored, and connected.

3. **You are "response-able" to them, not responsible for them.** You may be their boss or their mentor, but you are not responsible for their success. They are. You are "response-able" to lead them, to be direct and clear, to help them navigate their path, and to help them learn, fall down, get up, and become the best leader they can be. You are responsible for seeing them, hearing them, and being able to respond to them—but you are not responsible *for* them. If anything, you may be responsible for gifting them this message: if they want it, they must create it.

4. **You are a guide, an advocate, and a champion. You are not their guru who knows all the answers.** You do not have to know everything, and certainly not about them. They know themselves best. And they're on their own paths. That said, you may have mad skills that surpass where they are. You have sage wisdom, and you're their advocate. So lead, teach, guide, and give them feedback; think with them; learn with

them; direct as necessary; and help them find their own answers. One of the greatest gifts you can give people is teaching them they have their own answers.

5. **You must play. We all must play.** All work and no play makes everyone . . . exhausted, boring, and beige. Did you know that "in companies that stifle play, brainpower may actually decrease as it does in children with failure-to-thrive syndrome, a condition created by experientially deprived or abusive environments."[1] Yes. So play. Time-outs, field trips, days off, mosaic building adventures, hiking retreats—whatever feels like play, do that.

6. **You must be a model and catalyst for trust. Trust them and be trustworthy.** Trust between people stimulates oxytocin (a feel-good hormone and neurotransmitter), and oxytocin stimulates more trust. Then people feel safer and work together better. Not only does trust feel good, directing energy and attention in the right places; it's a highly productive and valuable leadership asset.

Throughout this book we've built congruency (with self and others) and integrated more behaviors and ways of being to support leadership trust and credibility, which include:

- Listening
- Being present
- Acknowledging each other (genuinely)
- Giving direct feedback
- Making risk taking safe
- Communicating intentionally
- Sharing information
- Naming it
- Showing vulnerability
- Being curious
- Setting each other up for success
- Asking for help
- Telling the truth
- Having a vision and clear intention
- Being in integrity with ourselves

These are just some of our resources for increasing trust and becoming more trustworthy. These skills, tools, and principles are embedded throughout this book, so if you're integrating, you're doing it.

#5. Let Them Lead

If you really want to grow your people, let them lead.

You want the members of your team to be smarter than you, faster than you, and better than you. You want them to lead, inspire, and enable their own future leaders. Your job as leader is not to be followed. It's to create, nourish, and grow other leaders. One of the ultimate forms of contagiousness is contagious leadership.

In order to do this you will need to take care of a few things:

- **Your ego (in the sense of your pride).** Your people being smarter than you, growing faster than you, and getting opportunities you would have loved is not a sign that you are a loser or that your job is at risk. It's a sign that you are a good leader who holds a big container.
- **Your own congruency.** The stronger and more solid you are, the easier it is to get out of the way and trust others to lead.
- **Your own growth.** Just because you are growing other leaders and handing off the baton, does not mean you are done. You may just be getting started. As you grow others and shift your role, you'll want to continuously grow yourself too. What's next for you? How can you serve in bigger ways? What scares you?
- **Your own mentorship.** Just like you mentor others, you need your own mentors and guides. Continue to do your work. The higher we get in our leadership roles and responsibilities, the more essential it is to have mentors and guides who push us too.
- **Your presence, your purpose, and your play.** Think back to Chapter 9 where we discussed the seven P's of personal burnout. Get in front of this one. Keep raising the bar proactively here. Up-level your presence and self-care, expand your purpose, and play even more. Life is long *and* life is short; be in it, play with it, and serve.

Fieldwork: Make It Real

Which of the ideas in this chapter are most important for you? Use them.

Here are some quick checkpoints to review this chapter:

- What is your intention of leadership? What/who are you being in service of?
- What is the size of the container you hold for the people you lead?
- How do you set people up for success?
- What feedback do you have for someone that will elevate his or her game? Work the model.
- Where can you elevate trust on your team or in your relationships?
- How are you seeing your humans?
- Do you let people lead? If not, what's getting in the way?
- What is your very next, even littlest, step after reading this chapter? Go.

CHAPTER 14

Honor and Accelerate Team Magic. Elevate and Propel Them.

We are better together when we show up.

You're positively contagious, your leadership is humming, and you're creating the impact you desire. Now what about your team? Team dynamics are a whole new ball game. How do you play this one? No worries; you've worked hard to get to this point, and if you've been showing up positively contagious and in service of the people you lead, your team will be right behind you with these practices and ways of being. If you've been reading this book with your team, this will be even easier. If not, you've still got this.

Remember, it only takes *one* person to shift the tone. And that's you. Your presence is your impact, so do a reboot, take a breath, set your intention to be in service of your team and its magic, and let's go.

Your Highly Contagious Team

The people on your team are contagious just like you are. They're contagious inside the team as they infect each other. And they're contagious outside the team as they influence the people around them who are constantly deciding if they want to work with, follow, trust, and model your team.

What kind of team do you have?

The Story of Two Teams: Team Chaos and Team Calm

Once upon a time there was a team, we'll call it *Team Chaos*.

The people on your Team Chaos showed up late for meetings, always had their phones in hand, talked behind each other's backs, hoarded information that would support others (because they wanted to have the upper hand), and ran from meeting to meeting without pause. They lived in the Drama Triangle (taking turns being Hero, Victim, and Perpetrator with each other), had wildly unproductive meetings, complained to others about their team, stayed late at work (because they weren't productive during the day), and turned into martyrs the next morning for being at work so late the night before.

Team Chaos's engagement scores were the lowest in the company, customer complaints about the team members were the highest, and their families were exhausted by the complaints their loved ones came home with every night.

When Team Chaos met with another team in the organization, the other team knew not to worry about being on time—so it too showed up late. It knew not to take the meeting too seriously—so its members were unprepared. And these members knew presence wasn't a big deal with Team Chaos—so they multitasked throughout. Everyone left the meeting unproductive, low vibe, and toxically contagious.

There was another team in the organization; we'll call it *Team Calm*.

The members of Team Calm set themselves up for success from the beginning. They got clear on the purpose of the team, why each was on the team, the core values of the team, and the value (and values) of each person. They were also clear on their energetic preferences on how they liked to work, their goals and intentions as a team, and their team agreements.

They had agreements for navigating conflict and for when agreements were broken. They integrated energy checks to tune in with each other and used the Five Steps to Intentional Impact to prepare for meetings and projects.

Finally, they got clear on the intended impact they wanted to have on each other, their clients, the teams around them, and even their families. They frequently asked themselves: "How do we want our families to experience us when we go home at night? What kind of container do we need to create as a team to make that so?"

It worked.

Team Calm showed up on time and present, phones were off, agreements were honored, and meetings were intentional and productive. The team started each meeting with an energy check, a quick review of core values and purpose, and a confirmation of the agenda and intended outcomes.

When the members of Team Calm had conflict, they went to each other directly. They wasted no time on triangulation or drama (if one of them tried to pull another team member into drama, the team member would remind him or her of their agreements and *then support the person* in "dialing direct").

They built in breaks between meetings and made their meetings 50 minutes long instead of 60 (they were so efficient, they often didn't need the full 50).

They sought ways to be helpful to other teams and each other providing information and opportunities that would make others shine.

And when they went home at night, they *went home* at night to be fully present with their lives.

Their engagement scores were the highest in the company, their complaints the lowest, their results on point, and when you asked people which team they trusted or would like to work with, Team Calm was named.

This is a composite of these teams; it doesn't always work out to these extremes on either side, and it paints a powerful picture.

Which team do you want to be?

If we put these two teams together, who would win? The lower-vibration team or the higher? You bet, Team Calm. The members are more grounded. If they hold their space, stay clear on their intent, model the behaviors they wish to see, and invite the other team to step up, Team Chaos will match *them.*

You create a strong and positively contagious team when, first, you do the work yourself personally, and second, you set your team up with foundational practices to support team health and the container. And when you work with a low-vibe team? You can change the tone—if you're willing to set it.

Any time is a great time to start this. If you're starting fresh as a new team, do this now. If your team has been together for years and no one is happy—do this now. A lovely way to enter this conversation is simply by asking the people on your team how they feel about the team dynamics, the quality of your meetings, and their state of being going home each night. This will likely open up a new level of conversation where you can bring these elements in.

Creating a Positively Contagious Team

There are several components I've found helpful in creating a positively contagious team. You can do one or all, and the more you do, the more impact there will be. This takes a bit of work up front and requires "going slow to go fast" at first. A pound of proactiveness *now* is worth a ton of cleaning stuff up later.

1. **The team's Essential You.** Just as we start your individual leadership from the inside out, the team works the same way. Is the vision of the team clear (do you all know where you're going)? Are your values clear, understood, and honored? Is your purpose clear, and is everyone on board and energized by it? Who are you as a team? The Essential You is at the core of the team; this *is* the team's identity. Every company I've known that has a strong core and positively contagious culture is very much in touch with the values and purpose of the team and organization. (Some even start meetings with a review of their values and purpose.) As you explore the Essential You, look at the team's presence and "brand."

What's your identity? How do others think of you? How do they experience you? What do you want to be known for? Why are you all together? And in service of what?

2. **The composition of the team.** Who's on the team and why? Are people in their best-suited roles doing what they have the energy, drive, competency, and capacity for? Are the roles and responsibilities clear? Does everyone know what he or she is accountable for and who's leading what? Does everyone know the charter of the team and the priorities? Whether you use a formal system or not, this element comes down to being super-clear about what and who the team is.

3. **The energy of the team.** What *is* the energy of the team? When your team comes together and all the team members are working their IEP and being conscious about how they show up, this is already being handled. You can rarely go wrong with people in their authentic energy, present, and holding positive intent. To support the energy of the team, there are assessments to help members identify qualities, preferences, and strengths that will help them do their best work *and* feel good doing it. You can look at the personality types, skills, competencies, and energetic preferences of each member individually and as a collective. Myers-Briggs Type Indicator® (MBTI®), DiSC®, StrengthsFinder®, Kolbe Indexes, WorkPlace Big Five Profile™, and many others are designed to help the individual and the team learn more about themselves and how to work together better. One of my favorites is the Simpli5® Assessment (by 5 Dynamics®, LLC)[1] as it measures the energetic preferences of the individual(s), and the team, doing the work. It's not about competence or personality, but rather supporting people to be optimized in their energetic preferences for thinking, working, and getting things done.

4. **The emotional health and safety of the team.** To set your team up beautifully, make sure you're addressing the emotional well-being and safety of the team. This is key if you want your people performing well and being positively

contagious. This includes physical safety and ensuring your work environment supports you mentally. It also includes emotional safety to ensure you all support each other. This is where naming team dynamics and creating healthy agreements come in. This is also where direct engagement, open and honest communication, productive feedback, and clean conflict navigation become extra important. The tools offered in Chapter 13 (and throughout Part 3) are all designed to support this element of teaming. Do not underestimate the importance of safety on your team. It is everything.

5. **The IEP of the team.** The IEP, the *intentions, energy, and presence* of the team, is fundamental to your team's well-being. You'll want to explore the following (see Chapters 5 and 6 for more on these):

- The team's *Physical and Environmental Energy* (Quadrant 1 of the IEP Model as referenced in Chapter 5): Are you set up for self-care, healthy food at meetings, an energizing environment? Are scheduling allowances to honor jet lag and personal care taken into account when the team travels? How do you intentionally handle the craziness of calendaring?

- The team's *Mental and Emotional Energy* (Quadrant 2): Is there safety for dialogue? Do you check your assumptions? Are you curious? Are you kind? Do you set intentions together, use conscious language, assume good, and believe in each other?

- The team's *Vibrational Energy* (Quadrant 3): Are you conscious of your presence? Do you do presence reboots? Are the teammates each responsible for the energy they bring into the room? Do you use the Energetic Xylophone to support team dynamics?

- The team's *Relational Energy* (Quadrant 4): Do you have agreements? Have you *decided* to be a team? Do you proactively design your relationships, love your nemesis, and navigate conflict with care?

6. **The structures of the team.** What structures do you use as a team to set yourself up for staying on track, staying connected, measuring impact, and being the most productive and effective possible? Structures include the quality of your team meetings, measurements and rewards (see "Structures That Support" below), using the IEP Sheet and the Five Steps to Intentional Impact framework as a team, building IEP moments into team meetings to support ongoing integration, scheduling and calendaring, and of course online systems like Slack, Dropbox, Evernote, Trello, 15Five®, Google, Todoist, and the many other platforms we have to support us in teaming. Choose the ones that work for you, agree upon them, stick with the plan, and be ready to up-level when they no longer serve you all now.

Structures That Support

Be intentional about the structures you create to measure results and how they'll impact your team dynamics. Are the rewards and measurement systems of your team and organization creating a culture of collaboration and care? Or a culture of competition and self-preservation? Do they motivate teams to succeed together or to watch their own back? Build your measurement systems so they reward and foster people supporting each other and helping them do well versus competing and working against each other. (More on this can be found in my book *Contagious Culture* in the Super 7 of Cultural Health.)

7. **The magic of the team.** What practices, rituals, or structures can you put in place to support the unique magic of your team? This may include meeting and team rituals, secret names, energizing competitions, shared impact goals, team events, and more. I've seen teams have secret names for each member (that only the team knows) to reflect what the

individual teammates care most about and what they want to step into every day. I've seen secret handshakes, regularly scheduled team outings, appreciation moments built into the last five minutes of the meeting to close on a great note, and Walls of Gratitude displayed on office walls (virtual and in person), and more. "Magic sauce" can be anything that is designed by your team that is life-giving and pleasurable and means something to each of you.

How Is Your Team Wired?

Since we're talking about energy and contagiousness throughout this book, I thought it'd be great to speak with Karen Gordon, CEO of 5 Dynamics, LLC,[2] an organization devoted to helping teams optimize their collective energy together by working in their energetic zones of ease through a suite of tools that essentially measures how we're wired and prefer to use our energy. I've shared 5 Dynamics (now named Simpli5) with clients since 2004 in this work, as it effectively helps people understand where they prefer to show up in any project or process.

When I asked Karen about her perspective on "being contagious" and the energetic dynamics at play, here's what she shared:

There are elements of leadership that come more naturally for some than for others. The key is in understanding your baseline and taking small, intentional steps to increase your focus in areas that do not come as naturally for you. For example, some people are naturally drawn to ideas and action and have lower energy for people and planning. Some are drawn to people and planning and have lower energy for ideas and action. None of us show up with high energy in all areas; however, all areas are equally important for optimal impact. If we truly want to be positively contagious, we need to be intentional about showing up in the areas that do not come as naturally, and we need to appreciate others who show up in ways that we don't.

One of the things Karen is speaking to here is part of what happens with the dynamics of "George" and "Mary." We all have different wiring and combinations of energetic flows for how we show up. The more we understand this about ourselves and appreciate it in others, the better we can all work together in positively contagious ways. We want to be conscious of the energetic dynamics and physiological processes at play. We all bring our own magic. Sometimes appreciating this requires a bit more curiosity, awareness, and rebooting to understand the different forms. Karen offers another way of framing this from a 5 Dynamics perspective:

When we understand how our energy flows through any project cycle: from idea, to engagement, to planning, to execution (the four areas), with evaluation taking place throughout each phase and at the end of the cycle, we are able to fine-tune our approach by being intentional in areas where we have lower natural energy flow. When we are intentional about showing up in all of the phases, we no longer dismiss others. We listen for all perspectives, and we begin to value cognitive diversity. We see people for who they are and value them for the gifts they bring.

When talking about the impact of IEP and some of the principles I've shared in this book as related to energetic preferences and contagiousness, Karen shares, "I know I set the tone for my team. I'm contagious. If my high-execute energy goes unchecked, I can bulldoze others. So, I need to be intentional about slowing down and being aware of what is happening in the room. From here I can create more of the impact I want."

What Karen is doing here is modeling awarenes and intention and working with her natural authentic energies in a way that enables her to bring all of herself to the table *while* meeting people where they are and honoring them—another act of leadership and being positively contagious.

Bringing Up the Lowest Vibration in the Room

I'm often asked, "How do I bring up the lowest vibration in the room when 'G' is devoted to bringing us down?"

You may avoid this issue all together if you and your team apply what I'm sharing in this book. You can also avoid it by starting your meeting with an energy check to get people "in the room," present, and aware of how they're showing up. (See "IEP Team Energy Check" below.)

If an energy check doesn't take care of it (or you choose to skip the check-in altogether), the answer to this question comes in five steps.

Step 1: Just Notice It: Hold Your Space and Don't Get Hooked

Your presence is your impact. Your mirror neurons are doing their thing—so staying congruent, high vibe, and present is your best bet of inviting others on your team to step up. Do not match the lowest vibration in the room (if you do, you'll lose the others quickly as well). Instead use your energetic presence as an invitation for others to match you. This often works, as presence begets presence. If this doesn't work, go to Step 2.

Step 2: Do the Energy Check

If it's not already part of your culture, simply say, "Let's give ourselves a minute to breathe, check in, and see where we are." Then do the check. If someone is at a "2" (low) and "not feeling it," or the person is fine being a "2" and doesn't want to change it, let that be OK. Don't try to fix it, talk the person out of it, or put any drama around it. Simply invite the person to take care, and if he or she would like support to ask for it. Remind people to notice their impact on the room and to be responsible (and "response-able") for it. This in itself will often shift the entire dynamic. If it doesn't, move to Step 3.

Step 3: Name It and Get Curious

"Hey G, how you doing? I'm noticing you're a little off. You OK? Need anything?" This inquiry, offered with genuine care and curiosity (not snark), can shift the energy in the room. People will either tell you what's up and what they need or say "Nope, all good," and shift. If that doesn't happen, on to Step 4.

Step 4: Call a Time-Out

If G is having a negative impact on the room and seemingly devoted to continue doing so, take a break. Check on G privately, give feedback, and see what's up. Is G aware of his or her impact? Is this the impact G wants to have on the room? What does G need in order to shift? This may do it. In the rare case that G is intent on having a negative impact on the room, or he or she is *not able* to shift . . . go to Step 5.

Step 5: Name It and Schedule the Bigger Conversation for Later

"G, we have a meeting to get back to. I'd really like you to be with us and contribute. We need you. I can't talk you into showing up well. If you choose to show up this way, that's your call, and be aware that it has impact. Your leadership credibility and influence are at stake. After this meeting let's sit down to talk about the bigger things at play here because I am pretty sure something else is going on. Let's explore that together." And then go back in (with or without G as you both decide).

Note: I've only seen this play to Step 5 *twice*. Both times great wisdom unfolded. Once, the employee needed support beyond what the organization could give, and was able to get that support after. The other time, there was a major issue with one of the team's projects, and while this situation was messy and uncomfortable, the conversation and learning for that team were priceless.

IEP Team Energy Check

Want to get your team present, "in the room," and conscious of how the team is showing up?

IEP Energy Check (5–10 minutes)

Everyone takes a breath, gets present, and gives himself or herself a minute for silence. Then, check in. (For a large group, have the individual members do this in silence or with a partner. If it's a small team, have each of the members share.)

Ask: "How's your energy on a scale of 0–10?" (0 being low and 10 being high)

- **Physical energy.** How are you feeling? How's your body?
- **Environmental energy.** How energized are you by this environment?
- **Mental energy.** How mentally present are you right now?
- **Emotional energy.** How is your emotional energy?
- **Vibrational energy.** What's your vibe? The quality of energy you've brought into this room?
- **Team energy.** How's it feel in here together? What's the energy of the team/group?

And then: "What's one thing you can do *right now* to bring it up?" From here you can do a presence reboot or take a break or whatever you sense best. Often just checking the energy and naming it *is* the reboot.

Quick IEP Energy Check (3 minutes)

Everyone takes a breath, gets present, and has 30 seconds to drop in. Then, check in:

- **What's the quality of your energetic presence right now?** How present are you? How's your energy? What are you bringing to this room? How are you showing up?

- **What do you need to do, be, or believe to bring it up?**
  Breathe, change my posture, change my mind, believe in this team and our work, set my intention, drink some water, etc.

They'll answer 0–10, share one thing to bring it up (often you'll hear, "Actually just naming it has made me more present!"), and then you're off!

TEAM MEETINGS THAT ROCK

Want to rock your next meeting? Follow this:

Before:

- Set the agenda; be clear on outcomes and who needs to be there.
- Set the environment up so it supports you to be present and humming on all cylinders: location, food, lighting, time zone/travel considerations, breaks, swag that supports (water bottles, flowers, good pens), and anything else that will impact the energy of the container.
- Send a reminder out 48 hours before and include: the agenda, outcomes, who's going to be there, and the dress code (if there is one), along with asking people to be on time, come prepared (do your Five Steps and any prep), be well rested—and anything else that will help people show up fully without the stress of ambiguity.

During:

- Get there on time! Start on time! Put phones away!
- Do an energy check.
- Do the Five Steps to Intentional Impact framework as a team (ideally they all did it for themselves before, and it's useful to check in on as a team to ground your IEP and the desired outcomes).

269

- Check agreements (or create them if you haven't already)
- Confirm finish time to ease any ambiguity or anxiety of running over.
- Go! *Note:* Make sure you table issues that are off-topic, saving them for a later date. You might use a "parking lot" system, have someone write things down as they come up, or have each person put their "off-topics" on Post-its as they go (to be collected and organized at the end). This will help you stay on track, honor time, stay present, and reboot as needed, without the anxiety of something important being missed.
- Recap next steps, agreements, and what needs to happen before the next meeting (including capturing any issues or off-topics that came up during this one).
- Close with appreciations and/or an IEP Moment that speaks to something in the IEP work you can all focus on for the week or something you're excited about (this can also be done at the beginning of the meeting).

After:

- Lock in what worked, what felt great, and what you want to do different or better next time.
- Follow through on action items and agreements.
- Continue your becoming as a team.

Fieldwork: Make It Real

Flag the ideas and practices from this chapter that you sense will support your team. Then, take both parts of this quiz. Your answers will point you to the areas that need extra TLC. (To accelerate results, do this as a team.)

Quiz: How Positively Contagious Is Our Team?

Your team is YOU and your team of people, so let's look at both.

Our Team

Rate 0–10 here (where 0 is nonexistent or totally unhealthy, and 10 is "We are rocking this!").

___ 1. We're on time.

___ 2. We have clean agreements.

___ 3. We are conscious about our IEP and making sure we take care of ourselves.

___ 4. Our meetings are *awesome*.

___ 5. People want to work with us.

___ 6. We have no gossip or backstabbing.

___ 7. People are excited about their work.

___ 8. We are able to say "I disagree," argue, and stay at the table to work through it (versus leaving and talking about it indirectly).

___ 9. We are low drama.

___ 10. We are focused on purpose, results, and doing our best.

Me on Our Team

Rate 0–10 here (where 0 is not true at all, and 10 is "so true and I am loving it!").

___ 1. I love my team and our dynamics.

___ 2. I feel I have influence over my team dynamics.

___ 3. I can't wait to get to work each day to be with my team.

___ 4. I spend no time stressing out about team drama (either at work or when I go home).

___ 5. I feel like I can speak openly on my team, make mistakes, and take risks.

___ 6. I feel like if I mess up, it's safe for me; my team has my back. (And I have their's.)

271

___ **7.** I feel I can be fully honest and authentic with my team.

___ **8.** I feel set up to succeed on this team.

___ **9.** I am clear about our mission, vision, and purpose.

___ **10.** I know what our team values are—and I love them.

Notes: (Noticings, where we're rocking it, TLC areas identified, next steps, etc.)

_____

_____

_____

_____

_____

_____

_____

_____

_____

_____

_____

_____

_____

_____

_____

_____

_____

_____

_____

_____

PART 5

CONTAGIOUS IMPACT: BE A FORCE FOR GOOD IN THE WORLD

CHAPTER 15

Create a (Positively) Contagious Culture. Live It.

If you build it, they will hum.

A contagious culture is simply a bunch of contagious yous being together.

You're contagious, present, and using your superpowers. Your relationships have new awareness, and your leadership has new range. Now we move into impact. If you're living Parts 1 through 4 of this book, impact is easy. It's happening. But is it sustainable? Is it real? And how do a bunch of contagious *yous* do it all together?

While this book is about you, we ultimately want to bring all that you're doing back to creating a contagious culture.

I spoke with organizations that have been integrating this work during the past few years, as well as revisited some I wrote about in *Contagious Culture*. Where are they now? How's this work been integrated? How's it grown? What works? What's been simplest? Most powerful? What's surprised you? Where else has it shown up?

I had many questions, and they had *many* answers.

I received 16,000 words of input from 13 organizations and 19 business leaders that were willing to share their stories, and provide best practices, wisdom bombs, and outcomes. In this chapter, I've compiled just *some* of their gems. (You can access more from their interviews in the *Contagious You Resource Kit* offered in Chapter 16.)

Hats off and hearts up to these organizations that continue to lean into the soft stuff (knowing that it's titanium) that makes their organizations, families, classrooms, students, patients, employees, and customers thrive even more.

With that, here we go.

Common Themes

In our discussions there were recurring themes with every person and organization. These themes boiled down to "beliefs and mindset" and "tools and principles." Before we dig into their stories, here are some of the most common.

Best-Practice Beliefs and Mindset

Almost every person I spoke with shared some form of belief, experience, or mindset frame in the following five areas.

1. Simple awareness, being present, knowing we're contagious, "seeing" people, acknowledging and honoring them, and taking a pause were part of the magic sauce that got them started and made this work real.

2. Taking care of themselves really did make them better for others. (Modeling self-care for their people was essential to making it contagious.)

3. Being a positively contagious culture didn't just stay at work—it followed people home, impacting their marriages, kids, families, and other aspects of their personal lives.

4. Little things mean a lot. It's often not a huge overhaul or initiative that's needed. Sometimes it's simply owning (and shifting) presence, connecting with intention, being kind, and/or choosing to integrate *one* idea at a time that makes the most real and sustainable changes.

5. It's a journey. Creating or changing culture takes intention, time, and practice. You've got to do the work, and the work starts with *you*.

Best-Practice Tools and Principles

I asked everyone I interviewed what tools or principles they found most useful, impactful, and easiest to implement in this work. The following nine showed up repeatedly:

1. Presence Reboots and Energy Checks
2. The Essential You (values, vision, purpose, and the bubble)
3. Changing their relationship with "self-care" and "self-kind"
4. Accessing (and staying connected to) intention
5. Using the Five Steps to Intentional Impact Framework and the IEP Sheet
6. Energetic Xylophone and reframing
7. Naming it and assuming good
8. Gratitude, curiosity, contribution, and service as state shifters
9. Conflict navigation, agreements, clean feedback, and creating healthy containers

The following sections tell *their* stories.

Case Studies, Shares, and Words of Wisdom from the Trenches

Please note that with all shares in this chapter, the words, learnings, and perspectives offered here are through the lens of the participants and organizations that shared their experiences. This is not a promotional chapter for me or the work; it is an offering of different ways of applying the content. This chapter also offers perspectives from other humans and organizations that may be similar to what you're going through, finding resistance in, or working on in your own organization right now. This is an important point for this chapter.

My intention for including these case studies is simple: it is to honor the care, effort, and experiences of each person sharing what was true for him or her, as well as to serve you in your own journey and application. Some organizations may have done a full IEP integration for years; others may have only read *Contagious Culture*, downloaded free tools, and attended (or hosted) an event. In all cases, the quality of their results and their experiences is reflective of their care for humans; their wisdom and heart in business; their willingness to dig deep and explore the ideas of contagiousness, ownership, impact, and the principles offered in this book; and finally their authentic application and due diligence in using the content as it resonated for them.

May their honesty and generosity serve you beautifully.

IDEO

IDEO is a design and innovation firm devoted to *creating positive and disproportionate impact through design*. If you read *Contagious Culture*, you know that IDEO and I go way back, having worked together since 2007. They've integrated this work into their organization in many ways; it's become a part of their language and processes, and they continue to integrate and practice as is authentic for their culture.

How do the people at IDEO create and *be* a positively contagious culture, not just *do* it? They live it. IDEO live their core values, stay connected to purpose, enroll their workforce and clients in what they stand for, and do phenomenal work. As a result, IDEO is one of the top firms in the world with a reputation for being a beautiful place to work and an organization that is honest and smart and in service of our future.

For this book I met with Duane Bray, Partner and Head of Global Talent, to understand the firm's success. In this ever-changing world where we're moving faster, innovation needs to be bigger and smarter, and we have more stress and demands than ever. How is IDEO not only keeping up with it all but thriving?

The Power of Ritual

IDEO found that nourishing its culture through ritual has been powerful. Duane talks about the power of ritual for storytelling, gathering people together in real time to share, transfer knowledge, and build an ever-evolving sense of community. The people at IDEO have rituals that are designed at a higher level such as "Fireside Chats" (conversations where they get real-real), their "Weekly WOW" (a weekly sharing of cultural inspiration from all studios, for all employees), and other location- and IDEO-wide specific rituals. They also have more grassroots rituals that happen every week such as "Make Time" where someone hosts and brings a topic, and people build something together. Making time to make and connect outside the context of day-to-day project work and take a minute to be together creates more community and brings teams back to the grassroots of identity and culture. In the case of IDEO, that means focusing on the culture as makers. The talent team devotes time to making rituals, stewarding, and creating conditions for people to model healthy and authentic behaviors and have a collaborative culture that celebrates the uniqueness of each person and the essentialness of the collective whole. When you look at the Essential You in the IEP Model, you'll see how these kinds of activities add to the identity of the organization as well as the core values of each member.

Another ritual? Project spaces. IDEO's work is project-based, so people are constantly beginning and ending new projects, building and completing teams, and building identities for the next project. This means they have to be facile, be present, and work together to truly honor the work, each member of the team, and the collective magic of the team as a whole. One of the most important cultural rituals, which goes back to their origin as being made up of designers and makers, is in creating the identity for the projects and workspaces. People name the project team, create agreements for how they'll work together, and design the team's workspace. The workspaces are unique to each project and range from flashing bright lights to album covers to artwork to drawings to anything the team fancies will reflect the energy and intention of the project. Building the identity of the team; staying connected to ritual, values, and each other; and being intentional about how they want to show up together builds a stronger sense of community, which ultimately creates a stronger culture and better results for their clients.

Showing Up and Managing Ambiguity

But . . . with all of the rituals and structures that are put in place to support culture and their becoming, none of them are as powerful if people aren't showing up well.

Duane shares:

The success of our rituals and practices has to do with role-modeling and making the space for each other. This is a really important point; people look to leaders and each other trying to get signals as to where things are going, how they're doing, and what's next. IDEO is a place that has a high degree of ambiguity and we're not going to take that away—the organization can't be made much simpler because that would defeat its purpose (ambiguity is necessary for innovation and making). But what we can do is give people the clarity to navigate in that ambiguity. Part of navigating ambiguity is in how leaders model, show up, and set the conditions. How people are being seen, how people understand that they are being seen, and helping them figure out what they need in order to be successful is essential to the being of our culture. This is also where our core values come in—they help identify and activate what we need to do and be in order to be successful.

In other words, the people at IDEO *celebrate* ambiguity and makes it work for them in service of the best results and project outcomes. And they *reduce* ambiguity (and help people navigate it) as much as possible when it comes to leadership, giving people the tools to navigate career growth and design, to collaborate and work through conflict more powerfully, and to show up well.

Tools and Principles

When asked to reflect on some of the most meaningful effective tools, ideas, and principles integrated from this work, Duane shares there are specific tools that have been helpful, including the basic philosophy of being contagious and creating your experience that can be game-changing. Being present, naming it, building agreements, and conflict navigation (through externalization and partnership) have been some of the core practices made most integral to their culture:

> You and I may have a conflict but instead of talking about "you versus me," we take the conflict and look at it and say, "Do we agree that this thing is there?" This combined with the ability to stay present in the conversation, name it, be in service of each other (and the issue at hand), and honor our agreements in the process have been core to effectively navigating the tensions and ambiguity often necessary in pushing edges, building teams, and making new things.

He also offers that there's another side to the IEP work that's more philosophical and that doesn't require you to go through a whole bunch of deep, deep courses or training or practice:

> You have control over your experience. Period. You can share with somebody in one discussion that if they take responsibility for their experience they can decide what they want to create. They can decide to have a good relationship or not. They can decide to be successful or not. It's a conscious contagious act. As soon as I even surface the idea that I am at choice and have a decision—I think and show up differently. If I'm modeling this, others are more likely to do the same in their own way.

Having worked together for years and having embedded these ideas into their culture, Duane says, they've found that they can make a quick impact with little effort:

> Within five minutes of a conversation with someone who holds these principles, you can get something practical to start with right away. All of the other tools and practices can come over time, but it's actually an orientation of having agency over

your own experience that is what's so powerful. As soon as people realize they have that, that unlocks a lot. This stance of ownership and agency is also contagious, so the more we live it and be it, the more it becomes a part of who we are.

Experience Creates Culture

As we close our conversation, Duane offers one more thought we can take with us:

> I think that the premise behind *Contagious You* is that taking a moment to prepare for how you're going to show up determines how people experience you and the impact you can have. That's the part that's so important for me—that I choose to show up. I could say nothing in a meeting, but people could have a powerful experience of me because of how I'm choosing to be in that room. A lot of people don't realize that it's not what you say, it's how you show up—and that's what's creating the culture. Your observable actions and the IEP you go into that room with are what people experience. The experience is what makes the result.

Large Financial Services Organization

Chris Burt is an Executive Human Resources Leader in a large financial services organization. To honor the organization's corporate guidelines, we are unable to name the organization. However, its story is powerful, and so I want to include parts of it here. The story Chris shares reflects the courage of doing something different and the impact possible when a large organization, traditionally focused on tangible results, numbers, and hard data, decides to embrace the "soft stuff." I've pulled excerpts from our discussion, leaving Chris's words intact as he tells his story and how using many of the ideas and principles in *Contagious Culture* and *Contagious You* have supported him and his organization in creating a more positively contagious culture.

What Inspired You to Embrace the "Soft Stuff" and Create a Positively Contagious Culture Using This Content?

Chris shares:

For years, business trainers have built curricula and models to inspire great individual and team leadership. In many respects, these models are brilliant, and have been skillfully delivered by training gurus in businesses around the globe— lots of "doing" and "skills building"—with minimal effect. The leadership gap in many organizations is wider than it has ever been. These models and the method in which they are delivered often don't stick. While participants may enjoy the content, and even intellectually grasp its significance, upon return to a workplace built around the status quo, the lessons fade. Little changes.

My experience across three decades suggests that people are simply overmanaged and under-led. Many business professionals have become supermanagers with superpowers to deliver results, do work, and manage projects, timelines, and budgets. But their leadership x-factor that taps into the individual discretionary effort of those working for them is lukewarm at best. The corporate "go-to" is often just to get them more and more training. The hope being that if "we train them, the results will come." Hope is a wonderful thing, but it's a lousy strategy for driving interpersonal change and translating that change into an improved business outcome.

Each in its own way, the leadership training models are valid and the delivery is entertaining and engaging. Yet something is still missing.

Enter IEP. The whole experience from my personal perspective "end-runs" traditional training models by creating experiences that drive "being" and ultimately translate into "doing." It seems esoteric, but I can only say that IEP in our organization got into people's work experiences, providing them with

283

a new framework, which drove new behaviors and ultimately better business results. IEP meets people as they are—wherever they are—and changes context for work and life. In a world of shrinking resources and ever-increasing business demands, it's proven to be the most effective method of tapping into the wonderful power of "discretionary effort"—that unique thing that can be given or withheld to achieve above and beyond results.

What Are Some of the Most Useful or Meaningful Ideas, Tools, or Principles You've Integrated to Make Your Culture Better?

Chris offers:

The idea that we are contagious and that our presence is our impact has been very important for us. I got this from reading your first book, but then, in the live session, there were two exercises in particular that were especially poignant for my team and me. Both were experiential and in the moment, working in collaboration with someone else (mostly in silence), and had me truly experience the energy I put into my team (or partner) and that they put into me. This highlighted for me the extraordinary power of my own Intentional Energetic Presence, and the impact it can have on my ability to drive business results.

I've realized that people's brains are hardwired to decode the energy and presence I transmit. If there is the slightest hint of insincerity, of hidden agendas or inauthenticity coming off me, I will limit that team's ability to operate at their best. They may be skeptical, cautious, or ambivalent and simply do nothing as result. Conversely, if what is coming off me includes hope and possibility, a sincere belief in the team's ability to achieve whatever it is I am asking of them, they will exceed my wildest expectations. These experiences, and the experience of using the principles in this work, have made me aware that the thought bubble above my head—which I think no one can see—actually speaks more than the words coming out of my mouth. And if they are in conflict, the team will pick up on it and results will be lukewarm at best.

More specifically, I've found great use in many of the tools, especially the ones that help us reboot in the moment and show up with intention. We've all had the experience of "not feeling it" on the job. We're all over-scheduled and likely have a backbreaking workload on any given day. I have been truly surprised by the power of Bubbling Up and how useful the Energetic Xylophone has been to help improve my energy and the energy of those I lead.

For example, many of us have meetings scheduled one after another with no break in between. Suppose my meeting at 9 a.m. doesn't go well, and is immediately followed by a meeting at 10 a.m. where I need to show up as motivational and inspirational. I could (and if unchecked, likely will) carry the negative energy from my 9 a.m. right into my 10 a.m. Because I don't want to do that—no one intentionally wants to be the guy that sucks the air out of the room—I can now take less than a minute and reset between the two meetings.

Often this exercise happens on the elevator ride to my next meeting. I acknowledge my energy from the 9 a.m., set an intention for my 10 a.m., and show up more congruently than I otherwise would have. The beauty of this is that it's authentic and it does not mean that I need to be "fake happy" at my 10 a.m. Strangely though, simply setting a new intention actually does raise my positive energy and enables me to be the most genuine version of me, which will significantly increase the likelihood that the desired outcome of my 10 a.m. will be achieved. It is this kind of "radical authenticity" that brings out the best in me and in those I lead. This exercise for me has proven to be the x-factor that has kept my leadership authentic—focused on business outcomes and not dependent upon the roller coaster of my day.

What Impact Have You Seen?

Chris says:

My organization had to scale up quickly and deliver on many enormous business outcomes. We did what most organizations do: hired the best and brightest; set them to work on tasks; and managed budgets, timelines, and resources along the way. A couple of years into this undertaking, even as we were delivering solid results, there was a growing amount of organizational strife that began to inhibit our ability to deliver. Where we were making progress before, progress slowed. Timelines slipped and our team fragmented into some pretty serious silos. At a minimum, people became less engaged and somewhat estranged from their leaders and from one another.

Traditional management tools were only scratching the surface, and I was wondering how a bunch of bright, talented, and well-intentioned people could arrive at this place. I began to see the negative energy wafting through my organization and knew that it was in that space that we needed some help if we were to get back on track. The IEP work shone a light on each of us in a caring and respectful way and helped us see how we were interdependent—and also accountable—as individuals and as teams. We were treating our work and our relationship with one another as a zero-sum game; my work got done at the expense of yours; my point of view was more valid than yours; etc. IEP brought a more holistic and highly personal perspective into the organization that created space where amazing results could flourish. We began to really "see" one another.

In addition, getting people in touch with their IEP and how they show up unlocked a greater ROI for us—not only on our results and feeling better working together—but on a lot of the training we'd invested in throughout the previous years. We realized in doing this work that one of the reasons we'd not been able to tap an optimal ROI for those engagements was because people were "doing" the training and the skills but

286

not "being" them and showing up at their best. This work and the ownership for our contagiousness unlocked a new level of cultural and business success.

Probility

Probility Physical Therapy in Michigan is "dedicated to making a difference in people's lives by providing outstanding therapy services in a welcoming atmosphere across 15 clinics." The main header on its website is "BeRemarkable." And the first person you see when you walk through the door is the "Director of First Impressions." Enough said. I spoke with Patrick Hoban, President of Probility, along with Kelly Poppaw, Clinic Director (and also an IEP-Certified Steward), to learn more about how this work has unfolded for the company over the past three years.

How Do You and Your Organization *Live* and *Be* a Contagious Culture Versus *Do* It?

According to Patrick:

> Probility teaches—from the moment that we interview someone, to orientation, training, and their daily work—a culture of love, caring, and service. We live this through only hiring people who display qualities like hope, joy, love, and humbleness. We show them on their first day they are a special part of our family by having every person have welcome gifts on their desk when they come in. We have programs that support and assist staff in being able to show gratitude and appreciation to each other at work as well as supporting our staff if they are in crisis. We create a culture where staff can consistently show we care about each other, that people can be their "whole self" while at work, and that we are a people/staff-first company. This is important: if the staff know we care about them significantly, they will then care about their patients in the same way.

Kelly offers:

One way we do this is by modeling culture—starting with leadership. We talk the talk *and* walk the walk. Just recently, Patrick granted our 14 Clinic Directors five extra hours of administrative time per week. He sent us an email titled "Living Our Core Values" and then described how by granting us more admin time, he wanted us to be able to feel more equipped to teach our staff and have time to get stuff done so we can go home and be present with ourselves and our families. This is an estimated $14,000 lost per week with patients. However, he believes we'll make up for it in our ability to invest more in our staff and leadership development. This was our President walking the talk, showing us that the quality of our people is the most important component of our growth. I've learned that companies that *live* and *be* a contagious culture focus on quality, quality, quality—in care, in service, in leadership, in their people, in everything.

What Are Some of the Most Useful, Simple, and Meaningful Ideas, Tools, and Principles You've Integrated to Make These Ideas Live and Your Culture Better?

Patrick shares:

I love doing the mental/emotional check-in with myself and setting the intention of how I want to show up before meetings—especially ones that are potentially challenging or stressful. I love the xylophone. When I'm low on the scale, I'll do something (a quick meditation, prayer, or something kind for someone else) to center myself and move up authentically. We provide personal growth opportunities through book clubs, leadership coaching that I do with every leader in the company (and that many of the leaders do with their staff), as well as sending them to seminars and workshops (like IEP Live!). Finally, we have a person on staff who is trained in IEP and goes from clinic to clinic to help improve people's intentionality.

Kelly says:

We know, live, and breathe our core values, which are at the heart of our culture. We don't just have them hanging on a wall in our lobby; our staff know them because they live them. We use them in our decision making and in how to respond and what action to take as various situations come up. As a leadership team, we intentionally reinforce them at our all-staff meetings by recognizing people across the organization for living each of our core values the best. These people stand in front of the whole company while Patrick reads cool stories about how they made a difference in people's lives. Then we name an overall champion and they get a golden apple core trophy that says, "You're Probility to the Core," which they keep at their desk until the next person is named.

The other principle we live by is that "we are contagious" and "how we show up, matters." Patrick tells us as Clinic Directors, "What you allow and what you don't allow is the culture you create." This ties to our core values of account-ability and greatness in our jobs. It's not just being great in the work we do, but being great human beings and servant leaders *inside* and *outside* the clinic. I can tell when one of my staff is not taking care of themselves as it has a huge effect on how they show up to work, how they interact with others (their vibrational energy), and their ability to be effective in their treatments with their patients. So, whenever I have a new hire come into my clinic, I get their permission from day one to hold them accountable for taking care of themselves. I've never had one person say no to me because I also ask them to hold me accountable for taking care of myself, too. I don't believe leadership is unidirectional; I ask my staff to hold me accountable, give me feedback, and assume positive intent. This opens up a conversation for me to do the same with them.

What Have You Been *Most* Surprised by in Terms of What It Takes to Create Culture and How People Respond to This Content?

Patrick's response:

This work has shown people they have the ability to impact their life, and not just have their external worlds impact them, which has been hugely impactful in creating more joy, happiness, and productivity here. The ripple effects at home and outside the clinic have been especially moving.

Kelly shares:

How little buy-in I get from staff when I make big grandiose gestures versus how *great* of buy-in I get when I pay attention and act on the little things. This can be as simple as turning my desk chair away from my computer screen and toward them so I'm facing them when they walk into my office. I give them my full presence. They leave my office feeling important and that they matter, which reflects in their patient care. There are also times when I change the cadence, tone, or volume of my voice to match what they need in the conversation. Or make sure I say hello and goodbye to each person, by name, when I see them in the morning and when I leave for the evening. These little things all have impact and are contagious, affecting whatever they do next.

What Impact Have You Seen?

According to Patrick:

Simply put—I have happier staff who are more aware of themselves, more emotionally intelligent, and who want to positively impact those around them. Probility has one of the highest employee satisfaction scores of any large department in our hospital system. The hospital has lots of good departments, and Probility is considered one of the happiest!

Kelly adds:

> We develop people in ways that they become leaders our staff *want* to follow, not just *have* to follow. We have our staff write visions, and we grow and develop them as people because we believe our staff are our biggest assets. We don't review or grade our staff on whether they are meeting productivity measures; we review and grade them on whether they are living our core values and *being* a contribution to our mission. We find that when we focus on these things, we're successful on all levels—the numbers and the results we want follow and we knock our budgets out of the water, showing huge profit margins—but it's not because we're driven by numbers or results. We honor and support the soft skills first.

imageOne

"It's a daily practice to live and be our culture," offers Rob Dube, Cofounder and President of imageOne, an organization offering a progressive approach to managed print. The organization's purpose? "To Deliver the X [DtX] to everyone, every day, every time. What is the X? The X is genuine care that consistently drives extraordinary energy, actions, and experiences."

It's working—imageOne was named to Forbes Small Giants 2017: America's Best Small Companies and also ranked the #1 Top Workplace in Michigan in 2018 by the *Detroit Free Press*. When you look at what the organization does—or rather its IEP and who the people are, you can see why.

Perspectives That Create a Highly Positively Contagious Culture

Rob shares:

> People are what drive and differentiate our company. What we do isn't any different than the thousands of competitors we have. So, it makes good business sense to take unbelievable care of them and the totality of their lives to set them up for

the greatest success possible, not to mention it's just the right thing to do. What's most important is that this care is genuine. Once we have the right mindset and intentions internally, it's easier to do it externally. Showing up well for each other, taking care of ourselves, and serving happens naturally.

Serving Customers, "Good" or "Bad"

Rob explains:

A common philosophy nowadays is that companies should only do business with customers they love and are in alignment with. For us, we challenge ourselves to do business with customers that *we* can *serve* . . . or, truly DtX. Some customers (simply other humans in other organizations that happen to need our services) are in miserable cultures. They can't help but not show up as their best. Our thought is, maybe we can bring a small light to their day. Or, in some cases, a very bright light. You never know the ripple effect this might have and what that might mean to that human.

When It Doesn't Work: Mindful Transitions

When it comes to culture? "Some people get it; some don't. It works for some, not for others. Don't take it personally," says Rob. He used to lose sleep over this, but through the years has shifted his mindset to see the organization and its culture "almost like a person—ever-evolving, always improving, imperfect, showing up in the world the best we can. Some days better than others."

For those who don't get it, aren't getting what they need, or aren't able to deliver what imageOne needs, he's learned to support them, incorporating what they call "mindful transitions" (an idea he learned from Robert Glazer at Acceleration Partners) instead:

It makes no sense for people to give a two-week notice of leaving a company, and it makes no sense for a human to be terminated and escorted out the door with a box containing their belongs (often containing pictures of their family—other humans who are about to be affected by this!). Instead, why can't we work together in a harmonious way to find what either is looking for? In the end, everyone wins.

Culture Takes Time

Rob's learned to be patient:

Cultures take time to shift. When we add new ideas and components to our culture, I focus on them for a good 12 months. Consistent communication has been key. I've learned to ask lots of questions and listen deeply to what really matters to people. Then ask some more. It's all about human relationships versus business relationships, showing up together, and working to make each other's day a bit brighter. That's how we create our culture.

15FIVE

Shane Metcalf, Cofounder and Chief Culture Officer of 15Five, an organization devoted to "unlocking the potential of every member of the global workforce" through the company's team communication suite of tools (which I also discussed in *Contagious Culture*), offers that the company continues to build systems and processes to reinforce its positive culture. From small rituals like beginning meetings with a one-word check-in to reinforce the value of people's internal emotional states (whatever they may be); to doing a full IEP Check-In at the beginning of leadership meetings to share where they are and where they *want* to be; to incorporating a list of questions related to these ideas in the company's quarterly *Best-Self Review* that help people reorient to their best self and what that means in both being and doing terms . . . These have all been easy and effective practices in helping their organization *be* a positively contagious culture.

Shane shares, "Normalizing these things so it takes zero effort or emotional courage to instigate them has been essential. This way they just happen and the conversations and awareness grow from there."

When asked what has surprised him most about creating culture and integrating the principles of this work, Shane said it was how hungry people are for this level of authentic relating in companies:

There may be some cynicism at first, but when you really get people connected to the benefit and the feeling of being seen by your peers, it's revelatory and life-changing. The impact is that people begin to relax into a far greater sense of belonging and psychological safety. Trust begets energy and energy is what leads to an enthusiastic life full of accomplishment and meaningful connection. By saying that we value the energetic presence of every person here and equipping them with the tools and resources to optimize themselves, we witness people regularly bloom into ever greater versions of themselves.

SAI ORGANIZATION

Dana Schon, Professional Learning Director (also now an IEP-Certified Steward), and Roark Horn, Executive Director of the School Administrators of Iowa, have found that living and being a contagious culture versus doing it is a lot simpler than many of the initiatives people often think about when they need to embark on a culture shift. They call this work "an invitation" because it's not prescriptive but rather invitational in nature, providing frameworks that are human, real, and easy to fit into anyone's life who wants to show up better.

Dana says:

People's connotations of the word "culture" often include tangible strategies that they'll engage their staff or team in doing in order to make a better culture, but much of culture is in our own choice as to how we show up. As leaders, we are in the best position to establish the culture we want to create and sustain in our organizations. Most people respond with surprise to the idea that we are contributing energy to the room all the time. When invited to think about how they contribute to their own culture and situation, they recognize the role they play in creating the results they have. This is an "aha."

So much of this work is about awareness. Once you have that, you can't be unaware. Recognizing that we have impact in how we choose to show up and that we're contagious has been a difference-maker in the quality of presence at the events, meetings, and learning opportunities we host. Our participants take their cue from us—when we show up high vibe and present, they do too. We've found we've been able to be more present, make better decisions, serve our buildings and districts better, manage our energy, and be more at choice in how we show up. This has had ripple effects throughout our organization. It's literally been contagious.

Roark remembers engaging in an "IEP Appreciation Bath" when this work was first brought into the organization. He claims that "bath" shifted the culture. "People said things no one had said before and affirmed each other. The idea of being present was incredibly important because when I assumed this role, people were still uncertain about my expectations. Through this IEP work, I felt more vulnerable and willing to engage in more authentic conversations."

After engaging in the work for a while, he shares he began to increase his awareness of his impact in all of his relationships. He says this awareness changed his relationships with his wife, mom, kids, and friends:

I'd catch myself not being present whereas before, I hadn't noticed. I wasn't aware. I became much more aware of the impact my presence had on others in the room. Now, I don't bring my phone into our events. I know what distracts me, and I eliminate those distractions. I recognize the power of my title in the room. It's been interesting to observe how others look to me when I am there as a participant. I realize that what I choose to do gives others permission to do. If I'm on my phone, then others feel it's OK to do the same. I recognize how contagious I am as a leader.

I have been most surprised by how effective it is and how easy it is to implement and what a difference it makes in how our members interact with each other. There is a presence, energy, connection, and empathy among those who have awareness of their presence as compared to those who don't.

Vivayic

Vivayic, a learning services company with the purpose of "building others' capacity to do good in the world," has been integrating the IEP Model over the past three years. Emily Kueker and Carrie Derner, two of the owners (and IEP Stewards), reflected on what they've learned to build a positively contagious culture for their team of 30-plus employees all working virtually.

Creating Awareness

"Creating awareness about the contagious nature of energy has been essential in giving us a common language to address the presence each of us brings into conversations," shares Emily. "We know we've been successful in establishing the IEP Method when a teammate volunteers, 'I need to reboot,' during a meeting. This means they're self-aware, and that they identify the need to be more intentional and know what to do to change their presence."

Naming It

"Employees have bought into 'naming it.' As owners, we have a deep commitment to each other, and we refuse to compromise on it," shares Carrie. "The freedom to name what we are sensing is beautiful. We don't play games. I feel comfortable naming most things with our team members, too. If they identify something that seems off, we work together to name it. This saves time, energy, and drama."

Integration, Accountability, and Making It Real

All new employees are introduced to IEP during the two-week onboarding process, and they attend a two-day live IEP event as quickly as possible. Components of the IEP Method are written into Vivayic competency models and creative operating procedures so that IEP will be part of ongoing processes, growth, and development conversations. Emily comments, "Our employees latch on to IEP quickly, and it really helps them understand our culture and the 'why' behind our language and habits."

The Five Steps to Intentional Impact

Vivayic uses the Five Steps to Intentional Impact before tough conversations, interviews, and meetings. Carrie explains:

Checking our intended impact has been priceless for Emily and me. Many times when discussing how to handle something, we stop and ask, "What are we hoping for as an outcome?" It's made a huge difference in how I approach situations. As a result, I'm a huge advocate of the 5 Steps with our team. I've been able to coach people through stressful situations and keep them focused on the intended impact.

The Results

The company has excellent employee engagement scores, which has led to extraordinary client engagement. The company recorded a Net Promoter Score of 82 in its most recent survey. This has led to Vivayic earning a spot on the Inc 5000 list for fastest-growing private companies four years in a row.

"We invest deeply in culture. We recognize the most important job we have as owners is to make Vivayic a place where people get a chance to be their best. The awareness and this work took us to another level," says Carrie, "The results speak for themselves."

Domaine Carneros

Shauna Sullivan of Domaine Carneros (DC), a phenomenal winery located in Napa Valley, California (also discussed in *Contagious Culture*), joined me for a check-in. After five years of integrating this work into the winery's culture, Domaine Carneros has created some lovely best practices and found the tricky and delightful parts of creating and sustaining a positively contagious culture.

Noticing

Shauna speaks to the power of "noticing" as part of continuing to stay present and create a culture that truly *is* positively contagious. "To become contagious you have to first notice that you are in fact contagious. Once you notice this, you can change it. Through this work we've embodied noticing the energies around us that shape our daily lives."

The Sunshine Committee

A few years back, Domaine Carneros created its own Sunshine Committee. The committee's charter: "To help create a workplace that intentionally thinks about their actions and impact within their employee culture." The committee creates spaces both physically and mentally where employees from different departments can interact, connect, become more aware of the energy they're emitting and taking on, and notice how it impacts the bigger picture of personal satisfaction, culture, influence, and their customers' experiences.

The winery has a core group of employees who hold the work with energy, spreading the good as much as possible. Shauna calls this core the "lifeblood" of the organization that serves all different employees and more deeply integrates the DC energetic culture.

Low-Hanging Fruit

DC has found that a little goes a long way and that there is low-hanging fruit everywhere around. The fruit? "Simply being present with and acknowledging our fellow employees so they feel seen and heard is easy and powerful. Paying attention to the whole person and expressing care and gratitude creates a pause in the busyness of their lives, making people feel valued and cared for. This is contagious," says Shauna.

Cultural Immersion

Shauna shares that it's taken time for a full cultural immersion:

It can take a good portion of time to get all employees to think about the impact they can have on their personal and work lives. What's helped us create that immersion has been the employees seeing a consistent, focused, and educational approach to living a more energetically aware life. Patience, modeling, and *being* culture are the most influential part of integrating a workplace culture to ensure that cultural immersion takes place.

Tasty Catering

Thomas J. Walter, Cofounder and Chief Culture Officer of Tasty Catering, holds that "the organization's culture is our biggest asset."

He's not kidding. Living Tasty Catering's core values, honoring its intentions for culture, holding culture as its biggest asset, and walking the talk in BEing and LIVing versus just doing culture have resulted in:

- Being named APA's Psychologically Healthiest Workplace (twice in the past four years)
- More than 90 percent employee engagement for the past 10 years
- Turnover of 4 percent
- Single-digit sales increases coupled with double-digit profit increases for the past four years
- 9,300 events last year and only 41 mistakes realized by the client
- 53 awards won for best place to work and happy people

But Tom shares that the company's most significant marker is happy people. A contagious culture is the root of their happiness: "Our staff go home happy at night and return happy in the morning."

How does Tasty Catering do this? With intention. Two of the most important cultural assets for being a positively contagious culture are the company's culture statement and its core values. (These were codesigned by the employees.) The culture statement and core values speak to who they *be* as an organization, how they show up together, and how they treat each other. The culture statements and values are posted throughout the building, and teams repeat the values before every meeting of five people or more. The values have become assumed behaviors for the organization with every leader modeling them—starting with Tom himself: "What is important is that I do live them. Leaders are always watched, listened to, talked about, and if I don't live the core values, the organization will be living a lie. Our values and who we are together has changed all of our lives for the better—including the lives of our families."

nuphoriq

Erin Walter, CEO of nuphoriq, a marketing firm outside Chicago, shared that when it comes to culture, nuphoriq doubles down on "authenticity" as its cultural beacon. "We simply choose to build an authentic culture. One that reflects who and what we really are. It's not about following rules, but more of a choice we make each day to show up. The whole idea is more than *do*-ing; it's making the choice to *be* our best selves each day."

The organization holds that authenticity is an idea that can apply to any culture. Instead of trying to show up as someone else, or looking externally to define themselves and their company, the employees look inward. She says, "It's about being us. It's incredibly powerful because it's naturally contagious. Once people experience it, they are inspired to live that way themselves."

Erin offered that the biggest surprise was discovering that the key to culture isn't a huge system:

It's about building a place where you can be you. Your deepest values become the company's values. Your why becomes the company's why. When you do that, culture spreads organically. The hard part ends with making the commitment to authenticity. After that, just be yourself.

Our team is more confident in who they are, what they bring to the table, and what we do together. Our office energy is high and positive, even dealing with the low moments of business. We attract external stakeholders who share our values, and naturally filter those who don't.

Altus Brands

Mimi Lemanski, owner of Altus Brands (and an IEP Steward), shares that her company has its agreements posted around the conference room, throughout the offices, and in the production facility. Before meetings, tough conversations, or overall planning, employees set intentions, reboot, and use the IEP Sheet to prepare. They lean into the concepts of "Assume Good" and "Who/what are you being in service of?" to support them in navigating conflict, making decisions, and reminding themselves that they're a team. Honoring the agreement of "direct engagement" has eliminated the "us versus them" mentality that they'd experienced in the past.

Mimi's been most surprised by how easy this work is to integrate when people *choose* to live it. "By embodying IEP, I've seen a shift in how people eat and speak to each other, and how we work as a team. It is in the authenticity of believing in IEP, and knowing that we're contagious and have a choice about that, that the transformation has taken place."

Their business results? Mimi says:

People are more engaged with each other and not guarded, which has helped productivity. Conversations that used to be seen as "adversarial" are now opportunities to come to solutions that work for everyone. Being driven by values and purpose, and being mindful of the four quadrants, has allowed us to really walk the IEP talk, take care of ourselves, and be clearer about what we're doing. Authenticity has been contagious, owning our thoughts and actions has helped us be more transparent and thoughtful, and with shared language and intentions we're better at celebrating wins and strategizing challenges.

5 Dynamics

Karen Gordon, CEO of 5 Dynamics, LLC (from Chapter 14), shared that the company has integrated components of this work into the organization by using things like the bubble and the Wall of Gratitude and by increasing the awareness and intentionality in how people show up with each other. "We are always 'bubbling up' around here. Anytime we begin to feel the stress welling up, we say 'Bubble up baby!,' and we all know what that means. Just naming it, saying it out loud, helps us to bring things back into perspective."

Being a frequent traveler, she also takes the power of intention and being positively contagious on the road. Karen adds: "It's easy to go to a negative place as you make your way through the hurdles of the travel experience. However, I set my intention before I show up. I go out of my way to be patient and kind. I look for opportunities to shift others' mindsets as well by doing something unexpected."

For example, when Karen travels by plane, she sits in the exit row a lot, which provides ample opportunities for making someone's day:

When a 6'7" guy boards the plane and is looking miserable, knowing that he is about to have to sit in a cramped space for three hours, I surprise him by offering him my seat. I love watching the shift in his energy and the energy of those who witness this. The smallest gestures make a big impact. Kindness and compassion have a ripple effect. When we commit one small act of kindness that is witnessed by others, they begin to reframe their thinking as well. It is a beautiful thing to watch unfold.

Tustin Unified School District

As shared in Chapter 4, Tustin Unified School District (TUSD) is the school district that has spent the past 18 months integrating this work into its system through IEP Stewardship and a series of engage-ments. I interviewed Greg Franklin, TUSD Superintendent, and Kathie Nielsen, Deputy Superintendent, for some of their insights and wisdom about what they've learned so far.

How Do You Live and Be a Contagious Culture?

Kathie and Greg offer collectively:

As a school district we recognized the deep need our stu-dents had for social and emotional support to thrive in our modern world. The surprise was the parallel need that our employees had for the same thing. *Contagious Culture* gave us a framework and vocabulary to reflect on our own inten-tionality, while supporting our students. It also made many of us more empathetic to the demands and pressures of our stu-dents because we recognize their struggles in our own lives. This has supported us in being more intentional about how we show up and take care of ourselves in order to be *be* that culture for each other and our students.

Greg and I explored a bit further:

- **What lessons have you learned?**
"That the work on self-development and organizational culture is never done."
- **What have been the most meaningful ideas, tools, or principles?**
"As a group, educators are extremely giving people and whole-heartedly in service of their students. One of the most mean-ingful insights and surprises from our work is that our teachers, principals, and counselors needed *permission* to take care of themselves—not out of selfishness—but in order to have a greater impact on their students."
- **Any surprises?**
"For many of our people this has been surprisingly emotional work. Unfortunately, in most of our work lives we do not take the time to reflect on the alignment of our values with the lives we lead and

303

decisions we make. Through that reflection our folks have experienced a more genuine connection to themselves, their colleagues, and their students. Some of our people have shared that the work with *Contagious Culture* has rejuvenated their careers."

- **What has been the impact?**
"The observable impacts of our work with *Contagious Culture* is an overt consciousness throughout the district of self-care, intentions, and impact. These appear on agendas, newsletters, and district podcasts. I hear conversations where folks are discussing these ideas openly. We spend a great deal of time on planning for impact, rather than simply managing tasks. Less overt, but perhaps more importantly, people are bringing their whole and true selves to the important work of preparing our students for the future."

And there you have it! In-the-trenches wisdom from leaders and organizations that have been working their IEP, building *contagious cultures*, and becoming more and more positively *contagious yous* in their own authentic ways. (More best practices, shares, and talking points from interviews with these organizations are available in the *Contagious You Resource Toolkit* at www.anesecavanaugh.com/cykresources/.)

What shares resonated for you? Where do you see yourself in them? What feels easy? Challenging? What's the littlest next thing you could do in your organization to make this real? Remember, one step at a time, one breath at a time, one awareness at a time, one action at a time, one moment of presence at a time, and . . . presence, not perfection.

Fieldwork: Make It Real

Circle three ideas/actions in this chapter that feel most compelling for you and your organization right now and create your plan.

CHAPTER 16

Create Impact and Real Results: Play the Game, Choose Your Cause. Be It.

Let's do this thing . . .

How do you apply everything you've just read in your real world?

Just do it. Live it. Play the game, choose your cause, and be it.

Maybe you want to create impact and results with your culture, life, personal relationships, money, health, or business success. Perhaps you want to solve big world problems or just hit that goal that feels super-important to you right now. Whatever you want to do, every single one of these has a common denominator: *you!*

You are it.

Choose what you want to be contagious for and get out there and lead.

In this chapter, I'll conclude this book with the core principles of being contagious, the magical Culture Lists you've been waiting for (two of them!), resources to carry on with (so you can be an even bigger carrier of positive contagions), and some closing thoughts.

You've done your work. Now it's time to live it.

15 Core Principles of Being Contagious

We've been immersed in core principles throughout this book. Below, I've distilled them down to 15 to help you bring it all together. These are not all-inclusive, of course; there are more. I encourage you to capture additional principles that have resonated for you—or that you've created for yourself while reading this book—in the margins here or throughout this chapter (*Note:* This entire chapter *IS* your fieldwork section. Enjoy!)

1. It starts with me—choice point after choice point—I choose. I contribute to helping things either go better or go worse; I set the tone; I can choose love or fear. Breathe.

2. I am contagious. Presence begets presence. Busy begets busy. Gratitude begets gratitude. Kindness begets kindness. Snark begets snark. I beget what I beget. How I show up is up to me. This is a moment-by-moment choice.

3. I get to choose and create my experience for myself. I can only influence the experience for another. (If you don't like your experience or influence, go back to #1.)

4. My body, mind, spirit, and heart all work together to help me create my experience and impact in the world. They must be nourished intentionally and held as sacred ground.

5. Self-care, self-kind, receiving, and asking for help are leadership skills. These are foundational for how much I can give of myself and how much I can hold for others. With this, honoring pain, pleasure, and what is true for me now is essential for having access to all of myself, living an authentic life, and being a congruently contagious leader.

6. My presence *is* my impact—in every meaning of the word. How present I am for me, for you, for my life, and *right now.*

7. Intuition, love, ownership, intention, devotion, gratitude, curiosity, breath, presence, and being "in service of" are all instant state shifters; when used in alignment, they are the ultimate force. Nourish the force.

8. Clarity of intention, true presence, powerful proclamation, commitment to service, and openness to magic open the Portal of Purpose for exuberant impact. Get in there.

9. Focusing on the negativity of the problem creates contraction—creating more problems. Focusing on the *gift* of the problem, or the solutions, creates expansion—creating healing and opportunity. (It still may be REALLY hard.)

10. Intention is everything. The strongest intention wins. When I am clear on my intention, it makes risk taking, truth telling, courage, vulnerability, showing up, and getting out of my comfort zones easier. I can stand my ground. When I'm not clear on my intention, risk taking, truth telling, courage, vulnerability, showing up, and getting out of my comfort zones are harder. And I'm more likely to be designed by my defaults or *other* people's intentions *for* me. Be clear.

11. Success and being better at leadership do not mean that problems go away or that things aren't hard. It means that problems become higher caliber as I get better at navigating and finding the gifts in them.

12. "No" is a complete sentence, silence is golden, and discernment is key. "Response-able" serves over "responsible" every time, and staying in my own lane and doing my best are magic.

13. When I am overwhelmed, lost, or unclear, *love* and the *intention of service* will reconnect me with my core, guide me toward what matters most, help me unleash the most potent version of myself in service of others, and contribute to the contagious good.

14. Devotion and magic go together to create more devotion and magic. We need both. (And a little pixie dust doesn't hurt either.)

15. Each of us is our best chance for "better." Loving collaboration makes the world go round. We are all mirrors for each other. We are the culture. I am the culture. And with that, we're back to #1 . . .

The Culture List: What to Do

As promised at the beginning of the book, here is the Culture Change List. (Did you jump ahead? It's OK; I knew you might.) Also as promised, you'll see how this list is only as powerful as the intentions, energy, and presence of the people delivering it, and only as effective as you are at being positively contagious.

Here's what to do.

YOU

Do these five things personally to build a stronger foundation for creating a positively contagious culture and the ultimate impact you all desire together.

1. Take absolute personal ownership and "response-ability" for your life, the culture, your experience, and the results you are creating. (Everything you do and be counts. *Everything.*)
2. Do your own IEP work and all you can for yourself to show up well, help things go right, take care of yourself, and come to the conversation as your best and most influential you.
3. Own your mistakes. Tell the truth. Ask for help. Do the right thing. Be kind. Stand strong. Honor your agreements. And be in integrity with yourself.
4. Model and be the change you want to see. (See the 15 Core Principles of Being Contagious listed above, especially #2.)
5. Be *with* people—not above them or below them—with them. "See" them. And serve.

Together as a Team/Organization

As a team or organization, define the culture you *truly* want to have. Write a vision for it:

- What success looks like
- How it feels
- What your employees say to others about their work, leaders, and what you're all up to (and what they say to their families when they go home at night)

- What people say about you in the world (include competitors and customers)
- Anything else that's important to you

With this picture in mind, create a map/strategy working backward from your vision. What do you need to put in place to create it? What needs to change? How can you support yourself individually and as a team?

Build your plan in stages; pull from the list below (as resonates for your timing and circumstances), make up your own, or combine.

Building Blocks for a Positively Contagious Culture

Now that you've established your foundation individually and as a team (in the previous two sections), build in actions and practices to support what you want to create. Here are 12 tangible focus areas and best practices, all discussed throughout this book, to move your cultural health, productivity, and power forward:

- Define your *cultural identity infrastructure* with your values, vision, and purpose.
- Define your *cultural heart and safety infrastructure* with agreements, structures, and rituals.
- Make your meetings more effective and life-giving.
- Up-level your feedback processes and norms.
- Create measurement and reward systems that inspire collaboration and the culture you desire.
- Create criteria for what you will and will not tolerate in behaviors as an organization. What are your deal breakers?
- Integrate Energy Checks, Reboots, the Five Steps to Intentional Impact, and Agreements into your meetings.
- Assess your Cultural IEP in all four quads and act accordingly. (Start with the Physical/Environmental for low-hanging fruit and to support your brain.)
- Create cultural space for self-care. Celebrate people taking care of themselves in their own authentic ways.

- Eliminate toxins: these can include pretending to be present or present-light listening, gossip, indirect engagement, fluff feedback, "bragging busy," and blame.
- Implement and practice accelerators: intentional presence, purpose, gratitude and acknowledgment, direct engagement, real feedback, impact crafting, and accountability.
- Make it safe to talk about the hard stuff, to say "I don't know," to ask for help, to have a bad moment, to take a minute, and to say "no" when something doesn't feel right.

Remember, *none* of this works best if you don't show up well. You can do all of these things and have crappy IEP—and you'll be frustrated (not to mention exhausted and ineffective). Your people will feel you doing culture, not being it. So *be* it and *do* it.

Putting these things in place will serve as support structures, reduce ambiguity and anxiety, and create more space for people to nourish their own IEP and show up better together.

The Personal IEP and Cultural Integration Check List

You'll want to craft a personal plan for yourself to keep working your IEP. And as you continue to create your culture, you'll want to maintain, strengthen, and expand it.

Any ideas or principles that you found useful and that resonate for you in this book can be built into your life and organization on a regular basis (see specific examples from organizations in Chapter 15). It simply takes intention, planning, doing (*and* being) the work, and owning it.

Here are some examples and suggested structures to support your ongoing implementation. Use these tools and practices, coupled with the others in this book, as they serve you the best.

Daily

Do any or all of these each day:

- Personal IEP practices (as discussed in the Essential You and Quadrants 1–4)

310

- The Five Steps to Intentional Impact, Energy Checks, and Team IEP Moments
- The daily (and moment-to-moment as needed!) following IEP check point questions (these can be used individually and also integrated into team inquiries):
  - What is my intention?
  - What is my intention in service of? Whom does it serve?
  - How am I showing up?
  - How am I taking care of myself? (Am I being self-kind?)
  - How have I set myself up for success?
  - What experience am I creating?
  - How am I contributing to this dynamic?
  - How am I contagious? What am I creating through what I'm projecting?
  - What can I shift (even slightly) right now to serve myself/others/this moment better?
  - What is the most generous thing I can do and be right now? (For myself and/or another?)
- The IEP Sheet

Weekly/Monthly/Quarterly

Do these weekly, monthly, or quarterly:

- Agreement check-ins
- Cultural and individual checkups (use assessments from Chapters 2 and 14)

Annually/Biannually

Do these once or twice a year:

- Engagement Survey
- IEP Cultural Assessment (combination of any assessments in this book and/or the formal IEP Cultural Assessment in *Contagious Culture*)

Deeper Integration, Scaling, and Sustainability

To take this work deeper and create integrated structures for ongoing support:

- Designate team and cultural IEP Champions to keep the work alive.
- Run book clubs with this book and *Contagious Culture*.
- Host or attend a live experience to integrate this work experientially.
- Train IEP Stewards and IEP Activators to bring this work and practices more deeply into your organization.
- Build IEP and contagiousness into performance reviews, measurements, and rewards formally and informally.

Resources to Continue On

Keeping this work alive and real in your daily life will accelerate its power exponentially. Keep coming back to it. This content will read differently each time you engage with it, because if you do your work, you'll be different.

To support you in carrying on and learning more, and as a gift for purchasing this book, I've created a special *Contagious You Resource Toolkit* accessible at www.anesecavanaugh.com/cykresources/.

In the kit you'll receive:

- Contagion Factor Formula examples and worksheet
- The IEP Sheet
- Bonus content that didn't make its way into the book
- Additional interview nuggets from organizations in Chapter 15
- A list of recommended reading and resources that support this work
- Information on our IEP Activator Program where you can get more tools, exercises, and videos for integration in your organization
- A subscription to my private communication list where I provide articles, resources, and exercises to support the content and principles in this body of work

This work is life's work—being contagious and growing your leadership is never done. Keep going!

It All Comes Back to Us

At the end of the day, no matter how many models I look at . . . or programs . . . or brilliant books . . . or bodies of work, I find that our best bet for leadership is us. It's "me" (*you*). It's being the change we want to see. It's leading ourselves so we can lead others. It's getting command of our state, thinking, and well-being. It's loving *ourselves* and *each other* so much that we can't help but show up and lead better. It's having a mindset that we are in service of others. It's being clear and rooted in our intention.

I believe it's the best way we can help things go well. It's the foundation.

Our foundation has to be strong:

When I lead me, and nourish me, with the intention for peace and also staying in service of *you*, I help things go well.

When I own my contagiousness and the tone I set in any moment, I create a better experience.

When I build my own resiliency and then encounter toxicity, I engage better, without becoming it.

When I am conscious of my presence, in command of my state, and well-resourced (versus "busy" or burnt out)—I communicate, support, serve, and collaborate with *you* better.

All of this is in service of leadership, joy, impact, and helping things go right.

So it becomes my primary job as leader to be responsible (*and* "response-able") for what I put out there energetically, to be conscious and protective of what I take on, to stay clear in my intentions, to stay present, and to take exquisite care of myself so I can become more powerfully and *helpfully* contagious.

Our culture is a result of all of us being contagious together (for good or bad).

So here we are. Creating culture. Together.

Let's make it a good one.

Becoming a Positively Contagious Force

Let's help each other become more positively contagious, shall we?

Let's make it OK, crucial even, to prioritize self-care, to balance it with the value of impact, and to stay focused on purpose and being a positive contribution. And then let's trust this will pay off in major dividends.

Let's make it OK to ask for help, to take time-outs, to eat well, to sleep, to take a minute, and to have some kind of balance that serves individuals in whatever way is most important to them.

Let's let it be OK to have negatively contagious "George" and "Georgette" moments (and even days), so we can be real, get the support we need, shift our contagiousness for good, and then pay it forward.

Let's make it OK to ask ourselves how are we *really*? How are our people? And what do we need? And then let's tell the truth.

And let's do what we need to do, and become who we need to become, to make more good in the world and unlock what's possible together.

There's so much good for us to do.
We don't have to take it on all at once.
One step at a time, one engagement at a time, one breath at a time, one kindness at a time, one act of courage and love at a time—keep showing up.
Please use this book for yourself in the ways that resonate.
Please pay it forward and make it positively contagious.
Please nourish and build more beautiful leaders.
Please use your superpowers for good.
Please help things go well.
And let's do this thing.
To your becoming,
To your impact,
To you . . .

Anese

314

NOTES

Foreword

1. Tracie McMillan, *Food and Wine* magazine, April 26, 2019, https://www.foodandwine.com/travel/restaurants/best-restaurants-work-jobs.
2. Peter Kropotkin, *Memoirs of a Revolutionist*, 1899, https://theanarchistlibrary.org/library/petr-kropotkin-memoirs-of-a-revolutionist.

The Cost of Disengagement

1. GALLUP, Inc. Gallup State of the American Workplace Report, 2017, https://www.gallup.com/workplace/238085/state-american-workplace-report-2017.aspx.
2. Ibid.
3. Ibid.
4. Ibid.
5. Jack Altman, "Don't Be Surprised When Your Employees Quit," *Forbes*, February 2017, https://www.forbes.com/sites/valleyvoices/2017/02/22/dont-be-surprised-when-your-employees-quit/#6df65aca325e.
6. Paul J. Zak, "The Neuroscience of Trust," *Harvard Business Review*, Special Issue, January 2019.
7. Ibid.
8. Judith E. Glaser and Richard D. Glaser, "The Neurochemistry of Positive Conversations," *Harvard Business Review*, Special Issue, January 2019.
9. Ibid.

Chapter 1

1. Wikipedia, https://en.wikipedia.org/wiki/First_impression _(psychology); *Sage Journals,* https://journals.sagepub.com/doi/ abs/10.1111/j.1467-9280.2006.01750.x?ssource=mfc&rss=1 and https://journals.sagepub.com/doi/10.1177/1948550617732388.
2. Princeton University, https://www.princeton.edu/news/2006/08/22/ snap-judgments-decide-faces-character-psychologist-finds.
3. Association for Psychological Science, https://www.psychological science.org/observer/how-many-seconds-to-a-first-impression.
4. Heart Math, https://www.heartmath.com/research/#eer and https://www.heartmath.org/research/science-of-the-heart/ energetic-communication/.

Chapter 7

1. Bruce H. Lipton, PhD, is an internationally recognized leader in bridging science and spirit, a stem cell biologist, and author of *The Biology of Belief* and additional books. More at https://www.brucelipton.com/.
2. Byron Katie created and teaches a world-renowned method of self-inquiry known as "The Work of Byron Katie," or simply as "The Work." More about her and her method, books, and training at https://thework.com/.

Chapter 8

1. Fundamentals of Neuroscience, https://en.wikiversity.org/wiki/ Fundamentals_of_Neuroscience.
2. M. Iacoboni, "Imitation, Empathy and Mirror Neurons," *Annu RevPsychol,* 2009, 60:653–670.
3. Sourya Acharya and Samarth Shukla, "Mirror Neurons: Enigma of the Metaphysical Modular Brain," *J Nat Sci Biol Med,* July–December 2012, 3(2):118–124.
4. Hyeonjin Jeon and Seung-Hwan Lee, "Neurons to Social Beings: Short Review of the Mirror Neuron System Research and Its Socio-Psychological and Psychiatric Implications," *Clin Psychopharmacol Neurosci,* 2018, 16(1):18–31.
5. Belanger et al., "Brain Energy Metabolism: Focus on Astrocyte-Neuron Metabolic Cooperation," *Cell Metabolism,* December 2011, 14(6, 7):724–738, https://www.sciencedirect.com/science/article/pii/ S1550413111004207 and https://www.ncbi.nlm.nih.gov/pubmed/ 22152301.
6. Ibid.
7. Parkinson et al., "Similar Neural Responses Predict Friendship," *Nature Communications,* 2018, (9):332.

8. Xie et al., "Sleep Drives Metabolite Clearance from the Adult Brain," *Science*, October 2013, (342)6156: 373–377.

9. Masaru Tateno and Toshikazu Saito, "Biological Studies on Alcohol-Induced Neuronal Damage," *Psychiatry Investing*, March 2008, 5(1): 21–27.

10. Saito et al., "Neonatal Ethanol Disturbs the Normal Maturation of Parvalbumin Interneurons Surrounded by Subsets of Perineuronal Nets in the Cerebral Cortex: Partial Reversal by Lithium," *Cerebral Cortex*, April 2019, 29(4): 1383–1397.

11. UCLA Newsroom, http://newsroom.ucla.edu/releases/the-teenage -brain-on-social-media.

12. Cacioppo et al., "The Negativity Bias: Conceptualization, Quantification, and Individual Differences," *Behavioral and Brain Sciences*, June 2014, 37(3): 309–310, https://www.ncbi.nlm.nih.gov/ pubmed/24970431.

13. *Neurosci Biobehav Review*, June 2014, (43): 48–73; doi: 10.1016/ j.neubiorev.2014.03.016; epub April 2014.

14. Lazar, et al., "Meditation Experience Is Associated with Increased Cortical Thickness," *Neuroreport*, 2005 (16): 1893–1897, https:// www.ncbi.nlm.nih.gov/pmc/articles/PMC1361002/.

15. Kim et al., "Antagonistic Negative and Positive Neurons of the Basolateral Amygdala," *Nat Neurosci*, December 2016, 19(12): 1636–1646.

Chapter 9

1. Gloria Mark of the University of California, Irvine, https:// www.nytimes.com/2013/05/05/opinion/sunday/a-focus-on -distraction.html.

Chapter 12

1. Brené Brown, PhD, LMSW, is a globally recognized thought leader, author, and research professor at the University of Houston, studying courage, vulnerability, shame, and empathy. "The Vault," as referenced in Chapter 12, is one of her "Seven Elements of Trust," which is about holding confidentiality and not sharing information or experiences that are not yours to share. More about her and her work, books, and training at www.brenebrown.com.

Chapter 13

1. R. Gilkey and C. Kilts, "Cognitive Fitness," *Harvard Business Review*, Special Neuroscience Edition, January 2019.

Chapter 14

1. The 5 Dynamics® Methodology is focused on team development and therefore not sold as individual assessments. More at https://www .simpli5.com/.
2. 5 Dynamics, LLC, https://www.simpli5.com/.

ACKNOWLEDGMENTS

It Takes a Powerful Positively Contagious Village

No part or chapter (or book!) could ever capture the words and sentiment required to thank the expansive list of people who make my life and this work possible. So thank you, everyone! Extra gratitude for those more deeply involved in this book and my process this year.

First and foremost, thank you to my kids, Jake and Izzy, for being awesome humans and my loves. It's my greatest privilege and role to be your mom and to watch you become. You are my full heart. I love you.

To Donya Dickerson, Nora Hennick, Amanda Muller, Amy Li, Daina Penikas, Jeff Weeks, and the good people at McGraw-Hill, thank you. It is an honor to do another book together. Donya, thank you for your wisdom, insight, and thoughtful editing, and for making this book show up at its best so it can be even more usefully contagious. Thank you Patty Wallenburg, Judy Duguid, and Sharon Honaker for your care and attention to detail, ensuring this book reads beautifully.

To Kristen Moeller and the team at Waterside Productions, thank you. Kristen, thank you for being my agent person. Deep gratitude for your belief, care, and intention for me and this book.

To the classy crew at Cave Henricks Communications—Barbara, Pam, Kim, and Nina—thank you for your teamwork and for helping us spread the word thoughtfully to help this book be contagious in the most meaningful ways.

To Carol Allen, thank you for your edits, support in storylines, and early reads as well as for helping shape this book and helping me write and serve readers better.

To Linda Sivertsen, thank you, Mamma, for your help on all books and *everything*. Our relationship is one of my most cherished. Too much to list here, so I'll only say: ODE, Remember, Magic, and are you ready for another? I love you.

To all the organizations and leaders who shared their experiences (whether identified or not) in this book, and to all who've attended our engagements posing great questions, sharing tremendous wisdom, and asking for this book—thank you. I made this for you.

To Dr. Seonok Lee, thank you for your guidance, expertise, and contributions in Chapter 8. Your grace, brilliance, and patience grew (and blew) my mind in so many beautiful ways. Thank you for showing us so eloquently how science supports this work and for so graciously and patiently digging into the magic of our brains with me.

To Dr. Victoria Stevens, thank you for your wisdom, diligence, advice, and care with this book, especially Chapter 11. Thank you for helping me honor the nuances of projection and therapy versus leadership, coaching, and development in order to best support the reader. For your support in my own life and in this body of work, your impact is *immeasurable*. I am deeply and forever grateful.

To Sandy Martini and Ashley Semberger, thank you for keeping things humming while I disappeared into "writing caves" and road trips. For being a stand for this work and for me and for helping me protect my time; for your wicked organizational skills; and for working so beautifully together to make things zoom. Sandy, for the many flowers that brightened my own environmental IEP while writing, and for calling me a "GHW." Thank you. (I am.)

To Jef Lear, many thanks for the graphics in this book, for being a stand for brand and truth in aesthetics, and for translating ideas into visuals that make meaning. It is an honor to work with you.

To our IEP Stewards, thank you for carrying this work forward. To SAI and TUSD, thank you for being the first in education to steward it. Deep gratitude to Kelly Poppaw, Dana Schon, Mimi Lemanski, Carrie Derner, and Emily Kueker who've been Stewards from the start. Thank you for your trust in me and the content and for caring about people as you do.

To my amazing partners, clients, and collaborators who are leading, being, becoming, and thinking with me—thank you for YOU.

Special thanks to Duane Bray, Heather Currier Hunt, and the IDEO crew, Chris Burt and Team, Mark Bernstein, Patrick Hoban, Mike Lalich, Janette Lampe, Lisa Brown, Karen Gordon, Kathie Nielsen, Greg Franklin, Deb Bielek, and Mary Spaeder for your support, for showing up, and for trusting me to show up with you.

To Terry McMillan, thank you for your sass, support, feedback, and belief. "An author should not be the same person she was when she started writing a book, as who she is when she finishes.." I have felt this daily; you were right. Not baaa'd! (The sheep are next!)

To Lois Harmon and Andrea Vieira, extra magic here. Thank you for being sisters in words and DWTS. Deeply grateful.

To Mike Robbins, Chip Conley, and Brad Meltzer, your impact and kindness ripples. I'll thank you each—forever.

To my CORE Leadership Community, North and South. Thank you for your support, love, championing, and grace while I birthed this baby. Your steadfast presence has taught me much. Soul-depth gratitude to Susan Mayginnes Howard, Sam Chan, Lisa Margulies, and Robin Graham for holding space, celebrating pixels, and sharing your unique support throughout. Sam, for the power of deeper intention and for being that safe space for me to lean into again and again, thank you.

To Ari Weinzweig, my gratitude has no bounds. Thank you for *you*. And for being an instant *yes* to this book, this work, and me. Your friendship, and intent for humans, has special residence in my heart.

Rob Dube, dear friend, champion, and C/EP. Our almost daily video exchanges are a documentary of this book and testament to the power of belief, craft, business, and doing nothing while doing something. Thank you for being.

Bo Burlingham, your words land deeply in my heart and have made a permanent imprint. Thank you for your support always.

To my Small Giants peeps (too many hearts to list) and every organization I'm a part of, my thanks. To every teacher, coach, advisor, therapist, or any kind of practitioner who's supported, guided, and taught me in any way, thereby contributing to this work, thank you.

To Dr. Josh Longo, Matt Williamson, and the training crew at LTF, thank you for helping me keep my body strong and my promise of exquisite self-care throughout this process intact.

To my neighbors for watching out for me so beautifully and being "family" to come home to after each trip. Linda, I've never loved twinkle lights so much.

Deepest love and gratitude for Aimee Leigh, Mandy Bryant, and Melissa Epperson for sistering and devotion, for daily calls and check-ins, for reading excerpts from this book via text, and for being a lifeline. I would not be me without you. I love you madly.

To Mom, thank you for nightly email check-ins and the intentions and heart behind them while I wrote. To my kids' dad, thank you—I feel blessed to walk this path of co-parenting with you. I am deeply grateful for every single chapter of our lives.

To all who supported me, my kids, this book, the business—*anything*, this past year especially—in your own unique ways, thank you.

Finally, to Alison Macondray, Matt Clark, Keather Roemhildt, Yanush Cherkis, Matt Beck, Jan Kamachi, Kevin Waldman, Adam Broidy, Marisa Smith, Kathryn Body, Nick Bryant, Aaron Centric, and Stephen Harms for extra presence, support, and nourishment during this book's unfolding—crucial to my life in ways I didn't even know I needed—until I had it.

Thank you *all* for showing up.

INDEX

Page numbers followed by *f* refer to figures.

ABOUT THE AUTHOR

Anese Cavanaugh is an award-winning speaker, teacher, advisor, and thinking partner to some of today's most innovative organizations and business leaders around the world. She is devoted to helping people show up and bring their best selves to the table in order to create significant positive impact in their lives and organizations (while feeling great doing so). In addition to creating and teaching the IEP Method® (Intentional Energetic Presence®), she speaks on leadership, showing up, being positively contagious, nourishing our relationship with ourselves, and creating a healthy culture.

As a leading voice on intention, energy, and presence in leadership and culture, she helps people clarify their intentions and intuition, transform "busy" and "burnout" into productive fuel, enjoy (and like) themselves more, and use their leadership superpowers for good in the world—all in service of unlocking greater leadership potential, collaboration, and impact.

Clients and program participants say that she "builds creative leaders," "brings love back into business," "gets people having real conversations," and "unlocks potential," and that she is "changing the conversation around self-care and self-kind in service of leadership and impact." Her work is based upon the premise that in order to show up and lead at our best, we must be present, show up for ourselves, be clear and clean in our intentions, and be in service of others.

She is the author of *Contagious Culture: Show Up, Set the Tone, and Intentionally Create an Organization that Thrives* and *The Leader You Will Be: An Invitation* (a leadership storybook).

She speaks regularly on stages around the country and has guest-lectured for law enforcement, at Stanford (business and d.school), at the University of Michigan, and for additional universities and educational organizations.

In addition to being an active entrepreneur, advisor, author, speaker, movement maker, and lover of the human spirit and impact, she is also mom to two amazing kids and two riley rescue dogs in Northern California.

You can find more from her on her blog, on podcasts, on Inc.com, and in publications such as the *Harvard Business Review, Huffington Post, Thrive Global, Forbes,* CEO.com, and others. You can also find additional resources to support you in your own leadership at:

www.anesecavanaugh.com

Twitter and LinkedIn: @anesecavanaugh

Want or Need More? My Team and I Are Here to Help

You have all you need in this book to help you fully up-level your very contagious leadership. If you wish for more, I invite you to download the special *Contagious You Resource Toolkit* (as mentioned in Chapter 16). Desire more? Wonderful. Read (or reread) *Contagious Culture*. More? Great! We're here to help. We have additional tools, resources, and programs to support your integration. These range from free resources on our site, to more books, to online trainings, to live sessions (public or private), to full organizational initiatives and rollouts.

Learn more at anesecavanaugh.com. While there, you'll find an invitation to subscribe to our mailing list to stay up-to-date on new articles, resources, events, and offerings as they become available. For speaking and engagement inquiries, requests, shares, notes, or just to say "Hi!" please contact me/my team at anesecavanaugh.com/contact/ or email direct at info@anesecavanaugh.com.

I look forward to being in the conversation with you!